Doing Business
For Dummies

Etiquette Tips

- **Familiarize yourself with religious holidays and customs.** Wish your colleagues Happy Diwali, Happy Pongal, or Id Mubarak at the appropriate times.

- **Use only the right hand to pick up, offer, or receive things.** Indians consider the left hand not as "pure" as the right.

- **Don't worry about the caste system.** The caste system doesn't impact how Westerners interact with locals. Ignoring it and treating people as equals, just as you always do, is fine.

- **Greet traditional Indians with a joined palms namaste.** *Namaste* means "I bow to the Divine in you." See Chapter 15 for an illustration.

- **Accept hospitality graciously.** *Athithi devo bhava* means "the guest is god," and it's an important tenet of Indian culture, so be prepared to be treated well and reciprocate hospitality.

Don't Be Surprised If Indians . . .

- **Offer a limp or weak handshake.** They're unused to shaking hands and it is a sign of respect to shake mildly.

- **Always say "yes."** "No" is a sign of deep disrespect, so Indians often prefer to please and give the answer "yes," hoping to accommodate what has been asked.

- **Don't make eye contact.** Indians are taught as a sign of respect to avert their eyes when talking to an older or superior person.

- **Move the head side to side, as if in disagreement, while listening to you.** This is a sign of extreme respect and showing involvement in the conversation and is a respectful acknowledgment of following you completely.

- **Nod the head to say "yes" when you're expecting a negative response.** This gesture really means "okay" and is again a sign of "I understand what you're saying."

For Dummies: Bestselling Book Series for Beginners

Doing Business in India For Dummies®

Indian Languages Demystified

India comes as close to the Tower of Babel as possible. There are at least 300 known languages, 24 of which have one million or more speakers.

Hindi is the national language of India and *Hindu* is a religion. Don't mix the two.

Here's a list of Indian states, their capitals, and the primary language of each:

State	Capital	Language(s)
Andhra Pradesh	Hyderabad	Telugu
Arunachal Pradesh	Itanagar	Assamese, Bengali, Hindi
Assam	Guwahati	Assamese, Bodo
Bihar	Patna	Hindi, Bihari
Chhattisgarh	Raipur	Hindi
Goa	Panaji	Konkani
Gujarat	Gandhinagar	Gujarati
Haryana	Chandigarh	Hindi
Himachal Pradesh	Shimla	Hindi, Pahari
Mizoram	Aizaw	Mizo, English
Jharkhand	Ranchi	Hindi
Jammu and Kashmir	Srinagar	Dogri, Kashmiri
Karnataka	Bangalore	Kannada
Kerala	Thiru-vanantha-puram	Malayalam
Madhya Pradesh	Bhopal	Hindi
Manipur	Imphal	Manipuri
Maharashtra	Mumbai	Marathi
Meghalaya	Shillong	Khasi, Garo
Nagaland	Kohima	Ao, Konyak, Angami, Sema, Lotha
Orissa	Bhubaneshwar	Oriya
Punjab	Chandigarh	Punjabi
Rajasthan	Jaipur	Hindi, Marwari, Mewari
Sikkim	Gangtok	Nepali
Tamil Nadu	Chennai	Tamil
Tripura	Agartala	Bengali, Tripuri, Manipuri, Kakborak
Uttar Pradesh	Lucknow	Hindi
Uttaranchal	Dehradun	Hindi
West Bengal	Kolkata	Bengali

For Dummies: Bestselling Book Series for Beginners

Doing Business in India

FOR DUMMIES®

by Ranjini Manian

BICENTENNIAL
1807
WILEY
2007
BICENTENNIAL

Wiley Publishing, Inc.

Doing Business in India For Dummies®

Published by
Wiley Publishing, Inc.
111 River St.
Hoboken, NJ 07030-5774
www.wiley.com

Copyright © 2007 by Wiley Publishing, Inc., Indianapolis, Indiana

Published by Wiley Publishing, Inc., Indianapolis, Indiana

Published simultaneously in Canada

WILEY

About the Author

Ranjini Manian is a linguist, pioneering businesswoman, and homemaker who lives in the southern Indian city of Chennai. She was raised in Mumbai, where she studied French Literature at Elphinstone College and attended the University of Sorbonne in Paris. Ranjini is fluent in French, Japanese, Spanish, English, and several Indian languages. She's traveled extensively, covering about 26 countries, for work as well as for the exploration of other cultures, making her a multicultural expert.

Ranjini founded Global Adjustments, India's leading destination and cross-cultural services company. She created and continues to be the editor of India's only free cultural magazine: *At A Glance – Understanding India.*

Under her leadership, Global Adjustments has been chosen as one of the top ten "cool companies" of India by *Business Today* and received several awards, including a commendation from the President of India.

In pursuit of their mission to ease people's passage to India, the Global Adjustments team has worked in the past dozen years with Fortune 500 companies and people from 70 different nationalities.

Ranjini is supported in her pursuits by her husband, son, and daughter.

Dedication

I dedicate this book to my husband, Chinnu Manian, my friend, philosopher, and guide, who taught me all about "doing business."

Author's Acknowledgments

Success can't be spelled without *u*. This book is a perfect example of the importance of so many who made this book succeed.

I gratefully acknowledge all the hours of tireless work of Susan Philip, my editorial coordinator, who kept the process going when others were losing their heads. She also made this book see light of day. She brought touches way beyond her role, and I could never have done it without her, all while managing a family of kids and two cats! We stressed out, laughed, sighed, and rejoiced all over *Doing Business in India For Dummies.* Thank you Susan for the pleasure of your company in this project.

Gopal was a very important player in this project too, bringing many valuable life experiences, collating ideas, and truly contributing, all while taking time out from his busy schedule of deep-sea diving around the world during the months we pulled together this book.

I am super thankful to my family: my husband, Chinnu Manian, my worst critic and my best guide; and my son Varun and daughter Rohini, who basically sacrificed any time with me during these past months as I dove into the book, running helter-skelter to collect data, interview leaders, and hammer away at the computer. (While writing this book, a stray kitten was adopted and grew into a cat, and I had no idea it happened in my own home. My daughter said to me when I discovered this just the other day, "What do you expect Mamma? You're always busy at your computer. Now Ginger is here and she has to stay!")

Many other folks helped in various chapters of the book, and I want to say a big thank you. In alphabetical order:

Arvind Datar, Gerard D'Cunha, Philip George, Sriram Iyer, Brian Jolley, George Koshy, Koshy M. Koshy, J. Krishnan, Vaidehi Krishnan, Jukka and Pia Lehtela , Norm Mainland, Tarkan Maner, Suzy McNeill, Rekha Murthy, Lakshmi Narayanan (Cognizant), M. Lakshmi Narayanan (Mico Bosch), Cesare Pagani, Sriram Panchu, Brittain Phillips, Radhakrishnan Pillai, Shanti Puducheri, Satish W. Pusegaonkar, N. Ram, Kamini Ramani, Rukmani Ramani (my dear mother), M. Rangaswamy, N. Ravi, Santhanam, Mallika Srinivasan, Gopal Surya, Hema Vijay, and C. N. Vishwanathan.

I would also like to thank the people on the Global Adjustments team: Rajeshwar Balasundaram, Nil, and Bindu.

And more thanks to the Wiley team: Stacy Kennedy, Tim Gallan, Alissa Schwipps, Carrie Burchfield, and Elizabeth Rea. Thank you for your contributions and willing help. If I have omitted any name I apologize in advance and thank you warmly.

I have used a hardworking taskforce to collect data and conduct interviews, and I wrote this book with only the best intentions. If, despite all efforts to capture the essence, I have committed any mistakes, I apologize in advance.

Publisher's Acknowledgments

We're proud of this book; please send us your comments through our Dummies online registration form located at www.dummies.com/register.

Some of the people who helped bring this book to market include the following:

Acquisitions, Editorial, and Media Development

Senior Project Editors: Tim Gallan, Alissa Schwipps

Acquisitions Editor: Stacy Kennedy

Copy Editor: Carrie A. Burchfield

Technical Editor: Gunjan Bagla, Amritt (www.amritt.com)

Editorial Manager: Christine Meloy Beck

Editorial Assistants: Erin Calligan Mooney, Joe Niesen, David Lutton, Leeann Harney

Cover Photo: Ashok Viswanathan

Cartoons: Rich Tennant (www.the5thwave.com)

Composition Services

Project Coordinator: Heather Kolter

Layout and Graphics: Carl Byers, Brooke Graczyk, Stephanie D. Jumper, Christine Williams

Anniversary Logo Design: Richard Pacifico

Proofreaders: Laura Albert, Aptara

Indexer: Aptara

Publishing and Editorial for Consumer Dummies

Diane Graves Steele, Vice President and Publisher, Consumer Dummies

Joyce Pepple, Acquisitions Director, Consumer Dummies

Kristin A. Cocks, Product Development Director, Consumer Dummies

Michael Spring, Vice President and Publisher, Travel

Kelly Regan, Editorial Director, Travel

Publishing for Technology Dummies

Andy Cummings, Vice President and Publisher, Dummies Technology/General User

Composition Services

Gerry Fahey, Vice President of Production Services

Debbie Stailey, Director of Composition Services

Contents at a Glance

Table of Contents

Introduction

*I*ndia is on the minds of many people all over the globe. The dizzying growth of several Asian economies has the business world standing up and taking notice, and India is one of the most promising prospects. Doing business in India is a top priority for many individuals and organizations, and if you're going to succeed in India, you have to survive in an environment very different from your own. No matter where you come from or where you have been, nothing is exactly like India.

I've written *Doing Business in India For Dummies* to help anyone who's interested in professional interaction with India. I want to help you make the most of your business's time in India, to help you prepare and plan, and to give you a better chance of success in a vibrant, booming economy. I offer you the Indian insights that I've gleaned as an insider and heard from the foreigners whom I've helped to spread their businesses to India with outstanding results.

About This Book

No book on doing business in India can tell you everything you need to know about the topic (unless it's so massive that you need an Indian elephant to haul it). In this book, I don't even try to be exhaustive. Instead, I offer a guide to the basics, including a bevy of useful information that you can really use as you make your Indian business plans. Are you wondering what works in India? How can you start up an operation there? How do you decide on a good location for your business? What do you need to know to manage an Indian team? Well, never fear; I tackle these questions and many more.

Each chapter is divided into sections, and each section contains information about some part of conducting business in India. Highlights include the following:

- How to create an effective business plan for your Indian venture
- What to consider when choosing an appropriate entity for your Indian business
- How to train your Indian team

- ✔ Where to find invaluable resources for setting up and growing your business
- ✔ What to expect as far as the broad rules and regulations that govern business in India
- ✔ How to communicate with your Indian colleagues, partners, and employees

This book distills the knowledge gained by many foreigners who have done business in India and also describes the tactics used by Indian residents who've succeeded in the thriving Indian economy. This combination of experiences is invaluable, and I hope it makes the prospect of doing business in India more manageable for you.

Conventions Used in This Book

The following conventions are used throughout the book to make things consistent and easy to understand:

- ✔ All Web addresses appear in `monofont`. Please note that at times a Web address may be long and may break over two lines. If this occurs, make sure to type the address in your Web browser exactly as it appears in the book without including extra spaces at the end of a line.
- ✔ New terms and Indian words appear in *italics* and are closely followed by an easy-to-understand definition.
- ✔ **Bold** text is used to highlight the important concepts of bulleted lists and the action steps of numbered lists.
- ✔ When I refer to Indian money, I use abbreviations. Rupees is abbreviated *Rs,* and it's always placed as before the numbers. For example, 700 rupees reads as Rs 700. For more about money, see Chapter 9.
- ✔ In this book you come across the terms *West* (a location) and *Westerner* (a person). I use the term *Westerner* as a more polite alternative for the word *foreigner,* which can carry negative connotations. My aim is surely not to offend anyone! The terms *West* and *Westerner* apply to anyone who's non-Indian (Americans, Easterners, Asians, and so on). I think of a Westerner as someone who's not of Indian origin, who lives and/or works in or with India.

What You're Not to Read

These *For Dummies* books are organized in a way that you don't have to read the whole thing. You can get in and get out and not have to wade through a bunch of information that you may not need. Actually, I'd love for you to read every word of this book, but if you don't, I've organized the text so you're able to find information easily and easily understand what you find.

I want to believe that you'll find every word fascinating, but I'm willing to cut you some slack if you're inclined to skip around. If you're going to jump around, keep in mind that although interesting, the sidebars sprinkled throughout the text aren't essential to your understanding of the material. Sidebars are contained within shaded boxes, and they often contain personal stories and other observations.

Foolish Assumptions

I wrote this book with some preconceived ideas about you, the reader, in mind. I've assumed the following:

- ✔ You want to do business in India.

- ✔ You're interested in doing business within India, or possibly planning to do it remotely.

- ✔ You're looking for opportunities and solutions so you can conduct your business effectively.

- ✔ You have little or no background knowledge on how to do business in India.

- ✔ You want a book that explains Indian business in simple terms — a book that you can easily understand and put to good use.

- ✔ You want some practical advice with do's and don'ts.

- ✔ You may already be doing business in India, but you want to expand it or look at more effective ways to continue.

- ✔ You don't have too much time to figure out the intricacies, and you need useful information — fast.

- ✔ You want to build positive and lasting Indian relationships and want to avoid faux pas.

How This Book Is Organized

This book is organized in such a way that you can read it either in parts or as a whole. If you're particularly interested in a specific area — say, the nitty-gritty of setting up a business in India — you'll find it all in one part (Part I). If you're aware of the basic requirements, but you need to know how to conduct yourself and your business in the most efficient way, you can find that information in a different part (Part IV), and so on.

Part I: Brushing Up on India Business Basics

In this part, I cover the past and current foundations of business in India. I include information about the ways that India has been doing business with the world for centuries. Then I focus on India's lively business climate today, and how the people and the land itself contribute to the growing economy. Also featured is information on the important ways that India has changed in recent years and how those changes basically equate to a big, wide-open door for foreign businesses and investment to enter the country.

Part II: Getting Your Business Up and Running

In the second part of the book, I take you through the various processes that you need to understand when getting your business started. I talk about the various business entities you can choose from and the basic rules that govern each. You have many choices to make — choosing a location, deciding what to include in your business plan, selecting your Indian team — and I offer helpful tips and guidance on how to make those decisions. I also give you an overview of money matters that are native to India and provide ideas on how best to deal with the powers that be (so you can avoid problems at all cost).

Part III: Going About Your Business in India

This part deals with the issues and concerns that you face after you get the ball rolling. I discuss India's strengths and idiosyncrasies in various fields, including marketing and manufacturing, and give you insight into the tactics and methods that work in India. (And, of course, the ones that *don't* work.) The combination of advice and examples from the collective experience of many who have walked the Indian business path before you makes it much easier for you to focus on the important aspects of running and growing your business in the country.

Part IV: Ensuring an Indian Success Story

Success in India doesn't always depend on cold, hard business logic. Success is also to a large extent about people skills and perspective. You may at times think that you've made an unwise decision by coming to India, suffering from culture shock and having difficulties managing or working with your Indian team. These types of problems have been the demise of many, but reading this part allows you to see many of those problems in advance and take steps to make sure they don't have a negative impact on you and your business. You also discover how to understand and relate to Indians better, getting key skills to work in such a unique country.

Part V: The Part of Tens

In this part, I give you some easy-to-digest tips on several topics. These areas include how to avoid treading on cultural toes, how to best manage your Indian workforce, and how to enjoy India's many wonders when you have a bit of downtime carved out during your visit. (It's not *all* about work, you know!) I also share with you the wisdom of an Indian business guru who lived some 2000 years ago but whose grasp of strategy is as relevant for you today as it was for his royal protégé two millennia ago.

Icons Used in This Book

This icon appears whenever an idea or item can save you time, money, or stress when doing business in India.

Anytime you see this icon, the information contained there is important (and sometimes worth reading more than once) and worth committing to memory.

This icon flags information that clues you in on dangers and potential pitfalls of doing business in India.

The Technical Stuff icon appears next to, well, technical information and specific examples. Good reading, but can be skipped if you're in a hurry.

For more than a decade I've run a relocation company that's helped thousands of people from 72 nationalities make their way in India. As a result, I'm able to condense the shared wisdom from hundreds of business associates into useful bits of essential knowledge that can make your business's entry into India a more rewarding and enjoyable experience. That information and wisdom is what you find attached to this icon.

Where to Go from Here

The great thing about this book is that it has been written with you in mind, as you stand on the cusp of a new business venture in an extraordinary foreign country. But I don't know what you already know or which areas you're particularly interested in, so I leave it to you to decide where to start and what to read first. The beauty of a functional reference book like this is that you can jump in, gain useful knowledge, and jump back out. Just head to the Table of Contents or the Index to find a good place to jump in with a topic that interests you, and go for it!

If you're not sure where you want to go, feel free to start at Part I. That part starts at the beginning. That section gives you all the basic info you need to understand the business climate in India and points to places where you can find more detailed information.

Want to know about retail or manufacturing, for example? Head to Chapters 11 and 12. If you're interested in how to build relationships with Indian associates, go to Chapter 14. If you want to understand a bit more about managing an India team and human resources topics, flip to Chapter 7 or 17, which discusses many aspects of handling this most valuable resource of people that make up your business. Chapter 15 on etiquette helps you deal with Indians and culture, too.

India is a fascinating country with as much potential for foreign businesses as anywhere else in the world. And there's no better time than now to get started! So jump right into this book, and *Swagath!* — welcome to India!

Part I
Brushing Up on India Business Basics

The 5th Wave   By Rich Tennant

"It's quite a business plan, Ms. Strunt. It's the first
one I've read whose mission statement says,
'...keeps me out of trouble'."

In this part . . .

India now has the largest number of billionaires among the world's top 20 after the United States. Thirty-six Indian billionaires with a total net worth of 191 billion dollars, according to the list of richest persons compiled by *Forbes* magazine, offer the world opportunities in collaborations. Also in this world of contrasts are many millions seeking and needing your ideas, and help to accelerate their progress. Both ends of the spectrum with unique Indian benefits and challenges are discussed in this part of knowing the India basics of geography, history, and economics. Feel the pulse of India here.

Chapter 1

So You Want to Do Business with India

In This Chapter

▶ Deciding to do business in India

▶ Getting started with your Indian business venture

▶ Fostering your business's growth and ensuring success in India

▶ Securing relationships for success

For more than a decade, I've helped businesspeople from abroad come to India and understand the key factors that can play a big part in determining whether their Indian story is one of success or failure. I've worked with thousands of people, and I've heard innumerable stories. In this book, I boil down the collective experience and serve it up like a big plate of *samosas* (an Indian food — see Chapter 15 for more on food and how to eat it at an Indian business dinner).

The growth of India's economy in the last decade has been truly remarkable. What was 50 years earlier a relatively quiet country intent on remaining economically isolated has quickly developed into a world power that's predicted to continue driving the dramatic growth that many expect to be one of the defining trends of the 21st century.

Much of India's economic boom can be attributed to the influence of foreign corporations and companies. You can barely read through a newspaper today and not see a mention of an exciting foreign business that's gearing up to establish some type of Indian presence.

But what's in it for you? How can you capitalize on the continuing success of India's economy and use its many resources to grow your business? In these pages, I provide you with a primer on what India has to offer and how you can take advantage of its economic bounty. You discover what makes India's business landscape so fertile and understand the specifics of what you need to do to sow your business's seeds and harvest a bumper profit.

So read on to glean the wisdom of the trail from those folks who've traveled it before. The info's all here, and you can use it however you need to.

Making the Decision to Come to India

If you're considering the possibilities of taking your business to India, know that many have walked the path before you and succeeded. After India made the decision to liberalize it's economy — enabling foreign influences to join the economy — in the early 1990s, countless numbers of businesses and investors from abroad have come to the country and most are very glad they did. And you can enjoy the same type of success if you know what you're getting into and know what to do once you get there.

You may be wondering why so many foreign businesses have set their sights on India. Sure, the opening up of their economy is a nice development, but scores of countries throughout the world wouldn't get much action from abroad at all if they threw open the gates for foreign industry and investment. So why has everyone rushed to India? The reasons include the following:

- ✔ **India has a population of more than one billion people.** That's one of the most important factors in India's success. Plenty of people work in a huge variety of businesses, and an increasing number of people are able to spend money on products and services from foreign companies.

- ✔ **Salaries in India are often much lower than elsewhere in the world, and the quality of the work done by Indians is good.** Companies can hire Indians to do one or many different tasks, save a bundle, increase profitability, and not miss a beat in terms of quality.

- ✔ **Natural resources are abundant in India.** The raw materials needed to fuel many different areas of industry can be found within India's borders (which should come as no surprise considering the fact that India is the world's seventh largest country).

- ✔ **Indians are hardworking, often well educated, and usually have some English language skills.** Over 300 million speak English in India, which is more than the population of the entire United States (U.S.). The English language skills make India particularly attractive for Western businesses.

- ✔ **India is an ancient civilization and a young nation.** The ancient touch gives its people a calmness and the young are in the majority in India. They even predict 550 million teens in India by 2015, which means India will have a workforce and consumer base long after many other leading countries would have grown old!

This list is just a sampling of the reasons why India is booming — you can read many more details in Chapter 2. And to get an idea of how to take advantage of India's positives, check out Chapter 3.

Setting up Shop in India

Doing business in India may seem like an easy proposition. After all, much of the educated population speaks English, and the legal foundation of the country is based on established European traditions. But the Indian way of life and the Indian way of communicating may take some getting used to, which can impact how you set up and grow your business in India. The following example illustrates this point:

> Some years ago, I invited a British associate to my Indian home for a visit, and gave him directions on how to get there. After listening to the string of instructions I provided, he politely asked, "Which left turn after the Chola Hotel do I need to take?" I thought about the answer to his question, and honestly didn't know.
>
> "I'm not sure. Maybe the third or fourth left. There's a tea stall at the end of the road," I said.
>
> "All right," he said, "I'll look for a tea stall then. I hope it's open when I get there so I don't miss it. And which house on the left is yours?" Again I thought about the answer, and again I wasn't completely sure. I knew which house was mine, but I didn't know how many other houses were on the same side of my street!
>
> "Hmm, let me think. First is the Appaji apartment, then there's an independent house, then another one or is it two?" I said. "Maybe it's the fourth or fifth house. I'm just not sure. Why don't you come to the Lifestyle store, which is near my house, and I'll pick you up there?" My associate agreed but then asked me how long I'd lived in that house.
>
> "Oh, 28 years," I said, and he couldn't believe it.

That incident made me realize that not everyone in India is completely adept at giving great directions — myself included. I realized how important providing clear, succinct instructions was, and that realization has stayed with me to this day.

Focused communications are extremely important in Part II of this book, where I go into detail about the things you need to know and do to get your Indian business ready to go. Setting up shop is difficult anywhere, but doing so in India, with all its business and cultural idiosyncrasies, can be particularly tricky if you don't know what you're getting into.

The key factors for getting started in India

So what do you need to consider as you devise and implement a plan for venturing into India? Well, for one thing, you obviously need a plan! Writing a business plan for an Indian business effort can be challenging because parts of the plan are the same as they'd be anywhere else in the world, but other parts need to be specifically catered for India. How much does your plan allow for the common obstacles that you may face while in India? How does it deal with funding issues? Throughout Chapter 4, I convey the important things to consider as you write your Indian business plan.

After you have your rough plan hashed out, you have some very big decisions to make — decisions that can make or break your burgeoning Indian enterprise. For example, what should you choose as your entry method? Should you consider a liaison office, or is a joint venture (JV) more appropriate for your situation in India? Where in India (geographically speaking) should you put down your business's roots? You can save a lot of money if you make a wise decision on that front. And how on earth are you going to go about hiring Indians for your staff when you don't know where or how to look?

See what I mean about big decisions? Fortunately for you, in Chapters 5 and 7, I provide all sorts of useful information to help you make the right choices for you and your business.

Many clients come to me in the early stages of their push into India with basic concerns that, as an Indian, I'd never thought of as confusing. They had trouble with the currency system or, more commonly, the system of counting in India that's very different from how the West counts. They also had very serious questions about the legal system in India (mainly how they could avoid it!) and how they handled their taxes. Talk about serious concerns! Working with them made it clear that these nuts and bolts issues weighed heavily on the minds of those people who are still in the early stages of doing business in India, so I provide you with plenty of useful info to cover those bases throughout Part II.

Oh, and what about that "o" word? Yes, you guessed it: *outsourcing.* That's one of the things that immediately comes to mind when Westerners think about business in India, and for good reason. India has quickly become back office to the world, offering business process outsourcing solutions that truly run the gamut. Don't worry, I include plenty of material on that topic for you to digest.

The importance of preparation

You can't underestimate the importance of preparation and studying up before jumping right into something. That's never been more clear to me than after I heard a story about the dangers of not being fully prepared when a Dane I got to know tried to get some investment interests off the ground in India:

> I know this poor guy was from Denmark, on his *fifth* trip to India, still trying to find the best way in. He knew about the prospects that India had to offer, and he came to the country 18 months earlier, armed only with some rough information on how to get started. He acted based on that info and ran into hurdle after hurdle. After four futile trips, his initial enthusiasm wore thin, and he sought solace in an Indian bar. That's when he met another foreigner who, unlike him, came to celebrate a recent business success. They talked about Indian business prospects, and the Danish man immediately realized that he'd been barking up the wrong tree. To his surprise, *two* methods existed for foreign direct investment (FDI) in India, and for so long he knew about only one. He never took the time to prepare and find out more, and he spent months floundering as a result. But that tip was all he needed. He adjusted his plan, got started, and it's been smooth sailing for him ever since.

Knowing what you're getting into and making the necessary preparations is absolutely critical for getting the ball rolling on your Indian business plans, so make the most of the information I convey in Part II. You and your bottom line will be very happy you did!

Keeping Your Indian Business Healthy and Growing

Well begun is half done, as the saying goes. Once your Indian business ball is rolling, you need to do as much as you can to ensure that it keeps rolling and that the profits keep rolling in until you're rolling in rupees (Rs)!

Successfully growing and developing your business in India is somewhat similar to what you'd expect in other countries, but remember that India is in many ways a world apart. You need to have Indian business wisdom and know some tricks of the trade if you're going to keep moving forward.

For example, getting a firm grasp of the intricacies of Indian human resources can be challenging for many Westerners. Indians can think and behave very differently than people from other countries, and you must know how to take that into account when making plans for them in your business.

So building and maintaining an Indian team can be tough, and the same is true of building and maintaining a sound manufacturing presence in the country, if you're interested in that angle. Part III of this book helps keep you on the right path.

Building Relationships for Success

Understanding the ins and outs of Indian business etiquette is very useful — personal relationships are paramount when doing business in the country. You really do get just one chance to make a first impression, and it's imperative that you do the most with it when the time comes to dealing with your Indian colleagues and partners. But don't sweat the pressure. Figuring out how to work in the Indian context can be fun, as I discuss in Part IV.

And on the Indian business road, you're sure to encounter your fair share of potholes: customs problems, labor issues, contract disputes, and more. Some of it may seem daunting, but always keep in mind that difficulties exist with doing business anywhere in the world, and rest assured that the advice in Part IV can help you avoid many of the most troublesome potholes.

The importance of attitude and perseverance

As you go about your business in India, you need to remember that going to work with the right attitude and making a commitment to persevering through rough patches can go a long way. One of my NRI (non-resident Indian) friends learned this fact recently when he came back to India to work after many years of working in the United States.

He came back to his native land and found himself in a foreign work culture. Fifteen-hour shifts were commonplace, and full weekends off were a distant memory! He had to set up a $40 million plant, and every minute counted, so he worked incredibly hard and kept smiling through long days and an uncertain future. The plant launched successfully, and it all worked out in the end.

That goes to show that the right work ethic and attitude paired with a healthy dose of know-how can go a long way in ensuring success. You're responsible for the work ethic and attitude, and this book can help you with the wisdom.

Chapter 2

Understanding Breaks and Brakes in Emergent India

In This Chapter

▶ Exploring the benefits of doing business in India

▶ Keeping an eye out for possible problems

---

*I*ndia is an ancient civilization but a young country. After gaining independence from British rule in 1947, India became a Republic (in 1950) and began planning the development of its economy. At first, the country focused on import substitution and export, but gradually India's eyes turned abroad, scanning the globe for business and investment.

You may expect India, with its cultural emphasis on *dharma* or duty, to give back to the rest of the world. More than ever before, India is doing just that, and one of its greatest recent gifts is a warm invitation to do business in its burgeoning economy, which is one of the world's fastest-growing. Now the country is determined to throw open its doors and establish itself as a world economic power. Sounds promising, right? Hey, one billion Indian citizens can't be wrong.

In this chapter, I explore India's budding economy and consider its vast potential for foreign investment. I also highlight the promising possibilities and potential pitfalls of setting up shop in a country half a world away. And because working with Indian citizens is a new proposition for many, I offer insight into the strengths and challenges of the Indian workforce.

Throughout history, India has received a great deal from the rest of the world. The many international influences include the country's name, which is the result of contributions from Persia and Greece. The origin was the river Sindh in the north. The Persians, who invaded the thriving settlement on the banks of the Sindh, converted the *S* sound to an *H* and referred to it as the land of the Hindh. From Persian, the word passed into Greek, where the *H* gave way to *I,* and from that was born India (at least phonetically)!

What Makes India an Attractive Place to Do Business

With one of the most promising economies in Asia (and the world!), India is on the minds and lips of many Western business owners and entrepreneurs. You can't read or watch a piece on international business without discovering an exciting new way in which businesses from a variety of foreign countries are capitalizing on India's bullish economy. So what's it about India that's causing companies and corporations all over the globe to look at it with eager, hopeful eyes?

Taking the time to understand all the positives India has to offer is a useful way to figure out what the country can have in store for you and your business. Check out the following sections for the basic reasons behind doing business in India.

Reduced business-related bureaucracy

India didn't always have its doors thrown open wide for international businesses. Much of the success enjoyed in the last few decades can be traced to shifts in the ways that India views and treats foreign business interests.

Liberalization to the rescue

Beginning in the early 1990s, India began taking an interest in market-oriented policies. The changes made by the Indian government during that period focused on creating export capabilities and building economic stability. Successive administrations have followed suit and carried on the reform process, regardless of their political affiliations.

Since the early '90s, these continued liberalization efforts have made for a consistently high economic growth rate and easier inroads to doing business in India. The economic self sufficiency that was emphasized for many years has given way to export-led growth and imports for a large and ready consumer base.

Prior to liberalization, foreign direct investment (FDI) was restricted by ceilings on equity participation, curbs on technology transfer, export obligations, and government approvals. However, under the new open door policy, total FDI is now possible in Indian ventures in many fields, and India's doing all it can to pave the way for international businessmen.

One example of the impact of India's new stance on FDI comes from the construction industry, which was given the green light for 100 percent FDI in

March 2005. Construction is now booming for townships, built-up infrastructure, and other projects such as housing, commercial buildings, hotels, resorts, hospitals, educational institutions, recreational facilities, and city- and regional-level infrastructures. Roads, highways, airstrips — you name it and it's being built in India by international companies. Some projects are even funded by the World Bank!

Foreign investment can be channeled freely into all sectors except retail trade, agriculture, plantations, atomic energy, gas pipelines, courier services, and gambling. In most sectors, foreign investors can go through the automatic route, sort of like the green channel in customs, for which approvals aren't required. The investor is merely required to keep the Reserve Bank of India (RBI), the country's apex bank, informed of the flow of funds and issue of shares. For more details, see Chapter 5.

Less red tape, more businesses in the black

One major improvement in encouraging FDI has come from a new Indian commitment to eliminating red tape. The rules are now far simpler. For starters, complicated governmental procedures for getting permissions have been replaced with investor-friendly single window facilities in many areas.

Licensing requirements have also been simplified and many restrictions on expansion have been lifted. Accessing foreign technology in India is now far easier, and even state-owned industries in certain sectors are being opened up to private participation.

The easing of investment norms in India has throngs of quality international corporations knocking at India's door. Corporations such as IBM, Hewlett-Packard, DuPont, GE, Intel, Eli Lilly, Microsoft, DaimlerChrysler, Bell Labs and Texas Instruments have set up Research and Development (R&D) centers in India. GE's R&D center in Bangalore is their largest outside the United States (U.S.). Surprised? I was too!

A booming economy

India's economy is mushrooming. Its gross domestic product (GDP) has grown by an average of 7 percent annually since 1994. The economy grew at the rate of 8.9 percent in the first quarter of the 2006–2007 financial year, and those people in the know predict the good times to continue.

Success in the service sector is the fuel for much of India's dizzying growth. A substantial portion of its GDP comes from services, and American firms account for almost $4 billion of investment in this sphere. Growth is the best antidote to poverty and helps Indians from the low side cross over to the high, steadily in an inclusive pattern.

Evidence of India's economic potential

India's economy has more positive indicators than a Bengal tiger has stripes. The following are just a few of the many examples:

- India has the third largest investor base in the world.

- Apart from the U.S. and Japan, India is the only other country to have built a super-computer all on its own.

- The country is a supply source for a vast list, ranging from traditional products like tea to cutting-edge software.

- India is the largest manufacturer of motor-cycles in the world.

- India ranks third in biotechnology develop-ment after Australia and China.

- The Indian entertainment industry, nick-named Bollywood (Bombay + Hollywood) because it's headquartered in the city the world knows as Bombay rather than Mumbai as it was re-christened some years ago, was recently valued at close to $5 billion. The forecasted growth rate is 18 percent.

- Thomson, the French television maker, is keen to be a long-term partner in India because the company realizes the potential for the edutainment and entertainment industry is a real commitment in Indian minds. They'll have achieved their goals if they become the preferred vendor in this area. "We can't afford not to be in India," their top brass say, echoing the thoughts of most manufacturing companies in the world.

- The country is a commercial launcher of satellites for both military and communica-tion purposes, nationally and internationally.

- Crude oil refining capacity in India is cur-rently 970,000 barrels per day.

- Travel and tourism is currently a 32 billion dollar per year industry and is growing at a rapid pace. As many as 5 million (roughly the population of Colorado) tourists visited India in 2005.

- India produces about 38 million tons of steel annually.

- India has the second largest cultivatable area in the world.

- The country's pharmaceutical industry is worth $9 billion.

- The Indian road network is more than 2 mil-lion miles long, making it the second largest in the world.

All this amazing business potential rests on a low-cost, high-quality model operated by a skilled, English-speaking workforce capable of utilizing indigenous know-how and having access to world-class R&D.

Business opportunities abound

Many Westerners are familiar with elaborate Indian buffets, and India's econ-omy offers that same type of bountiful variety. The menu is bountiful: agricul-ture, textiles, manufacturing, handicrafts, and a diverse array of services. Infrastructure upgrades are undertaken at a brisk pace, and a sense of excite-ment is everywhere, boosted by a very bullish stock market, which bounces back even if it takes an occasional beating. The economy is indeed sustainable.

Although a high level of potential exists across the board, a number of industries have enjoyed a phenomenal amount of success in India in the past decade. The following list of industries have shown the fastest growth and most potential for foreign business ventures in India:

- ✔ Automobiles and auto components
- ✔ Business process outsourcing
- ✔ Communications
- ✔ Healthcare
- ✔ Hospitality
- ✔ Information technology — IT — (software and hardware)
- ✔ Infrastructure development

Based on estimates by the Federation of Indian Chambers of Commerce and Industry, the following areas are also sure to be long-term growth industries:

- ✔ Biotech and bioinformatics
- ✔ Food processing
- ✔ Metals and minerals
- ✔ Oil and gas

Special incentives and tax breaks are given for certain sectors such as power, electronics, telecom, software, hydrocarbons, R&D, and exports. These incentives differ from state to state, and the government has its own terms and conditions, too. If you're interested in exploring business opportunities in one of these industries, check out more information on policy and concessions by visiting the Web sites of each Indian state (listed in Chapter 5).

A banking system you can count on

India's extensive and efficient banking system is one of the factors that has enhanced its attractiveness in the eyes of the business world. The international big guns of banking — Deutsche Bank, Citibank, HSBC, and more — all have major operations in multiple locations in India.

Since liberalization efforts began, many positive changes have occurred in the Indian banking sector. A wide variety of services are now available under the current banking systems. Investors can find a range of different types of accounts and loans, easy access to plastic money, and a smooth path to international transfers. The banks are fully aware of the potential, and they make doing business a breeze for investors.

The law of the land

The Indian legal system is based on English common law, a vestige from India's time as a British colony. Familiar to most Westerners, this system simplifies the business process for many entrepreneurs for whom an understanding of local law is a necessity.

Even if you're armed with a basic understanding of Indian law, you can still run into a sticky legal situation. Be sure to talk to others who've walked this trail before you, read the fine print, watch out for multiple interpretations, and involve local experts when necessary. (See Chapter 7 for more information on using consultants.)

Open foreign policy

India adopted an international policy of non-alignment soon after it earned independence from British rule. This policy dictates that India doesn't cast its lot with any major international bloc.

A non-alignment policy is an advantage for India from a business perspective. It allows companies from countries like the U.S., China, Saudi Arabia, Israel, Cuba, Burma, and South Africa — a politically explosive cocktail in most other contexts — to operate with equal ease in the gigantic Indian business melting pot.

A favorable time zone and geographic location

India's time zone and geographic location are also in its favor and have made the country even more attractive post-liberalization. An office located in India can, during working hours, communicate and conduct business with Australians in the morning, Europeans in the afternoon, and Americans at the end of the day. Who needs 80 days when you can go around the world in an eight-hour workday?

Although India spans roughly 1,200 miles from east to west, the entire country uses only one time zone: Indian Standard Time (IST). The difference between Greenwich Mean Time (GMT) and IST is five and a half hours. Yes, five and *a half!* India shares this oddity with Iran and parts of Australia. The reason? Put simply, India had to straddle two time zones and it chose to split the difference!

India on the mind

Recently, leading players had interesting things to say about business in India. Check out these quotes:

✔ "India is an emerging market, one of the fastest growing markets. It has displayed consistent growth, its huge middle class has great purchasing power, and the retail sector is set to change consumer behavior here. Its hardworking and educated workforce gives the country an edge." — Mr. Lakshmi Narayanan of Cognizant, leading IT player, won the best small companies of America award and rang the NASDAQ bell remotely from India.

✔ "India has sustained advantages and offers a long-term competitive edge. Its strengths in the IT and BPO (Business Process Outsourcing) sectors are well known; there's been a revolution in the manufacturing sector, and investments have been flowing in, particularly in the automobile and auto component sectors." — Mallika Srinivasan, Head of Tractors and Farm Equipment, awarded Woman Entrepreneur of India by Economic Times.

✔ "India's exuding confidence. The GDP is consistent; forex [foreign-exchange market] reserves are good. The quality and stability of the government is an advantage. People show a willingness to adapt; they're flexible. Keeping to time is of course a problem, but if you persist, output will happen." — Sreeram Iyer, Head of Scope International (Standard Chartered Bank's BPO).

✔ "There's a good measure of political stability here. The UPA (United Progressive Alliance) is a stable alliance, the Common Minimum Program is holding, and we have a fine Prime Minister; he has enormous experience, and he's a big asset." — N. Ram, Editor in Chief, *The Hindu,* among India's leading newspapers with over a million circulation.

The country shares borders with Pakistan, Bhutan, Nepal, Bangladesh, Myanmar, Tibet, and China. In terms of transport logistics, the location is outstanding. Add to this 334 (and counting) serviceable airports, 12 of which are international. Top it off with a vast coastline of more than 4,300 miles, hugging large and small ports, and India becomes an intriguing central cog in a worldwide supply-chain model.

A billion reasons to set up shop in India

India is packed with not only opportunities but also with people! With a population of more than one billion, India is the world's second most populous country (after China). And it's still growing at the rate of 1.38 percent each year!

Up and coming portions of the population

The population's age demographics can be segmented as follows:

- ✓ 0-14 years old = 31%
- ✓ 15-64 years old = 64%
- ✓ over 65 years old = 5%

That colossal middle segment of the population includes the prime working age range, meaning that India has a truly enormous workforce from which the rest of the world can draw.

In addition, what's intriguing to marketing experts is that the median age is 25 years! Women make up 48.6 percent of the total population, according to World Bank statistics for 2004. And women account for 28 percent of the Indian workforce, which is 427 million strong! Each year, more and more women join the salary ranks, which means more power — spending and otherwise — for the fairer sex. Can you see the marketing opportunities opening up?

India's burgeoning population was once a major source of concern, because planners feared that the growing millions would overwhelm its economic resources. But with India's focus on a strong, stable economy, its population annoyance has turned to an advantage.

They speak English

An unbelievable variety of languages and dialects are spoken in India. They vary from state to state and from district to district within each state. The constitution recognizes 23 languages, including Hindi, Bengali, Gujarati, Marathi, Kannada, Tamil, Telugu, Malayalam, and Urdu (not to mention English). Each language has its own script. In a world where communication is one of the most important keys to success, the language barrier may seem an insurmountable problem. But that's not the case, however, and the reason is that Indians can communicate effectively in English. This spoken English with the language of digits sets Indians well on the road to growth.

The English skills of India's population are far better than most Asian countries, again due to the long period India spent as a British colony. English is the business language and is also used for most government communications. This advantage is huge to Westerners wanting to set up shop in India.

You still may have difficulty understanding some of your Indian business partners. While most professionals are proficient in English, other people on the job may not be as fluent. Check out "Breaking through the language barrier" later in this chapter for tips on communicating effectively.

They've hit the books

The intelligence of Indians is a no-brainer. They have a well-deserved reputation for excelling in the fields of technology and mathematics. And Indians are also renowned for their driven, ambitious nature.

I have often been asked, "Why don't Indians dislike Westerners even though they were under British rule for centuries?" Indians know they have the British to thank for their outstanding educational system. India has a well-organized system with internationally recognized excellence in certain areas of higher education. Over 250 universities and in excess of 13,000 higher educational institutions exist in India. This mammoth system generates nearly 2.5 million graduates each year, including more than 300,000 engineers and 150,000 IT professionals. India boasts the world's largest pool of IT professionals, and the second largest amount of scientists, engineers, and accountants.

Although the overall number of graduates is high, not all are readily employable. Soft skills, communication, and the ability to apply theory to practical work situations are areas that sometimes require additional training.

In India's version of the Ivy League, the top schools are the Indian Institutes of Technology (IIT) and the Indian Institutes of Management (IIM), which today symbolize internationally recognized excellence. Graduates from both institutes are highly sought after and typically command substantial salaries upon entering the working world.

University-based research in India is also world class. India has over 1,500 research facilities, and just about every cutting edge technology known to humankind is represented. For example, stem cell research in India is today among the most advanced in the world.

When you advertise for an open position, thousands of résumés may pour in and sifting through them can be a monumental task. Consider using a placement agency for your Indian hires. (For more details, see Chapter 7.)

Silicon Valley, India

Bangalore, in southern India, has developed a well-deserved reputation as a global IT center. Bangalore alone boasts 150,000 IT professionals, as compared to about 120,000 in California's Silicon Valley. A quick drive around the city (or others in the south like Hyderabad or Chennai) reveals many sleek glass and steel structures, dotting India's IT corridors. Many of the world's major IT corporations — including Microsoft, Google, and IBM — have a major presence in Bangalore, and others join the ranks all the time.

They're returning from abroad with a world of experience and expertise

According to World Bank statistics from 2000, 1.04 million Indian-born people educated past secondary school lived in the world's 30 richest countries. The brain drain was a major problem for India. These educated young Indians were lured overseas by high salaries and incomparably high standards of living, not to mention superior research facilities. But thanks to dramatic improvements at home, the tide is slowly turning.

A few years ago, it would've seemed hard to imagine that Indians who'd enjoyed a taste of life in the West would want to return home. But that's exactly what's happening now. The non-resident Indian (NRI) finds that not only have living conditions improved beyond recognition back home, but also his salary goes much further here. (Not to mention the appeal of being able to raise his kids in the vibrant culture of his origin.)

These returning NRIs are extremely attractive from a business standpoint. They're well equipped to identify new market opportunities, raise capital, build work teams, and establish partnerships both locally and overseas. They're able to help Westerners better understand the Indian way of doing business. If you happen to meet a NRI, consider how he can fit into your Indian business plan!

For Indian entrepreneurs, these "foreign-returned" professionals represent new sources of skill, technology, and capital and serve as role models and mentors. They provide insight into the methods of working — the structure and discipline — of a Western business. They also provide the momentum necessary for the Indian businessman to move out of the traditional and hierarchical business pattern into a more flexible and profitable, albeit risky mode.

The returning Indian professional is also invaluable to domestic policymakers, who can pick his brain to make financial and regulatory bodies as well as infrastructure more attractive to the foreign investor.

Worldwatch on India

The Worldwatch Institute is a Washington, D.C.-based research group that focuses on social and environmental concerns. In its 2006 State of the World report, Worldwatch said, "The dramatic rise of China and India presents one of the gravest threats — and greatest opportunities — facing the world today. The choices these countries make in the next few years will lead the world either toward a future beset by growing ecological and political instability — or down a development path based on efficient technologies and better stewardship of resources." Take these words of wisdom to heart and make efforts to ensure that your dealings in India have a positive impact on the social and environmental situations there.

Potential Pitfalls

The outlook for doing business in India is grand, and although the positives far outweigh the negatives, concerns can develop into problems for your Indian business ventures. Many of these concerns are merely growing pains, which will lessen as India continues to settle into its role as an international economic powerhouse.

In this section, I explain two of the major hindrances to doing business in India and offer help on how to make these problems turn into pebbles, not potholes, on your business road to India.

Cutting through the remaining red tape

Although much progress has been made in reducing business-related bureacracy, some processes are still slow and several are the subject of political debate. Many paths are clear, but yours may still involve a trail of paperwork!

Don't be discouraged by the bureaucracy. Although certain hoops, such as obtaining electricity connections, environmental clearances, and land approvals can be difficult to jump through, the red tape is less of a hindrance in India than in other parts of the world. See Chapter 8 for tips on how to deal with Indian bureaucracy.

According to a recent study conducted by the global consultancy firm Grant Thornton International, India's red tape is no worse than China's and is actually much less problematic than Europe's.

Each year, the end of February marks the announcement of the annual budget. At this time the Indian governmental rules and policies on key issues may change. Pencil this date (February 28th or 29th) into your calendar, and remember that you may need to make adjustments in early March.

Breaking through the language barrier

The literacy rate in India averages about 60 percent (this rate is defined by using anyone above the age of 15 who can read and write). Although this rate can be better, the Indian government is taking steps to improve the literacy rate, including a massive campaign called *Sarva Siksha Abhiyan* (education for all) that launched in 2000. The goal of that effort is to achieve universal primary literacy in India by the year 2010, and the government is investing heavily to build new schools, upgrade existing facilities, recruit and train more teachers, and revise syllabi.

You can also find several levels of English language proficiency:

- ✔ The top level consists of well-educated Indians with English as a language of instruction. They speak, act, and think in English. They speak English at home and use their mother tongue only with older family members.

- ✔ The next level doesn't speak English at home and has various accented intonations with a different speed of speech.

- ✔ Indians from regional language schools (schools where the local language is taught and English can be a bit of an afterthought) find English a challenge because they tend to translate conversation to Indian languages in their heads, formulate a response, and translate back into English before speaking.

- ✔ The "man in the street" understands, and responds with varying degrees of proficiency in English.

The English language abilities of Indians are improving all the time. Indian industries are spending considerable time and resources to improve cross-cultural communications to create more global Indians. You can cash in on their efforts when you find a sharp, receptive pool of Indian partners and employees.

Although you may be distracted initially by the language problem of Indian accents coming through in English, don't let this issue be an obstacle. With a little practice and patience, you can understand and make yourself understood easily. If you want to hurdle the language barrier, check out the following tips:

- ✔ **Adapt to accents temporarily.** When you notice that the locals pronounce a word in a particular way, temporarily adopting their pronunciation can sometimes be simpler, even if you know it's wrong. It may also be useful to use a word that's of Indian origin. For example, asking an Indian if you can *prepone* a meeting is more easily understood than asking them to *advance* the same meeting.

- ✔ **Allow others to tune in their ears.** Indian English requires you to retune your ear, but your listeners are likely to find it just as tough to figure out your accent. Slow down and have patience. Stressing all syllables and avoiding lazy pronunciations can help a great deal.

- ✔ **Ask for confirmation.** Don't presume that the listener understood your meaning. This case is especially true of requests. When you finish giving a set of instructions, don't hesitate to ask for the information to be repeated. For example, after asking your assistant to take a CD to the office manager, ask, "What are you going to do?"

Communicate ASAP (as simply as possible)

In India, simplicity and brevity are key when conveying a point across the language barrier. Following a new accent and a new vocabulary can be tough, but if you keep your language simple and your instructions short and to the point, you're more easily understood. Don't talk down to your Indian counterparts, but do what you can to keep it simple. This example illustrates how one long-winded businessman from Leicester learned his lesson:

> I had some copies to make, so I asked Ramu, my office boy, "Do you have a lot to do now, or would you mind terribly making a copy of this report for me Ramu?" (22 words)

> Ramu looked at me blankly. Yesterday, Mary, my Indian secretary, who'd hired him, had said he understood English and spoke it. So why was he giving me this look now?

> "Again, sir please," he said tentatively.

> "Oh, I'm sorry. I just asked if it would be okay for you to please take a Xerox copy of this report now?" (23 words)

> "Why sorry Sir? Nothing wrong!" he exclaimed with a look of horror.

> "No, no, nothing wrong, I just wanted a copy of this taken, but don't bother, I'll get Mary to do it."

> "Madam gone out for lunch Sir. We have copier here," he said with a smile.

> "Yes — could I have this copied please?" (7 words)

> "Oh, Sir want copy?"

> "Yes, that's what I was wondering."

> "Sir? Copy?"

> "Please?"

> "Copy wanting?"

> "Yes pleasing, I mean please."

> Off he went, carrying the report I had wasted so many words on, and was back in the wink of an eye, with a Xeroxed copy. Ramu continued to work with us throughout my stay in India, and I figured out not to use my long British sentences . . . "Ramu, copy please." Three words did the trick!

If you can be mindful of the language barrier and take simple steps to overcome it, you quickly see that it's more of a speed bump than a major obstacle.

✔ **Differentiate yes from no.** When body language is confusing and you don't know if your staff just nodded yes or no, it's completely acceptable to ask again for confirmation. For example: "Will you come to work tomorrow? Please say yes or no." It's better to be clear instead of getting what you didn't expect.

✔ **Prune down your sentences.** Use short sentences with easily understood words. Instead of saying, "What education system do you follow for your children?" ask, "Which school do your children go to?"

✔ **Speak the lingo.** Some words have connotations that may be different from those you're used to back home. For example, to *table* something in many Western contexts means to put it on hold. But in India *tabling* something means that it's presented or dealt with immediately.

✔ **Tune in your ear.** To get used to the local accents, listen very carefully. Indian languages, especially southern ones, are spoken at high speed. The tongue is used in all sorts of ways for special sounds in dialects like Tamil, Telugu, and Malayalam. English spoken by Indians whose native language is one of these dialects includes some strange sounds. Listen carefully and soon you can hear a pattern. For example, *M* and *N* are pronounced as *yem* and *yen.*

Chapter 3

Making Sense of India: A Business Viewpoint

In This Chapter

▶ Understanding the influences of geography on business in India

▶ Studying how the economic past shaped present-day business

▶ Ordering the communities in India

▶ Realizing the potential of India's diverse classes

You may imagine India as an exotic land of coconut trees and mountains, tigers and snakes. And then you hear of poverty, dirt, and disease in India. So why's the business world suddenly flocking to this place? Because the country is booming! It's a vast land with varied geography, plentiful resources, and a unique history of commerce. Sure, the challenges are diverse, but as a business destination India looks good!

To make a success of your business venture in India, you need to understand the inner workings of India: its land, its people, and even parts of its past. The country is made up of so many pieces, but once you have an idea of how the pieces fit together, making savvy business decisions is a cinch!

This chapter helps you put together the vibrant jigsaw puzzle that's India, so you can zero in on just the right focus for your business.

Getting the Lay of the Land

Give the globe a twist, twirl to Asia, and look at the lower end of the continent. And there you see that India stretches down into the Indian Ocean, toward the equator in the northern hemisphere. India is an immense country (more than 1.2 million square miles) comprising many different geographic regions. The triangular part of the country is India's Deccan Plateau. The lands of India rise from the ocean to that plateau and on up to the majestic

Himalayas in the north. Its various landscapes and resources can support a breadth of industries, and the players in those industries that take full advantage of what India has to offer can truly flourish.

India shares extensive land boundaries with its neighbors Bangladesh, Bhutan, China, Nepal, and Pakistan. India's coasts are lapped by the waters of the Arabian Sea, the Indian Ocean, and the Bay of Bengal. In total, India has over 4,300 miles of coastline. The massive coastline leaves plenty of room for major ports, and India has 11 of them, creating an attractive port capacity for shipping.

But don't let India's size worry you about transportation and shipping concerns. The country has an excellent rail transport system, built on the backbone of the tracks laid by the British during the colonial era. Freight can also be transported to the farthest nook and the highest reaches of India by long stretches of roadways reaching from Kashmir in the north to Kanyakumari in the south, and from Gujarat in the west to the eastern states of Assam and Manipur.

Pointing out the geographic regions of India

India's landscape is a fascinating mix of different terrain. The country can be divided into the following geographic regions:

- **Coastal plains:** Between the Western Ghats and the Arabian Sea is a rich coastal plain, which makes up most of the state of Kerala.

- **The Deccan plateau:** The Vindhya range of mountains bisects the country, and the southern part, peninsular India, is geologically the oldest area. The original inhabitants of the land, the Dravidians, were pushed back by the invading Aryans in the North and settled here. The Dravidian language of Tamil is among the oldest in the world, arguably also the fastest spoken.

- **The Himalayan mountain range:** The Himalayan mountain range in the north has some of the highest peaks in the world. However, contrary to popular belief, the world's highest mountain — Mount Everest — is *not* in India. (It lies within the borders of neighboring Nepal.) These mountains are interspersed with plateaus and valleys and account for about a sixth of India's total land area.

- **Thar Desert:** In the west of India lies the great Thar Desert, contained primarily in the state of Rajasthan.

- **The Indo-Gangetic Plain:** This area lies in central India and is a great flat stretch of one of the richest deposits of sedimentary soil in the world. This soil is delivered by three mighty rivers: the Sind (now known as the

Indus), the Ganga or Ganges, and the Brahmaputra. Each of these rivers traverses the region, and some of the most important historic and economic development of India took place here. It is one of the most densely populated and intensely cultivated regions in the world.

✔ **Western and Eastern Ghats:** The Deccan plateau is flanked by the Eastern and Western Ghats — mountain ranges that meet in the south in the Nilgiris or Blue Mountains.

India's geographic diversity makes it a tour operator's dream. Visitors to India can scuba dive in the Andamans, bump along on a camel safari in the Thar desert, drift on houseboats along Kerala's waterways, and even ski on the snow clad slopes of Kashmir. You can take advantage of this while you're in India on business (see Chapter 10 for more info on enjoying your stay in India) or *as* your business: Tourism and hospitality are two of India's fastest growing industries!

Discovering India's 28 great states

India has 28 states and 7 union territories or centrally administered territories. The states are divided according to linguistic distinctions, and consequently some are large and others small, some are highly industrialized, others rural. Some are highly developed and literate, and others still have some way to go in this respect.

Here are a few interesting tidbits:

✔ India's commercial capital, Bangalore in the southern Indian state of Karnataka, is India's answer to the Silicon Valley.

✔ The southern Indian state of Kerala was the first among Indian states to achieve 100 percent literacy.

✔ In the northeast, the bunch of seven states known as the seven sisters are largely undeveloped and their people retain their tribal legacy to a large extent.

✔ West Bengal in the east has a communist political atmosphere and is a cultural goldmine.

✔ Rajasthan in the west is a desert state, a land of history and courage.

✔ Up in the north, the mountain state of Jammu and Kashmir is a tourist paradise and also the source of a border dispute between India and Pakistan.

For more information on India's states, check out Table 3-1.

Table 3-1			An Overview of India's States		
States	**Capital**	**Language**	**International Airports**	**Industries**	
Andhra Pradesh	Hyderabad	Telugu	Hyderabad	Automobile manufacturing, pharmaceuticals, Information Technology (IT), textiles, mineral mining	
Arunachal Pradesh	Itanagar	Monpa, Miji		Oil and Natural Gas, Tourism	
Assam	Guwahati Guwahati,	Assamese, Bodo		Tea, Handicrafts	
Bihar	Patna	Hindi, Bihari			
Chhattisgarh	Raipur	Hindi		Iron and steel, cement, rice	
Goa	Panaji	Konkani	Vasco da Gama	Fisheries, mining, electronics, handicrafts	
Gujarat	Gandhinagar	Gujarati	Ahmedabad	IT, pharmaceuticals, biotechnology, jewelry, textiles, tourism	
Haryana	Chandigarh	Hindi		Electronics, automobile manufacturing, IT, medical equipment	
Himachal Pradesh	Shimla	Hindi, Pahari		Agriculture, horticulture, tourism	
Mizoram	Aizaw	Mizo, English			
Jharkhand	Ranchi	Hindi		Iron and steel, cement, coal, ceramics	
Jammu and Kashmir	Srinagar	Dogri, Kashmiri		Tourism, handicrafts, textiles	
Karnataka	Bangalore	Kannada	Bangalore	IT, electronics, telecommunications, automobile manufacturing, textiles	

States	Capital	Language	International Airports	Industries
Kerala	Thiruvananthapuram	Malayalam	Thiruvananthapuram, Kochi	Marine products, textiles, spices, minerals, software biotechnology, rubber, tourism
Madhya Pradesh	Bhopal	Hindi		biotechnology, produce, tourism
Maharashtra	Mumbai	Marathi	Mumbai	Automobile manufacturing, textiles, food processing, leather, floriculture
Manipur	Imphal	Manipuri		Agriculture, horticulture, handicrafts, tourism
Meghalaya	Shillong	Khasi, Garo		Cement, horticulture, agriculture-based industries, minerals
Nagaland	Kohima	Ao, Konyak, Angami, Sema and Lotha		Farming, petroleum, handicrafts, tourism
Orissa	Bhubaneshwar	Oriya		Pharmaceuticals, aluminum, gems and jewelry, petrochemicals, automobile manufacturing
Punjab	Chandigarh	Punjabi	Amritsar	Agriculture, animal husbandry, electronics, pharmaceuticals, white goods, textiles, machinery
Rajasthan	Jaipur	Hindi, Marwari, Mewari		Mineral-based industries, tourism
Sikkim	Gangtok	Nepali		Liquor and tourism

(continued)

Table 3-1 (continued)

States	Capital	Language	International Airports	Industries
Tamil Nadu	Chennai	Tamil	Chennai	IT, pharmaceuticals, textiles, automobile and auto component manufacturing, mineral-based industries, leather, chemicals, petrochemicals
Tripura	Agartala	Bengali, Tripuri, Manipuri, Kakborak		Rubber, horticulture
Uttar Pradesh	Lucknow	Hindi		Agriculture, horticulture, textiles, engineering goods, leather
Uttarakhand	Dehradun	Hindi		Biotechnology, food processing, tea, tourism
West Bengal	Kolkata	Benagli	Kolkata	Jute, automobile manufacturing, pharmaceuticals, chemicals, aluminum, ceramics

Tsunami!

India was among the countries in the path of the brutal tsunami that struck Asia on December 26, 2004 and left a horrifying trail of death and destruction. As one of the most devastating natural disasters in history, the tsunami had a considerable impact on much of the continent, including India's coast. The eastern and southern coastal areas were hit the hardest. Despite the damage, however, India was fortunate to rally quickly from the disaster, and the country's strong economy scarcely missed a step.

Feeling the weather in India

India has a tropical climate, largely speaking. But of course, India has a myriad of weather conditions — brilliant sunshine, freezing snow, a heavy downpour, or a great howling storm. Because many businesses can benefit or suffer from different kinds of weather, this section touches on a few Indian climate tidbits to keep in mind.

The four seasons in India

India's climate features four seasons with one different one from the West. India doesn't really have fall or autumn as a distinctive time. India has spring, summer, monsoon, and winter. Generally speaking, the northern half of the country is prone to extreme temperatures, with temperatures over 104°F in the summer and plunging to around 40°F in the winter. In the south, as you get closer and closer to the equator, the weather is much more consistent. It stays pretty hot in that part of India, and the joke is that there are only three seasons in the south: hot, hotter, and hottest!

The rainy season

The monsoon is India's most dramatic season. The skies scowl at you and lob thunderclaps and lightning bolts, while drenching you with torrential rains. Two kinds of monsoon winds exist in India:

- ✔ The **southwest monsoon** blows in from the sea to the land from June to September.

- ✔ The **northeast monsoon** moves in the reverse direction between October and November.

These monsoons cause considerable disruption to normal life, particularly urban life. But India's economy can soar or dip on these temperamental winds. India still has a very strong agricultural base, and the prosperity of virtually all the country's crops depends on the monsoon rains — their punctuality as well as their abundance. So pay close attention when the weathermen make predictions on the life of India's next monsoon.

Understanding India's Economic History

India can lay claim to one of the world's oldest civilizations, and its economic history is truly long and complicated. The present can't be divorced from the past, and you can better understand today's India if you have an idea of where it came from, economically speaking. This section focuses on the history of economy and trade in India.

India's beginnings and pre-colonial times

India is ancient. The Indus Valley civilization, an urbanized society that thrived between 2800 BC and 1800 BC, was economically very sound. The city-states of Mohenjo, Daro, and Harappa were well-planned and apparently carried on a flourishing trade with other civilizations like the Mesopotamians, Sumerians, and Egyptians. So doing business with foreign countries is nothing new to India.

Rudimentary forms of today's corporations also developed in ancient India. These corporations were known as *nigams, sangams,* and *srenis* and were basically organizations of merchants and traders common from around the 8th century BC to the 10th century AD. They covered virtually every aspect of business life.

Throughout India's early history, a number of empires and dynasties rose and fell. Economically speaking, the most notable dynasty was the Mauryas. They united most of the subcontinent between 321 and 185 BC. The Mauryas established a common currency, and trade flourished.

The Maurya dynasty owes its existence to a man named Chanakya, scholar-politician, who wrote a renowned book on the science of material gain called *Arthasasthra.* This early economic whiz is still talked about today (and you can find out more about him in Chapter 19).

Under the Mauryas, ancient India had numerous private commercial bodies dedicated solely to commerce. The Mauryas introduced the world to Indian products like muslin, calico, the pashmina shawls of Kashmir, and exotic spices. These commodities continue to be hot ticket items in the world of trade more than 2,000 years later.

After centuries of rule by various groups, prominent among them being the Moghuls, Portuguese explorer Vasco de Gama visited India in 1498. An influx of Europeans, including the Dutch, French, and British, continued until the 17th century, when the British East India Company established itself in the country, setting in motion a chain of events that resulted in India's inclusion in the British Empire.

Colonial India: Under the Union Jack

From the self-sustaining village-centric economy it had followed in ancient times, the land had gradually moved to new and different market systems. Many rulers minted their own currency, and no common monetary system existed in the subcontinent. Trade was based on barter or on the exchange of goods for precious metals.

With crusading skill, the British soon changed things. When the British came to India, they found a traditional rural economy, driven by a strong commercial network, but it was hampered by poor technology. So they introduced infrastructure, which included building road and rail networks (many of which survive to this day, along with British names for streets, bridges, and even townships), set up factories and communication systems to facilitate trade and commerce, and brought in a uniform currency. Trade prospered, but the balance was decidedly skewed.

The assets of the British East India Company became so huge that the British government decided to step in. India was made a colony, and Queen Victoria was named Empress of India. From a small trading outpost, India became the jewel in the British crown.

But the focus of the British was on exploiting the resources of India for its own material gain, which meant that India itself was unable to benefit from the many opportunities that opened up in the changing world order. The country remained economically backward, fettered by poverty, illiteracy, and disease. The trauma of the partition of the land into the two nations of Pakistan and India added to the burdens of an already impoverished country.

When India gained its independence in 1947, it was one of the world's poorest economies. Sixty years after independence, all that is history. Check out the next section for more information.

Post-colonial era: Independent India

India has metamorphosed beyond imagination since gaining its independence, but the change has been most dramatic in the last decade or so.

Immediately after its independence, India focused on nurturing the country's economy based on agriculture with an emphasis on self-sufficiency. The doors for international trade were mostly closed. But in the 1950s, the country faced huge trade deficits, and the problem grew with passing years. Faced with major difficulties, the government finally decided that the time had come to take a new look at policies, and it began to look outward.

The change was gradual, and even as late as 1990, India had a fixed exchange rate system, where the rupee (India's monetary unit) was dependent on the value of a basket of currencies of major trading partners. But a policy of liberalization was ushered in, and the doors to international commerce have been swinging open ever since. Check out Chapter 2 for more info on the effects of liberalization.

DISTILLED WISDOM

This is India!

Time was when an expatriate's biggest attraction in getting an India posting was the "hardship" allowance he was entitled to in view of the "hardships" he would have to endure here. Even back then, it wasn't much of a hardship to be waited on hand and foot by an army of servants and driven about in air-conditioned cars, Westerners tell me, but CEOs now line up to have first-hand experience of an India project.

Global headquarters of many companies worldwide will soon be in India, the output is becoming world class and the success model is sustainable with reduced cost wooing them continuously. Cisco has its chief globalization officer relocated and posted in Bangalore, India. Manufacturing, research and development and all such crucial departments have their top brass operating out of India. HR, finance, sales, customer support — all happen out of India across locations. This growing presence as the action shifts, and soon one-fifth of Cisco's top management will be located out of India!

One of my expatriate clients, Norm Mainland from Canada, wrote me this note:

> When I first started going to India in the mid-1990's, the phrase, "This is India," was commonly heard. It was said with a sigh, in resignation, in an attitude of acceptance, as an expletive, as an explanation and an excuse for why plans and activities had gone awry. The train is late (excessively!) — This is India. The expected visitor doesn't arrive. This is India!

> The repair is unsatisfactory — This is India!

> Telephone quality was poor; transportation and information difficult to obtain. The list went on.

> But this WAS India.

> On my most recent visit after a seven-year gap, I was astounded at how things had changed. This is India can still be said, but with pride and assertiveness. Sure, it is still a big country with many problems, but things work here!

> Society is being modernized. You can now summon an autorickshaw (a three-wheeler taxi) by calling the driver on his cell phone. There is ready access to bank machines and easy acceptance of credit cards. All this wasn't there then years ago. It was a surprise and delight to find such progress.

> "This is India," a massive country with a fantastically complex society, but a country becoming one of the economic pillars of the international world.

Classifying the Community

Despite being the world's largest democracy, India is a hierarchical society. It is a country full of complex social community structures that can be found throughout the spectrum of social and business environments.

Understanding the basics of these communities and how they're structured can be a big help as you work your way into India. In this section, I give you the rundown on India's community.

India's caste system

Many Westerners have heard of the caste system, but a thorough understanding of its ins and outs is still relatively uncommon. The next sections highlight the nitty-gritty of the caste system.

What's the caste system?

Broadly speaking, a *caste system* is a process of placing people in occupational groups and has pervaded several aspects of Indian society for centuries. Rooted in religion and based on a division of labor, the caste system, among other things, dictates the type of occupations a person can pursue and the social interactions that she may have. Castes are an aspect of Hindu religion. Other religions in India do not follow this system.

Castes and groups are ranked in hierarchical order (the origin wasn't to have any hierarchy based on occupation or birth but purely on personality, this has got skewed somehow over time), which determine the behavior of one member of society over another. Even in a modern business setting, where caste isn't an openly acknowledged issue, there may be a subtle observance of village or family-style ranking. For instance, a young official may address a senior person, not necessarily his superior, as *chachaji,* a respectful term for a paternal uncle.

How it's structured

India's caste system has four main classes (also called *varnas*) based originally on personality, profession and birth. In descending order, the classes are as follows:

- **Brahmana (now more commonly spelled Brahmin):** Consists of those engaged in scriptural education and teaching, essential for the continuation of knowledge.
- **Kshatriya:** Takes on all forms of public service, including administration, maintenance of law and order, and defense.

- ✔ **Vaishya:** Engage in commercial activity as businessmen.
- ✔ **Shudra:** Work as semi- and unskilled laborers.

The most obvious problem in this system was that under its rigidity, the lower castes were prevented from aspiring to climb higher, and, therefore, economic progress was restricted. But India is aware of the problem.

Mahatma Gandhi, the father of modern India, made the lower castes and untouchables a fifth, lowly class with the name of *Harijan* or children of God. You see many references to SC and ST in India, in newspapers, government notifications, and so on. These initials refer to Scheduled Castes and Scheduled Tribes — scheduled is what Harijan is translated into today. The government is sensitive about reserving seats in colleges and job opportunities as well for them. But the government has legislation to make up for the past suppression and oppression of the lower castes.

For more information on the emerging class structure (as opposed to caste structure), see "Diversifying India's Classes," later in this chapter.

How it works

Castes still rarely intermarry and are definitely not changeable. In urban India though, where you interact mostly in business, people of all castes meet socially or for business. Discriminating against anyone because of their caste for things like club memberships and so on is against the law. People can even be arrested for using the word *shudra* against anyone. You would do well to ignore this fact of Indian society.

Though caste and community are facts of Indian life, foreigners are not expected to behave differently toward any caste.

Business communities in India

Business communities in India are a remnant of the caste system. Certain classes and communities of people have been traditionally involved in different fields and have acquired skills in these fields, passed down from generation to generation. These communities are based not only on the caste system but also on ethnic criteria and religion because some religions were traditionally associated with different trades.

Modern day business communities are offshoots of the Vaishyas, the third of the four original major caste clusters in ancient India. Even in olden days, money was concentrated in the hands of this community. As time rolled on, the Vaishyas transformed into various manifestations and consolidated wealth and power.

People in different regions are experts in the trade and business that dominate that area. For instance, some are traditionally farmers, others are bankers, and others have a knack for doing business with overseas partners. These skills have been honed over centuries and can be leveraged with great results today.

To help you identify various business communities, pay attention to Indian surnames (last names). Surnames can tell you a lot about someone's ancestors, breeding, and background. Membership is determined by birth, not choice or payment. The following is a bird's eye view of the important business communities in India:

- **The Baniyas:** This trading community was originally concentrated along the west coast of India. They still wield power as bankers and money-lenders. Surnames here are like the Gujarati.

- **The Brahmins:** This community mainly consists of traditional priests and has turned its age-old inclination for knowledge to financial gain. Their forefathers were knowledge workers in spiritual pursuits, and they continue to be knowledge workers in information technology and finance. They're forces to contend with in these fields. Surnames such as Iyer or Iyengar in the south are common.

- **The Chettiars:** This Tamil community, traditionally merchants and money-lenders, provide the finance for newly established shopkeepers and businessmen. Surnames ending in *appan* or *aiah* are common: Meyappan, Chettiappan, Subbaiah, or Muthaiah.

- **The Christians of Kerala:** They're the leading business community of this southern Indian state. They can have anglicized last names such as Philip, Thomas, or John.

- **The Ezhavas:** In the State of Kerala, the Ezhavas, who follow a matriarchal form of society, are one of the strongest communities as far as numbers go. They've made a name for themselves as merchants, landowners, and cultivators. Panicker or Ashan are some Ezhava surnames, although they really don't use any distinctive ones.

- **The Gujaratis:** This group is essentially business minded. They've done well for themselves as businessmen abroad. The diamond trade attracted many Gujaratis to Belgium. Gujarati last names are Shah or Mehta.

- **The Jains:** This religious community is fairly widespread in India and is one of the country's most prosperous trading and business groups. They use Jain as their last names often as in the case of the family that owns India's largest newspaper — The Times of India.

- **The Jats:** Agriculturists by tradition, this community is the official farming class of Punjab. Agriculture is big business in this northern State, and the Jats are a prosperous lot. Common surnames include Chauhan or Dalal.

✔ **The Marwaris:** A community of entrepreneurs originally from Rajasthan in the north. They've now settled all over India. Commerce, finance, and industrial manufacturing are their areas of preference. The socioeconomic and sociocultural role of the Marwari community can be compared to that of the Jewish trading communities of Europe. Surname examples are Goenka or Jhaver.

✔ **The Mudaliars:** They run successful private business in Tamil Nadu. They're known to use the community title as their last names — for example, Mudaliar.

✔ **The Muslims:** In coastal India, the Islamic community has made a name for itself as traders. In the north, they've long been known for their artisanship with materials like leather, brass, glass, and silk. Modern India has seen the rise of many Muslim industrialists. Last names can include Hussain or Khan.

✔ **The Nadars:** Translates as *Lords of the land.* They're based in Tamil Nadu. Today they're primarily businesspeople and merchants, and they are universally known to be hard working. Nadar is a last name they use, such as the famous founder of HCL computers.

✔ **The Sikhs:** They constitute less than 2 percent of the population of India and are the turbaned Indians that the world sees as a stereotype. They play a disproportionately large role in the economy (and armed forces) of the country because as a community they're known for reliability and fair dealing. Punjab, their home state, has some of the best infrastructure in the country. Sikhs have an aptitude for agriculture-based or mechanically-oriented industries. Last names often end in Singh.

✔ **The Sindhis:** They're known for their business savvy. Originally from the Sindh region in the north, now mainly in Pakistan, they've made a mark in the field of textiles all over the country and abroad. Their last names often end in *ani* — for example, Thadani or Sangtani.

✔ **The businessmen from across the seas:** India has nearly always welcomed business wizards from other nations and religions. The Memons and Bohras, two foreign religious groups, and the Zoroastrians all thought India was a good place to work in. The Zoroastrians, also known as Parsees, were leading industrialists in India and the Tata family is a leading example. There are a few Jews too. They all came to trade and stayed on. That was centuries ago, and the 21st century is just as welcoming!

The joint family system

The family is by tradition a hallowed institution in India. And the family, as ancient India knew it, wasn't restricted to just a father, mother, and their children. It embraced a wide spread group of patriarchs, uncles, aunts, cousins, siblings, children, grandchildren, and great grandchildren. This extended unit is known as the *joint family,* and it functions as a very effective support system both in the personal and the business spheres.

Joint families at home are less common now, thanks to growing urbanization and a system of employment that takes younger generations away from the family hearth. But families still thrive in the world of business. For example, India's biggest business houses are family enterprises — the Tatas and Birlas.

Under the joint family system, the members of a family put their talents and resources together for the greater good of the family. In business terms, this means there's more to invest and draw from, which is a distinct advantage. The system is still fairly popular, and many of the big business houses of India subscribe to the theory of united as a family we stand. Young members of the family are given special training to keep up with the times, and the wisdom and experience of the older generation is always available.

Diversifying India's Classes

To take advantage of the opportunities in India for your business, you need to fully understand the socioeconomic diversity of the Indian population. After all, your customers, clients, colleagues, and employees all lie in this vast population.

If you've been reading this entire chapter, you may have run across the earlier section that discussed the structure of the Indian caste system (see "Classifying the Community"). The caste system is becoming less prevalent as time goes on. And in its place, India's population divides instead into classes, similar in many respects to the socioeconomic classes in the West.

Indian ties: They're bound to last

Considering India's widespread fondness for the bonds of communities, it's no surprise that family communities in India are large and tightly knit, often including a whole clan. This extended family has very strong claims on individual Indians, which can be a double-edged sword in business.

For example, Westerners may often feel frustrated by an Indian's propensity to take off for a wedding, funeral, or naming ceremony of a second cousin twice removed, located in a faraway corner of the country. These occasions may seem like questionable reasons to miss work, but in India these commitments are honored. The good news is that these community ties can be used in your favor when you need your business community — your employees — to pull together to finish a project or something similar.

If you're looking to do business in India, forget about the caste system and look at the class system, which comprises four socioeconomic classes covered in this section. Knowing each class helps you make smart business decisions about the market for your product or service or even gives you a new idea for a product you can invent for the classes specifically.

The upper crust

Members of the upper class are also called high net worth individuals (HNI). The Indian economy benefits from the foresight and generosity of the upper class. These folks are largely community oriented, and chances are they set up industries in the state of their own origin or the city where they're headquartered. The job creation and corporate social responsibility are aimed at building up their own state and community. Use this sense of loyalty to your advantage when seeking out business opportunities. A business proposition that benefits an HNI's home area can be very attractive!

Upper class Indians are also often educated overseas, and many of their children are in the process of earning foreign degrees. Many are alumni of Ivy League schools. They may be leaders of massive IT companies, manufacturers of automobiles, or owners of diverse businesses ranging from alcohol to airlines or telecommunications to oil rigs. They may also be owners of large construction houses, textile mills, or even movie producers.

The upper crust love to spend their money. Here are a couple of business areas you may want to tap into if you're considering business in India:

- ✔ **Luxury goods:** With India's upper class population spending more and more within the country, the market for luxury goods is estimated to reach $452 million in the coming years. Some examples of these types of goods include Bombardier aircraft or Louis Vuitton bags.

- ✔ **Weddings:** These occasions are lavish affairs. Some families have their children married on ships, in private jets, or even at the Palace of Versailles! The total costs can reach more than $2 million, not including the cash, jewelry, and other valuables often given as gifts on the occasion. If your business is event planning — or more specifically wedding planning — keep this goldmine in mind!

The middle layer

India's middle class has arisen mostly from the IT and BPO (Business Process Outsourcing) boom. This sector drives India's phenomenal growth. The size of India's middle class population — an estimated 300 million — exceeds the population of the United States, and represents a powerful and growing consumer market.

The earning and spending power of these people are directly proportionate to the wages paid by multinational businesses who are generous yet come out winners when they compare their Indian operating costs to the costs they face back home.

The Indian middle class includes accountants, doctors, engineers, designers, and software professionals, just to name a few. They spend their money on property, cars, computers, and devices to improve their standard of living and status in life.

Members of the Indian middle class are also

- ✔ **Consciously Indian:** They buy products that are tailored to Indian culture, so if you're planning on bringing a global name to India — in clothing, accessories, white goods, or otherwise — be sure that you're mindful of their tastes.

- ✔ **Consumer oriented:** They purchase goods in a $286 billion retail market. (Read more about retailing in India in Chapter 11.)

- ✔ **Young and gadget savvy:** The market for devices like mobile phones and personal computers is large and growing.

The worker bees

Directly below the middle class on the socioeconomic scale are the ordinary farmers, trades people, artisans, and workers. Members of this Indian working class have had some schooling, understand some English, and are industrious and quick learners.

These people live in MIG (middle income group as the government calls them) apartments in the larger cities. They often have a home base in a nearby village, and their families live there while the earning member works in the cities. The worker bees are the people who work in your factories. They're the plumbers, electricians, domestic staff, and the petty vendors on the streets. They may run their own vegetable stalls, nurse in the hospital, or teach in a government school.

To get the best for yourself and also for the members of the working class that help fuel your business ventures, do think of ways to add value to this part of the population. Remember that they may need some improvements in basic necessities like sanitation and daily supplies, and that they also like to spend on entertainment.

India's mobile phone boom

India's mobile phone market is booming: Recent estimates indicate that more than a million Indians sign up for cell phone service each month. Part of that boom can be attributed to demand among working class Indians who can easily justify the expense with an increase in earning capacity.

For example, an Indian employed as a driver earning Rs 7,000 month also runs a courier businesses that employs two boys who deliver mail door to door on bicycles. The man manages his employees via mobile phone while his full-time driving job ensures him a steady income. Or take the case of the real estate agent who lives in a cement and mud dwelling with only a motorbike to commute. He suddenly found that he could put through more deals in the seasonal business thanks to his wise investment in a cell phone.

So you can see that the market is vast for handy gadgets and devices. India is a cell phone company's paradise.

Below the poverty line

At the bottom of the scale are India's estimated 320 million poor who have no access to adequate jobs, food, shelter, or clothing. They're uneducated and often even illiterate, and the Indian government sets aside many funds for them, but the path isn't smooth in this redistribution of wealth.

If your business venture can be geared toward assisting this portion of the Indian population, you can immediately get help and benefits from the Indian government. Eight-hundred million people are said to live on less than $2 a day. Moving them up the value chain is the goal because they sharply contrast the country that also houses 36 of *Forbes* richest people.

Part II
Getting Your Business Up and Running

The 5th Wave   By Rich Tennant

In this part . . .

Y ou discover new and uncharted territory as part of doing business in India. Practically speaking, the advice here helps you handle your business all the way from scratch to a successful establishment, including tips on dealing with people and stuff that matters in between.

You figure out how to put a business plan together and start that plan successfully. You also massage the relationship of doing business from afar. Don't forget to focus on your Indian specifics — info about teambuilding, dealing with the higher Indian powers, and managing your money.

Chapter 4

Putting Together a Business Plan

· ·

· ·

So you like what you've seen and heard of India, and you want a slice of the Indian economic pie. Well, you can have it. But wait! First you have to convince the Indians to let you in on the feast. In other words, prepare a business plan, India style.

To prepare an effective plan you also need to know what works best in India. You need to get the hang of the Indian slant to business to make a plan that meets with the approval of potential partners who are able to secure loans from Indian sources, apart from the funds you bring into the country yourself. Many issues exist in the business to which you may never have thought of, but you have to negotiate them Indian style, not Western style, if you want to succeed.

In this chapter I present you with ideas on how to draw up plans for your business venture in India that both look good to the Indians you're trying to impress and work well in an environment that is unfamiliar to you.

The Importance of Creating a Business Plan

Like any journey into unfamiliar territory, your business's voyage into India can be much more successful if it has a precise map that shows where you've been, where you are, and where you're going. That map should come in the form of a well thought out business plan. Without an extensive, thoughtful plan, minor bumps in your business's journey can seem as tall as Kanchenjunga (India's highest peak).

In this section, you discover a few reasons why you should approach your Indian business plan a bit differently than you would in the West. Take note of the important factors for you in coming up with the map for your business in India, and you'll clearly understand why a business plan is so crucial to your success.

A few things to keep in mind

You may be a veteran business plan writer in your own country, having authored many success stories. But when you're working on a business plan for India, remember that you're on someone else's turf, and you have a lot to learn *and* unlearn:

- ✔ **Audience:** Study your target Indian audience thoroughly, and get to know its quirks before formulating your business plan. Market surveys, for example, can be an invaluable tool when it comes time to focus in on a particular target audience. (Check out "What need does your product or service propose to fulfill?" later in this chapter for more info on market surveys.)

- ✔ **Basic nuts and bolts stuff:** If you're writing a plan to set up a manufacturing unit at a specific place in India and market your product across the country, keep in mind different tax rates, entry rules, and varying levels of infrastructure availability in the many Indian states. This process is something you may not have to do back home. Logistics have a far greater emphasis here than in the West.

- ✔ **Language clarity:** Clarity is key. Keep in mind that your plan is used for your reference *and* to convince prospective partners and prospective financiers of the soundness of your proposed venture in India. Make sure that there's no room for misinterpretation in your wording.

A few core questions

Before you begin formulating your Indian business plan you should consider several basic key questions. These questions are covered in the sections to follow.

What's the product or service that your business proposes to provide?

Not to state the obvious, but you need to figure out what product your business provides. So what's your big idea, your grand product? That question may sound outrageously obvious, but it's one you need to take very seriously. Set out your answer clearly, whether you're thinking of a revolutionary new concept or a simple product.

For example, if you plan to start a smoothie bar in India, you should explain in your plan exactly what a smoothie is. Just because everyone is familiar with a smoothie in your part of the world, doesn't mean smoothies are as well known in India. Actually, they're not, and that could be the case with a variety of products. For all you know, an Indian reading your smoothie bar business plan may think you want to start a pub!

What need does your product or service propose to fulfill?

If you use the smoothie bar example (from the previous section), ask yourself a few questions: Does India need a smoothie bar? Will Indians go for it? How do you know? A market survey is the best way to find out.

Market surveys are very common in India. A market survey is a questionnaire that you can use to ask Indians specific questions. It speaks to a section of the target audience live, or via e-mail, and gets responses so informed decisions can be made. To carry out these surveys, you can employ young men and women to do the door-to-door asking. Then you can get management students to analyze the answers to these questions as part of their course projects; and presto! you have a market survey on which to base your business plan. If those options don't sound appealing to you, try out world class market research companies (like the Indian Market Research Bureau) who can design, administer, and evaluate such surveys.

Who are your potential customers and why do you think they'll buy your product?

To know your market culturally is key. Looking at India as your market is like looking at all of Europe with differences in language, lifestyle, dress, cuisines, and temperaments. So no generalizations truly work. The assertive and status conscious Northerner versus the low key and more traditional Southerner may well be your target audience for two completely different kinds of cars or homes or lifestyle products. Take the time to understand these subtleties, which we do in this book in Chapter 14.

When identifying your potential customers, don't put too much emphasis on vague statistics. For instance, Westerners sometimes hear about India's gargantuan population and assume that surely the market for their product can be found within that mass of one billion Indians. But that statistic (and many others) doesn't mean anything unless you view it against the backdrop of Indian culture.

For example, the seller should identify needs, based on culture and lifestyle rather than on demographics alone. Take the vacuum cleaner — an ever-present item in the West. It's a good example of how statistics can be deceiving. Statistically speaking, tens of millions of Indian households make up the potential market for a vacuum cleaner manufacturer. But have tens of millions of these gadgets been sold in India? No! That's because in India, vacuum cleaners aren't everywhere, maids are. If you confront an Indian with a sales pitch, he may think, "Sure, I can afford to buy one. But why should I? The maid is doing a good enough job with broom and mop!" (Plus, most Indian homes aren't carpeted and vacuum cleaners aren't so effective on hard floors.) Population *statistics* say that vacuum cleaners would have a huge market in India, but Indian *culture* says otherwise.

India is a complicated market. Don't assume that just because the potential customer figures you've been presented are humongous, you'll see a long, long line of Indians with cash in hand, eager to pay for your product or service.

How will you reach your potential customers?

Half the battle of setting up a successful business venture is letting the target market know about what your business has to offer. In this regard, India is no different than any other country. It helps, though, that India is an advertiser's paradise. To help get your business's message to the masses, you can have your pick from the top global advertisement agencies that have set up shop in India, or you can go with a well established Indian company, depending on your advertising budget and goals. I provide more information on this opportunity in Chapter 11.

Keeping your ears to the ground for financial resources to last

As you come to India, you bring money into the country, so don't expect to find easy sources to fund your India business. You're expected to bring your wallet along. But if you think you can't do it alone, you can of course look for joint venture (JV) partners, who help with the funding by getting loans from various avenues like banks and venture capitalists in India itself. See Chapter 5, where I outline modes of entry into India, including JVs.

But it's important to consider how other India-specific factors can affect your capital. Will the money you raise for the first year of your business's life be enough to keep things moving along if you run into regulatory delays? Could a change in the pricing of raw materials quickly deplete the cash you've raised through debt and equity? Make sure your cash flow plans are well informed by India's challenges and quirks! The Indian tax structures and subsidy systems are prone to change and could affect pricing, so it's wise to keep abreast of economic developments through the media and through your Indian agent/contact. I explore more financial considerations in Chapter 9.

As a planning tool, your business plan should

✔ Guide you through the various phases of your business

✔ Help you identify roadblocks and obstacles and establish alternatives

These two functions of a business plan take on a distinct hue in India. The main reason is the very size and diversity of the country, which can impact different phases of your business in terms of both time and money and present roadblocks unless you plan each phase thoughtfully.

Meticulous attention to detail when planning makes life easier down the road. For example, make sure your plan takes the challenges presented by supply chain management into account. India's ports are many and varied, but your mindset shouldn't be "any port in a storm," and your plan should reflect that. Take note of the droughts, yearly tidal cycles, rainfall seasons, port equipment, local port holidays, and land transportation available near the port. Strive to be that thorough with all aspects of your plan, and your business's agility and adaptability will shine.

Creating a Business Plan

Think of your venture like building a house in unfamiliar territory. Your architect's plan needs to take into account the peculiarities of the terrain and the climatic conditions and resources available and then tailor them to best fit your needs and build the best possible house. Drawing up a plan for a business venture in India should be done in the same way. In this section I fill you in on some important items and concerns that shouldn't be ignored when writing up your business plan.

Do your homework before starting your business plan. Chapters 2 and 3 of this book give you a good overview of what you need to know about the fundamentals of India, and Chapter 5 tells you about the possible entry strategies.

Making sure your plan is versatile

Though the components of a solid business plan are roughly the same everywhere in the world, India has its own take on everything. Your Indian business plan needs to be versatile enough to serve as an effective means of communication, management, and planning. The next three sections explain the nuances from the Indian perspective.

Promotion

Your business plan needs to communicate important information to a variety of different parties. For example, your plan needs to do the following:

✓ **Assist in courting joint venture partners and strategic business partners (key service providers, vendors, and so on).** To woo joint venture partners, you must make your plan attractive in terms of viability and also in terms of what your prospective partner can get out of it. So get your math right — show them what you project the bottom line to be.

To successfully attract key business partners of any hue, make certain that you get the language of your business plan just right. Keep your language simple, but don't overdo it and risk a plan that sounds condescending. Flowery language or oversimplification can only confuse the issue, and both parties are likely to cry foul at a later stage.

✔ **Attract the authorities and smooth the permission channel.** Indian authorities are savvy. When you seek the requisite permissions to set up a business, officials are armed with data across various disciplines of business. Don't try to pass off a plan for a power back-up system by merely saying that you intend to invest a particular sum of money in it — they want you to justify the power load requirements, provide data on the power situation/stability in target area, explain the technical viability of your own particular system, and much more. With any venture, be sure to dig beneath the surface and explore all angles before getting yourself measured for a new suit for that ground-breaking ceremony.

Include a write-up of the background of your company, with details on how it got started. And give them numbers — how your profits have grown, where you see your company in the next five years, and so on.

✔ **Have proof that you've thought of possible problems with your venture and decided on potential alternatives.** Factor in your plan several problems that may occur and present possible solutions. Those notations may convince readers that you've done your homework, are aware of the risks, and are confident that you can handle them. This small step not only weighs heavily in your favor when seeking to attract capital but also puts you in good standing if things do go wrong.

If possible, make a personal visit to India as you work on your plan. Scout around and see how things look to you. Explore the logistics, talk to others that have done similar businesses, and get input on what works and what doesn't from Indian and expatriate businesspeople. Then engage an expert to show you the ropes — a cultural mediator is a must for your India business plan.

Management

Indians are comfortable doing business with people from other countries. They admire the management processes you employ. Having a foreign partner is even a status symbol, so you'll be welcomed. If carefully conceived, your business plan can serve as a management tool and can help you do the following:

✔ **Inform your budgetary evaluations and adjustments.** Your plan should also include a thorough cash flow projection. Knowing the amount of capital you plan to have at any given point is useful when determining whether you need to tighten your belt or grow your business.

Collections in India is a challenge as in any other part of the world. In India, giving a credit line of 60 or even 90 days, and not asking too directly for monies in order to save face, are nuances that you would have to factor in to stay in the well-oiled path of cash flow.

✔ **Provide blueprints to keep your business on track.** In the course of doing business in India, you may be tempted with situations that take you off course. If you have a solid plan of action prepared for the future, resisting the tangent temptation can be easier and keep you on track.

For instance an offshoot of your main product may have meteoric sales, but don't let that dilute your real goal. After the main product is well established you can then promote the additions. One company that sells music systems found this with their universal remotes. They focused and now have a market share for both.

✔ **Track, monitor, and evaluate your progress.** You can manage the forward progress of your business if you review your plan at a glance to estimate where you've fallen short and where you can capitalize on windfalls.

If your plan is strong on the management angle, it not only serves you well during the course of your business relationship with India but also impresses prospective partners, backers, and financiers.

Covering the important financial concerns

For your business plan to have the desired positive impact on your Indian business partners, you need to do an outstanding job of outlining the important financial matters. While the product overview, track record, and market analysis in your plan tell your prospective vendors, service providers, and customers what they need to know, your Indian business partners want to know a lot more about the money matters.

The following sections outline the information that you need to provide for your Indian business partners.

Financial planning

Your financial plan should provide project cost and means of finance. It needs to include

✔ Clear details of the pricing structure and comparative prices of competitors' products

✔ Details of the costs involved, and if those costs will change if the business performs well or poorly, and the minimum sales required to recover your costs

Many capital and operating costs are the same in India as in the West. As you may imagine, the biggest cost differences come in human resources. Experts indicate that salaries are 50 to 60 percent lower in India.

Financial projections

When drawing up your India blueprint, pay attention to your profit and loss account, and give thought to the factors that negatively impact your bottom line:

- **Logistics:** Logistics play a major role in cost for any business plan, but its role is particularly large in India. India is vast, and although its transportation systems are constantly improving, there's more to it than checking train timetables. Every state has entry check posts at its borders. Given that laws differ from state to state, you could get stuck in sticky situations — for example a perfectly legitimate cargo of bottled beer being trucked from Mumbai to its northern neighbor, Jaipur. The truck route has to completely bypass the interim state of Gujarat, where both transportation and consumption of alcohol is banned! The route you choose impacts your cost.

- **Variable projections:** Key costs — power and consumables — could go up by 5 to 10 percent. Rate hikes are quite common in India, especially in the energy sector. There's not really a predictable pattern to such hikes, so to be on the safe side, factor a 3 to 5 percent escalation every year in such costs.

   Customs duties are import/export costs imposed by the government. Check out Chapter 9 for more details. These duties are liable to change every year in India as well and significantly impact costs. If your business involves importing equipment, for example, you should include this factor when drawing up your business plan.

In developing countries like India, make sure to examine the social impact of a business venture. Businesses in India have a long tradition of altruistic projects; successful businesses recognize the extent of the division in society between rich and poor and take it on themselves to do something about it. The Ambani group, which runs Reliance petrochemicals or Telecom, are building whole new satellite cities to bridge the rural urban divide, which is the need in today's India to get the one side over to the other. India is capitalist, but with a strong social conscience, be aware of this and consider ways to contribute in your business plan. I offer more details on this in Chapter 14.

Taking other considerations into account

Making a favorable first impression is half the battle in India. But how can you make a good impression with your business plan, and make the most of it? Check out the following sections for your game plan.

Getting the timing right

Indians have a strong sense of tradition and an equally strong belief in religion and superstition. And those traditions go hand in hand with certain times of the day, month, year, and so on. When you come up with the timeline for your business venture, consider the good and bad times to do business.

Coming up with a winner

In India, certain times of the year inspire businesses to offer discounts on their products and services. Diwali (an important Indian festival) is a perfect example. Many employees in India receive bonuses around Diwali time, so spending power is high. Your businesses can capitalize by offering discounts, to boost sales during this time.

Particular sales of precious metals, consumer goods, and automobiles peak and buying these items during Diwali is considered lucky. Indians even buy stocks on this day, in total disregard of market trends and prices, so that the first entry in the book of accounts is blessed! This is called *muhurat trading* (auspicious trading). Think about how timing your venture's launch with Diwali can pay rich dividends.

Striking out

There are also bad times to launch a new venture in India. Indians avoid embarking on new ventures during the waning phase of the moon. Also, each day has a 90-minute period called *Rahu Kaalam* that's considered inauspicious (or an unpromising time to do business). This period occurs at a different time each day of the week. See Table 4-1 for a full list of days and times of Rahu Kaalam. If you schedule a crucial business event during these times, you're going to hear disapproval.

Table 4-1	Charting Rahu Kaalam
90-minute inauspicious period	*Day of the week*
7:30 a.m. to 9:00 a.m.	Monday
9:00 a.m. to 10:30 a.m.	Saturday
10:30 a.m. to noon	Friday
noon to 1:30 p.m.	Wednesday
1:30 p.m. to 3:00 p.m.	Tuesday
3:00 p.m. to 4:30 p.m.	Thursday
4:30 p.m. to 6:00 p.m.	Sunday

You can remember the daily changes of these bad times with this mnemonic device: **M**other (Monday) **S**aw (Saturday) **F**ather (Friday) **W**earing (Wednesday) **T**he (Tuesday) **T**urban (Thursday) **S**uddenly (Sunday). Also, in general, Tuesdays are considered to be bad days to start a new venture in many places throughout India.

Dropping names

Dropping names, both personal and corporate, is a great way to help build your reputation in India. Your chances with bankers, venture capitalists, vendors, state agencies, and more may improve if you include in your management/partner team at least one recognizable name. Some good PR work is essential, and getting a local partner or agent who knows the names to rope in are key. The American Chamber of Commerce (Amcham) or the Confederation of Indian Industries (CII) or even the Federation of Industries (FICCI) are good places to start networking.

You should also cultivate relationships at the appropriate levels on the corporate ladder. As your relationships form with colleagues at your level in a particular company or partnership, your CEO should also foster a relationship with his or her counterpart at the same company.

Relationship building is best done by personal visits, luncheons, and entertaining. Seek advice and also seek to serve a good other than your own — give your time and true attention; the rest follows automatically.

Using publicity to your advantage

Publicity carries a great deal of weight in India. As part of your business plan, include positive media clippings about members of your team or your partners to impress your audience.

Alternatively, you can contact relevant trade publications to get media coverage regarding your business idea, too. Be sure to include those clippings in your business plan presentation as well. And the positive press doesn't have to be India-specific: Using it to demonstrate that you have a profile outside India helps, too.

Involving your Indian colleagues early and often

Involve key employees from your Indian team as early as possible when you're drawing up your plan. The more they're involved, the more they feel like they have a stake in the project, and their level of commitment will go up proportionately.

During the process, be sure to show that you have trust in your Indian partners. Large Indian businesses have faith, loyalty, and trust as the cornerstone of their enterprise and would expect the same from their foreign partners.

One way to show that you trust your Indian partners is to not dwell only on the letter of the written document you share but instead an amicable and healthy respectful relationship. Spend time with them, seek their approval and advice, be inclusive, and ask for their opinion genuinely. After the partner feels respected and knows of your sincerity, this relationship will go much further than any documents and legalese you go over with a fine tooth comb.

Here are a couple of pieces of advice:

✔ When firming up a business plan for a joint venture, be very transparent with your Indian business partner about your investment plans over a reasonable period — say, five years. This piece of info helps him plan his finances, because historically the foreign partner has deeper pockets than the Indian one.

✔ Consider running a pilot project if possible that can reveal any previously unconsidered stumbling blocks or hurdles, which can then be more easily ironed out. If you choose to go national directly, be prepared for surprising turns and bends in the road.

Identifying and Avoiding Common Obstacles

When you're planning for a journey into unfamiliar territory, you'll be working in the dark to some extent. But just because the course that lies ahead is unfamiliar doesn't mean that it's uncharted. In this section, I expose some of the rough terrain that you may encounter and clue you in on how to avoid it with adjustments to your business plan.

Following your assumptions

You're probably excited about your business prospects in India, and that's natural, but don't make assumptions in your business plan that show your endeavor getting started and growing too quickly. For example, clearance from a pollution control board or getting your water and electrical connections established immediately may not be as swift and comprehensive as you think. Such assumptions can leave you disappointed or in a bind later. India is buzzing with economic activity, but some processes still take longer than in the West. Also, consult your Indian partners — don't take them for granted.

Ken Green, a seasoned businessman, had been running a successful enterprise with an Indian partner for a while. He wanted to diversify into a related field, using a special raw material that he knew the Indian company made. He assumed the company would be happy to support him and didn't take the precaution of checking with them. He prepared a detailed business plan and managed to get the backing of financiers, too. However, when the partners were presented with the project, they weighed the costs and benefits and found that the costs were way too high. Ken was left high and dry.

Assessing the legal angles

Sure, India's laws are being liberalized. But there's fine print everywhere, and you need to keep an eye out for it as you work on your business plan. Make certain you pay special attention to the possible forms your business is permitted to take in India (proprietorship, partnership, corporation, franchise, and so on). Each has certain legal limitations, and you can avoid such costly mistakes by making a thorough study of the laws and by-laws relevant to your business before writing your plan. I've included details on these options in Chapter 5.

One U.S.-based investor tied up with an Indian manufacturer to set up a manufacturing unit using imported technology. The business plan set out a number of product lines based on technology the foreign partner was able to provide. Timeframes were drawn up, and costing and profits were estimated. However, at the approvals stage, while some of the required technology could be transferred, others needed specific approvals from the central government. As a result, the business volumes and values projections for the first year went out the window. More capital was required to keep the unit going.

Keep a contingency plan ready for changes and/or differences of opinion between India's central and state governments. India has a federal system of government, and the central government's ruling party may not be the same as those in power at state levels. Several states may be ruled by parties that oppose the party in power at the Indian Parliament, and, to complicate matters, elections to the central and state governments aren't always held simultaneously. Don't take it for granted that development projects in the states that need the Union Government's backing will be smooth sailing. You have to factor in possible roadblocks and even detours along the way.

Identifying and planning for competition

As in any business scenario, competition is a vital factor you need to consider in India. If your competition is a local, he has a big advantage over you because he has first-hand knowledge of the market and possibly a local network. He also knows people who can put in a good word. *Your* strength is your systems and your managerial expertise, so be sure to take advantage of those strengths when accounting for competition in your business plan.

If your competition isn't local then the person who does his homework best and partners up with the most appropriate local businesspeople wins. So again preparation and planning is key.

You need time and intuition to get a finger on a market's pulse, especially in a market, which swings up and down (as it's known to do in India). Hire professionals to make an analysis and identify your competition for you. In the liberalized Indian business scenario, professional assessments can be easily obtained.

Allowing for the emotion of Indian business

To Westerners, business logic dominates the assessment of a proposition or negotiation. In India you may, however, find that either emotion or individual personality has a greater bearing, leaving you confused as to why "sound logic" hasn't prevailed.

For example, a business could make a windfall profit because of reasons out of anyone's control, such as a commodity price movement. When the division of the windfall earnings are discussed, Western business logic says that the rules of the contract are the final word, whereas Eastern business logic says that the good fortune was never visualized when the contract was put together and so the division of the earnings should be different.

Don't take the Indian emphasis on emotion to mean that Indians are a soft people or that they let their hearts rule their heads. Indian businesspeople are savvy, and if they sometimes seem overly emotional, it's just that they see things from a different perspective.

For example, Indians are a mix between scientific and spiritual; they were even in the old days merchants and monks. So they may believe in something that seems like superstition to you, or they may take something that happens or is said personally rather than professionally. See their side; realize there's a background, and seek to get clarity from them before you proceed. Don't throw in the towel too early! Keep this in mind, and realize that you can use the Indian tendencies to your advantage by being accommodating and trying to see business situations through Indian eyes.

Here's one more thing to keep in mind: Indians are highly optimistic. Sometimes, when your prospective Indian partner presents you with a business plan or working blueprint, his enthusiasm may seem over the top. You may feel like slamming your foot down on the brakes, but be sure to take a closer look because your hesitation could be a mistake. Maybe the optimism isn't misplaced at all. When in doubt, use a SWOT (Strengths, Weaknesses, Opportunities, Threats) analysis and try to imagine the proposition in the Indian market before condemning it.

If you want more information on SWOT analyses, check out *Strategic Planning For Dummies* by Erica Olsen (Wiley).

Implementing Your Indian Business Plan

Even the best laid plans are of no use if they aren't properly implemented. You need to utilize your Indian business plan long after it's written to ensure that what has been planned for the venture is carried out in reality.

It's important to assign parts of the plan to various team members who follow some sort of reporting structure. Clarity of roles and expectations are key in getting business plans and all aspects of your India business to succeed. Measurable goal setting and following time tables for implementation and even contingencies if parts of the plan aren't working are all part of the Western Realism, which is needed to guide your India project. This combined with Eastern Wisdom is bound to get India, the world, and even the planet to succeed according to many great leaders today.

Referring back to your plan and monitoring progress

Taking the time to look back at your plan is well worth the effort after you've started down the Indian business road. If you're the acting CEO, know that a good monitoring system based on your business plan sets the achievement standards for each segment, so take a few actions to make sure the plan is working:

✔ Require a continuous flow of information from key team members to monitor the progress of your plan.

✔ Take corrective measures in the plan when necessary.

✔ Keep an eye on reports from the areas of finance, production, marketing, and human resources.

✔ Review performances periodically to assess them against what's outlined in your plan.

Most companies are comfortable with a monthly analysis. Normally, a fixed date in a month is set aside for the submission/transmission of the above bulleted information. It's a good idea to require the head of each of the four major departments to report to the top Indian manager, who turns in the report to you.

No one facet of your business is more important than the others — all of the components need to operate together because each one impacts your bottom line. When it becomes clear that an area (or areas) is performing differently than what you'd planned, circle the wagons and call in your key staff members to discuss whether it makes sense to review and possibly change the goals set out in your plan.

Reviewing and making changes to your plan

While you have times that you need to do standard reviews of goals in your business plan, some India-specific events call for a review of your business plan that may result in necessary changes. Check out the following sections for these instances.

Changes to tax structure

Traditionally in India, changes in taxation are announced when the national budget is presented in Parliament by the Finance Minister. This occasion happens each year on February 28th, but taxes can be altered on other dates. Keep a close watch on the news items in the papers and on television. Do hire a tax consultant or chartered accountant to keep you updated because tax changes can easily cause a variance in your plan.

Exchange rates and laws

Exchange rates and laws have significant influences on your company's operations in India. Because currency conversions are involved, exchange rate fluctuations need to be monitored.

Have your finance specialist hold a monthly meeting with the local banker to get his views on currency movements. This tactic then becomes an excellent input for devising a currency hedge plan, which is a method to safeguard against factors like volatility of the exchange rate and is a risk management tool. It works chiefly on currency futures.

National and state politics

The two levels of government in India don't need to have the same party in power, so this difference also contributes to variances. Make sure to keep a finger on the political pulse of the country, so you can be warned when changes are afoot that may have a bearing on your business future.

Monsoons

The rains are another India-specific factor that you need to consider. The Indian economy is still primarily agricultural, and a billion Indians must be fed each day. Due to the adoption of new scientific methods, research, and hard work, India has been self sufficient in grain production over the last few decades. But Indian agriculture still depends on timely and adequate monsoon rains. A bad monsoon can have a domino effect on countless factors that impact food prices, loan repayments, fertilizer requirements, supply movements, retail demand, and so on. So depending on your area of business, keep an eye on the monsoons to consider how they may impact your plan. (Desalination plants are underway though to solve problems of water starved parts of India so this may relieve matters a bit shortly.)

International treaties

Some global deals that India participates in may also have an impact on your plan. India commits in various world forums to adhere to and change a few key issues. For example, India is committed to bring down custom fees to between 5 and 10 percent ad valorem (in proportion to the value) for all imports by 2010. Needless to say, such policy changes can impact your business in India.

Check out www.commerce.nic.in for more information. Also look at www.finance.indiamart.com/taxation/taxtreaties.html for info on double taxation treaties.

Special trade treaties

India signs trade treaties with various countries from time to time. These pacts can include a far-reaching nuclear energy scheme with the United States, a defense supply deal with Russia, or an oil pipeline contract with Iran. There are also treaties signed for duty-free or reduced-duty trade with a few countries such as Sri Lanka and Thailand.

Watch for news on these types of treaties and think about how you may have to adjust your business plan based on their effects. Visit www.commerce.nic.in or www.finance.indiamart.com/taxation/taxtreaties.html for more info.

Policy changes by the Reserve Bank of India

Needless to say, any company operating in India needs to be completely tuned to all the various policy changes made by this central bank. The Reserve Bank of India (RBI) is the one that mints the rupee and is also the top bank that governs India's financial moves. The Governor of the RBI works closely with the finance ministry of India. There are specialist RBI consultants you can hire to get further and up-to-date information.

Terrorism

For the last few decades, India has had two trouble spots in terms of terrorist activity: Kashmir and Assam. The former is a political legacy from the days of independence. The latter is more recent and perhaps of more concern from a business perspective.

India has a fair amount of onshore oil deposits and pipelines in the northeast that are sometimes attacked by rebels who call themselves United Liberation Front of Assam (ULFA). While all efforts are being made to contain and resolve the issue, this issue negatively influences the stability of the economy.

Health concerns

One area that's a high priority in the West but is prioritized in India is the health of employees. Periodic health checkups for staff are advisable and a review of major problems is useful. Recently, a wave of mosquito-borne diseases swept the country, primarily the debilitating Chikungunya and the potentially life-threatening Dengue Fever. Both diseases caused significant loss of workdays, which can affect your work efficiency and your business plan.

Be proactive! Some foreign-based companies took the initiative of researching these essentially tropical diseases and circulating information about prevention and cures among their Indian employees. If you do the same, you may be able to prevent the loss of work days from your employees, and you'll show that you care about the welfare of your employees.

Chapter 5

Starting Up in India

· ·

In This Chapter

▶ Figuring out investment options

▶ Deciding on a location

▶ Getting familiar with the entry vehicles

▶ Setting your plan in motion

· ·

*T*he inviting aroma from the sumptuous Indian economic banquet is attracting a variety of hungry international business diners. The question, just like when you're faced with an extensive spread of any sort, is how and where to begin.

The blueprint for industry in India was first drawn up in the Industrial Policy Resolution way back in 1956 — less than a decade after independence from British control. Incredibly enough, this doctrine remained almost entirely untouched for 35 years, giving a fascinating snapshot of how much the Indian economy was protected. The long overdue change in approach came in 1991 with the Statement of Industrial Policy. The procedures and approvals for investment and doing business in India have been simplified, and the Indian government says this progress is ongoing and proactive. Chapter 2 explores the most notable reforms.

As you chart your course for doing business in India, here are three key questions to ask yourself:

✔ What type of investment works best for me and my business?

✔ Where's the best location for my business office?

✔ What's the most viable entry vehicle or start-up mode for my business?

This chapter helps you explore your choices and answer these questions about the business you want to start in India. The information you find in this chapter also explains the steps you need to take to make your dream a reality.

Understanding the Investment Routes

You can make a business entry into India in various ways. Some routes are still closed to traffic, while others are only partially open, but for the most part, it's a clear road ahead.

In this section, you first look at those areas that are out of bounds, and then those that have been opened up only in part, so you know your limits. From there, consider the avenues by which the government of India permits overseas investment and see how the world has taken up its offer.

Exploring your options for investment

Generally speaking, overseas investment is permitted in virtually every sector. Exceptions are those areas that the government views as being of strategic, political, or religious concern. (Sorry, risqué magazines can't be sold in India, so that's one route I don't explore here.) Here are some other sectors you can regard as investment no-no's:

- Atomic energy
- Arms and ammunition
- Railway transport
- Mining of certain materials including iron, manganese, chrome, gypsum, gold, diamonds, copper and zinc

India wants to keep the control of these vital and sensitive industries in-house because of concerns regarding internal security and sovereignty. However, the investment blocks are few and far between. India permits 100 percent foreign equity in most industries. But sector-specific caps on foreign equity do exist in some industries. The Indian government has imposed ceilings on these areas of investment. Table 5-1 gives you a bird's eye view of the investment limits in some popular areas.

If you want to start an iron mining business in India for instance, you have to partner with Indian investors or a government body, because you as a foreign investor can only own 49 percent of the business.

Table 5-1	Investment Caps by Sector
Sector	*Foreign Investment Ceiling Percentages*
Refining	26
Investment companies	40
Mining	49
Petroleum (other than refining)	49
Telecom	49
Private sector banking	50
Broadcasting	51
Defense industry	51
Atomic mineral mining	60
Coal & lignite mining	74
Domestic airlines	74
Computer hardware manufacturing	74
Insurance	74

Seeking approval for your business

In keeping with its open-door policy, India has greatly simplified the process of foreign investment in the country. The government of India allows Foreign Direct Investment (FDI) through two routes: automatic and government approval. The automatic route is now available in all except a few sectors where a ceiling exists on FDI. Government approval is required for those sectors falling outside the range of operation of the automatic route.

Filing for automatic approval: AAR for your FDI without the RBI

Overseas companies can basically set up 100 percent subsidiaries in India without any prior approval from the Reserve Bank of India (RBI), except for certain specified industries (see Table 5-1 for examples). This mode of investment is the Automatic Approval Route (AAR).

The AAR is the easiest for foreign investors because companies aren't required to obtain permission from the government or the RBI before investing. The only condition is that you submit information to the RBI within 30 days of inward remittances or issue of shares to foreign investors. Some tried-and-true AAR sectors include manufacturing, infrastructure, and services. Even where there are sector-specific caps such as those listed in Table 5-1, proposals for equity stakes in those sectors up to their respective ceilings are automatically approved in most cases.

In sectors where automatic clearance for FDI is already granted, you can also set up wholly-owned subsidiaries of foreign companies rather easily. You don't even need prior approval from the Foreign Investment Promotion Board (FIPB), which is a governmental entity set up to advise and facilitate overseas investment. This, however, doesn't include the purchase of shares from existing shareholders, which is a separate — although still easy — transaction that allows the government to track ownership patterns.

Foreign investment in India is governed by FDI policy and the Foreign Exchange Management Act (FEMA). FEMA's predecessor was the Foreign Exchange Regulation Act (FERA). The operative words *regulation* and *management* signify the sea change in India's stance on international trade. For more details on FDI and cash flow regulations, see Chapter 9.

Automatic approval isn't available for proposals in a few areas that the government considers to be strategic, including asset reconstruction, atomic energy, broadcasting, courier services, defense industries, public-sector petroleum-refining companies, print media, certain types of trading activities, satellites, and investing companies in infrastructure and service sectors. Foreign investments in these areas are scrutinized.

Applying for government approval: An-OK from the FIPB

Investment proposals that don't qualify for automatic approval (see the preceding section) must be submitted to the FIPB. Proposals seeking industrial license and technical collaborations along with permission for foreign investment are given governmental package clearance — the industrial license, technical collaboration, and investment are cleared all at once. This method is preferred for most multinational corporations that have big plans for India. Indian companies taking the FIPB route don't require any further clearance from the RBI to receive inward remittances and issue shares to foreign investors.

When submitting proposals to the FIPB, note whether you currently have or have had a financial/technical collaboration or trademark agreement in India in the same or allied field for which you've sought approval. If you have, provide details and justify the need for your new proposal.

You can submit applications from abroad to the Indian Missions, who then forwards them to the Department of Economic Affairs (DEA). Proposals received by the DEA are placed before the FIPB within 15 days. For project proposals involving a total investment of up to six billion rupees (roughly $1.33 million U.S. dollars — the U.S. dollar is approximately Rs 45), the FIPB's recommendations are considered and approved by the Finance Minister. For projects involving more than that amount, the Cabinet Committee on Economic Affairs is consulted. In either case, you should receive a decision within 30 days.

Taking a look at how others are investing in India

You can see results of the streamlined approval process in the high levels of FDI in dozens of Indian industries. Table 5-2 reveals some of the notable examples.

Table 5-2	FDI Inflows (in millions USD)		
Industry	*02-03*	*03-04*	*04-05*
Computer services	297	166	372
Construction	237	172	209
Electricity	48	90	14
Financing/insurance/biz services	223	206	363
Fisheries	9	2	10
Food & dairy products	39	64	183
Health & medical services	28	15	25
Manufacturing	480	426	924
Mining	9	18	11
Other services	236	215	110
Trade, Hotels, Restaurants	39	67	22
Transport	12	20	70
Total	1,657	1,461	2,313

Counting every rupee

Incredibly enough, in the era before liberalization in India, any corporate body or individual had to provide an explanation for funds received in Indian bank accounts from overseas. For example, a $100 check from an uncle in Boston to his favorite niece in Bombay invited the wrath of the RBI! Of course, if the check was sent as a birthday or wedding gift, that was okay with the RBI as long as a copy of the birthday card or the wedding invitation was produced on demand.

The system has thankfully changed since liberalization. When foreign exchange comes into India, the receiving bank issues a certificate called the Foreign Inward Remittance Certificate (FIRC). This form is issued in triplicate: one copy for the bank, one for the person receiving the funds, and the last to the RBI for its records.

The increased levels of FDI across numerous sectors give you an idea of the quality of the returns on those investments. But where in the world are all of those investments coming from? Table 5-3 holds the answers.

Table 5-3	Top Sources of FDI Inflow (in millions of USD)		
Country	*02-03*	*03-04*	*04-05*
Germany	103	69	143
Japan	66	67	122
Mauritius	534	381	820
Netherlands	94	197	196
South Korea	15	22	14
United States	268	297	469
Total	1,658	1,462	2,320

The tiny island nation of Mauritius is responsible for the highest inflows of FDI into India (see Table 5-3). This African country has a special taxation treaty with India. The treaty grants Mauritian corporations significant tax benefits on investments in India. Mauritius is to India what the Bahamas or other Caribbean islands are to the Western investment fraternity.

In addition to overseas investment in Indian industry, Indian capital markets are also now open to Foreign Institutional Investors (FIIs) This area has seen significant growth of late (not surprising when you consider the strength of returns on Indian investments over the last few years).

The Government has set up entities to help, monitor, and encourage overseas investment into India. Foremost among them is the Secretariat for Industrial Assistance (SIA). This division is a specific division within the Ministry of Commerce and Industry that facilitates all issues related to investments that need government approval. The SIA is extremely tech-savvy: It responds to investor e-mails within 24 hours and has set times for investor help chat sessions online. Check it out at www.dipp.gov.in. You can also seek help from the Foreign Investment Implementation Authority (FIIA). It helps foreign investors obtain necessary approvals, iron out operational and procedural difficulties, and seek intra-governmental solutions.

Choosing a Business Address

New Delhi, India's capital, is a premier business destination. It happens to be adjacent to the city of Agra, the home of the Taj Mahal, which is one of the wonders of the modern world. The dazzling white marble structure is actually a tomb that a Moghul Emperor built in memory of his beloved queen.

So wouldn't a view of the Taj be nice? Well, yes it would, but unfortunately, you can't see the Taj Mahal from any office window in New Delhi, but it's still an amazing business hub. And many other Indian cities throughout the country are equally or even more popular with overseas businesspeople. These locations are attractive for logistic factors as well as financial considerations (many offer tax concessions) and also for the availability of a skilled workforce. Choosing a site with the best business view is vital for success in India.

In this section, you gain a closer understanding of the cities of India from a business point of view, what they're called — the old names and the new and what their advantages are.

Exploring India's business landscape

The Indian government classifies India's cities as Tier I, II, or III, based primarily on population, infrastructure, and spending power. However, this classification system can change a bit based on other business-related criteria such as investment concessions, work culture, manpower, and raw material availability. For instance, even large cities like Kolkata and Ahmedabad, which should fall under the Tier I category by virtue of population, have been tagged Tier II or III because of labor and economy issues.

India is on a back-to-its-roots spree. It has changed the anglicized names given to many cities by the British back to the Indian versions. For instance, Madras is now Chennai, Bombay is Mumbai, and Calcutta is Kolkata. This process is ongoing, and many Indians find it tough to remember the new names, persistently calling them by the old British names. But for official purposes and even for travel arrangements, the Indian names are now the rule. So when you're talking destinations, double check to make sure, or you can land in the wrong place!

The issue of location has become increasingly fluid, with communications having significantly improved and with most multinational companies investing heavily in Intranet systems. The choice of a business location in India is now dictated almost exclusively by essential business considerations. In this section, you find out what makes a city fall into a specific tier and whether you want to do business in a Tier I, II, or III city.

Considering Tier 1 cities

Tier I cities provide the largest and most qualified labor pools, the best infrastructure, and feature the most modern buildings. Traditionally, overseas companies tend to park their Indian operations in well-known cities like Mumbai, New Delhi, Chennai, Bangalore, and Hyderabad. These cities have attracted a significant proportion of FDI and are also referred to as the Metros.

Bangalore in the south of India is known the "Silicon Valley of India" because of the high concentration of IT-based companies there. Chennai, also in the South, is known as the Detroit of India because it is highly favored by automobile manufacturers.

The Tier I cities are the ones with infrastructure well in place, because they've been attracting investment for a while now. Because of overcrowding, tiers II and III are being developed (see the next section). Though infrastructure and other facilities like lifestyle comforts may not be as good in these areas, you have the advantage of cost and also of getting in at the start.

Weighing the benefits of Tier II and Tier III cities

As business costs rise in Tier I cities, labor shortages surface, and familiarity with India as a business location improves, more domestic and foreign firms are now considering Tier II and Tier III cities for expansion, or even for establishing their first Indian foothold.

Many second- and third-tier cities focus on one industry or another — a very welcome business development. Some remote areas have even found themselves catapulted onto the international business scene because governmental factors can benefit particular projects in certain areas. The Enron power project in Dabhol, in the state of Maharashtra, is one example.

Pune, near Mumbai, with its competitive business environment, human resources availability, telecommunications connectivity, quality infrastructure, and availability of real estate is one example of a promising Tier II city. Tier III cities on the rise include Kolkata and Ahmedabad. Foreign IT-enabled services (ITeS) companies like IBM, Microsoft, and Dell are leading the charge into Tier III cities.

These cities can offer advantages:

- ✔ Competitive infrastructure
- ✔ Good quality of life
- ✔ Highly educated population
- ✔ Proximity to primary cities

Consider the following up-and-coming cities of business destinations:

- ✔ Bhubaneshwar in the east
- ✔ Chandigarh and Jaipur in the north of India
- ✔ Kochi and Thiruvananthapuram in the southern state of Kerala
- ✔ Mangalore and Mysore in the south

Evaluating potential sites

Your choice of location should be based on the following criteria:

- ✔ **Access to and the cost of utilities:** Check on power, water, and modern conveniences. Don't take availability for granted because it can change from state to state and even within a state. Costs can vary, too. Do your homework before you hang out your shingle.

- ✔ **Availability of infrastructure:** Road, rail, and port connectivity should be kept in mind when weighing the pros and cons of a particular business address.

- ✔ **Availability of skilled manpower:** It's tough to get Indians to pull up their roots. So if the kind of personnel you need — software wizards, for example — aren't already plentiful in the proposed town or city, you're in trouble. Take the mountain to Mohammed. It's well worth your while!

- ✔ **Proximity to resources:** Depending on the nature of your proposed business venture, read up on the availability of resources you need in the vicinity of the location you're considering. For instance, if you're planning to set up an automobile manufacturing unit, see if the area you're considering has easy access to components and hardware.

Be sure to check out the work culture in your target area because some states are more prone than others to labor unrest, strikes, *bandhs,* and *hartals* (both protest demonstrations). These disturbances can wreak havoc with your deadlines because you may lose days of productivity due to the workers protest and sometimes if it gets violent there is also a potential danger to products, because people can burn things as a sign of protest. The protests can really be about anything, by anybody. Check out Chapter 16 for more info on protests.

Every state government is competing for business, and each offers an array of incentives intended to maximize returns on investment. These incentives need to be carefully examined as they do, in most cases, have a significant impact on project costs and profits. Here are a few examples:

- ✔ A project/investment can be exempt from payment of any power tariff.
- ✔ A project/investment can be eligible for a concessional tariff.
- ✔ There can also be a waiver or reduction in local taxes on a particular manufactured product.
- ✔ There can even be a buy back arrangement.

Incentives essentially vary from state to state. When looking at possible locations, research the state governments to determine the policies and incentives they offer.

Taking advantage of the benefits of location

If your business exports products from India, check out the various programs geared toward offering advantages based on the location of your facilities. These programs are designed to fundamentally alter the investment geography of India and promote more balanced growth. The Indian government is keen to drive the development of certain areas, so be sure to investigate how you can benefit from setting up shop in a particular spot.

Special economic zones

A special economic zone (SEZ) is an area that's been designed to provide a globally competitive, duty free, cost-effective environment to export-oriented businesses such as manufacturing, trade, and services. SEZs feature many benefits:

✔ Good infrastructure including roads, water supply, drainage, and electricity

✔ Developed land and buildings that conform to certain general standards

✔ Customs clearance facilities available on site

✔ Tax advantages also available (Chapter 9 has additional details)

Approvals for setting up operations in an SEZ are granted by the development commissioner for that zone. The commissioner is also responsible for any necessary post-approval formalities. Businesses in SEZs must be total foreign exchange earners, and certain zones allow only specific industries to reap benefits. But the corporate structure of companies operating out of these zones can be public, private, joint, or government.

There are currently eleven SEZs operational in India at the following locations (in parentheses are the names of the states they're found in):

✔ Chennai (Tamil Nadu)

✔ Falta, Manikanchan-Salt Lake (West Bengal)

✔ Indore (Madhya Pradesh)

✔ Jaipur (Rajasthan)

✔ Kandla, Surat (Gujarat)

✔ Kochi (Kerala)

✔ Noida (Uttar Pradesh)

✔ Santa Cruz (Maharashtra)

✔ Visakhapatnam (Andhra Pradesh)

Over 40 new SEZs have been approved by the government and are under various stages of completion. The following are just a few of the Indian business locales of the future:

✔ Bhadohi, Kanpur, Greater Noida (Uttar Pradesh)

✔ Dronagiri (Maharashtra)

✔ Hassan (Karnataka)

✔ Kakinada (Andhra Pradesh)

✔ Kulpi (West Bengal)

✔ Paradeep (Orissa)

Export oriented units and parks

Export oriented units (EOUs) are another option for businesses looking to cash in on location-specific benefits within India. EOUs offer a host of advantages, many of which are the same as those afforded by SEZs (see the preceding section). They can also provide a technological skills pool and an industrial base.

EOUs can be found in a much wider range of locations, but the rules differ from SEZs, so be sure to investigate which is most appropriate for your business (the Web sites listed at the end of this chapter in the section "Putting your Plan into Play" are a great place to start).

Business parks such as software and technology parks can also provide an attractive situation for some companies. These parks are strewn across India and offer various infrastructure benefits and other perks.

Choosing an Entry Route

You can utilize a variety of entry methods and strategies to start your business in India. Getting off to a good start is critical, so your entry method decision should be a sound one.

The most important factor in choosing an entry route should be the type of industry you're in, because the service determines the functions your business needs to be able to perform in India. The nature of some industries requires that an Indian office be extremely versatile in the number and range of actions it can take, while other industries require little more than a nameplate in India to take care of the appropriate business dealings.

In this section, I highlight several entry routes to fill you in on your options. Whether you choose to enter India with a branch office, liaison office, project office, joint venture, or a 100 percent foreign-owned company, you need to be familiar with the features and limitations of the various routes. Check with someone in your industry who's conducted business in India before and made the same choices, and you can also discuss the options with a consultant (see Chapter 7 for more information on using consultants).

Liaison/representative office

The liaison/representative office option is the simplest and quickest way of dipping your toe into the Indian business pool. A liaison office acts as a communication channel between foreign businesses and Indian consumers. It promotes the businesses by spreading product awareness and explores opportunities for setting up a more permanent presence in India.

A liaison office must be funded exclusively by its foreign business office through normal banking channels. Liaison offices pay no taxes and their accounts aren't audited. All that's needed is a formal approval from the RBI. The approval is normally granted within a few weeks of submitting the formal application, and it's typically good for an initial period of three years. Renewal is just as easy.

Such an office or entity can't undertake any commercial, trading, or industrial activity directly or indirectly. Essentially, it has a mandate to do the following:

✔ Be your representative in India

✔ Look after your interests

✔ Give publicity to your products

✔ Keep an eye open for other areas where you can do business

✔ Work to step up both exports and imports

✔ Promote technical and financial collaborations

✔ Take steps to encourage joint efforts in terms of both money and technology

✔ Enhance communication channels between the parent company and Indian companies

✔ Keep the communication going between your company back home and the Indian outfit

Although liaison offices can't undertake any commercial, trading, or industrial activities, they can act on behalf of their overseas offices for purposes such as exporting orders with Indian companies and carrying on normal activities related to exports.

This entry method was, till the recent past, highly underrated and often overlooked by overseas companies. But a slew of top Japanese, Swiss, and German trading companies, banks, and technical consultants have all utilized this model over the last decade or so, and their successes serve as solid proof that using a liaison office is a smart move.

Branch office

A branch office is an establishment that undertakes the same mainline business activity as its head office. Setting up a branch office in India requires the approval of the RBI. Interestingly enough, the scope of activities a branch office can carry out is quite restrictive, but if your business is interested in an entry into India that's simple and straightforward, this option is worth considering. Branch offices are permitted to engage in the following business activities only:

 ✔ Exporting/importing of goods

 ✔ Rendering professional/consultancy services

 ✔ Carrying on research work initiated by the head office

 ✔ Encouraging partnerships vis-à-vis technology and finance

 ✔ Working as the head office's buying or selling agent here

 ✔ Developing software and IT services

 ✔ Providing technical product support

If you're setting up a branch or a representative or liaison office for a foreign company in India, you must register it with the Registrar of Companies. You must also file your annual financial statements (covering Indian and world-wide operations) and a number of other documents. You must also keep the Registrar informed of changes in the registered/principal office of the parent firm, such as changes in the director or secretary, changes in its charter, statute, or memorandum, and articles of association.

Project office

Project offices are a basic, pared-down option for foreign companies looking to execute extremely specific projects in India. Under Indian law, a project office can carry out only the specific project for which it was set up — nothing more. That sounds like a limiting situation, but if your firm doesn't require any functionality for its Indian office beyond one particular activity then a project office is an attractive option.

When a parent company is awarded a project in India for a limited time, it often sets up a project office. Project offices don't require prior permission from the RBI, but they're required to furnish regular reports to a regional RBI office. And like branch offices (see the preceding section), project offices are funded directly from abroad. Examples of foreign companies that commonly take advantage of the project office option include those specializing in turnkey construction or installation.

Joint ventures

A joint venture (JV) is a financial or technical collaboration that can take many forms, including an alliance with an Indian firm, a greenfield project (which is a project built from scratch), or a takeover. As a foreign company looking to begin conducting business in India, a joint venture can be appealing because it uses a powerful synergy. A good example comes from the mining industry, where foreign companies that specialize in the mining of bauxite (a key mineral in manufacturing aluminum) form JVs with existing Indian aluminum smelters, thereby creating robust players in aluminum production.

JVs have many benefits, which include warehousing, transportation, and built-in distribution. In India, joint ventures can take the form of companies, partnerships, or joint working agreements.

When signing a JV in India, pay special attention to the following points:

- ✔ **Contribution by the two parties:** Work out the fine print about the monetary implications in advance, including the equity and other resources each brings to the business, and aspects like transferability. Get everything signed and countersigned. Remember, money is the root of all evil and has spelled out the end of many JVs.

- ✔ **Exercise of control:** Who has the control? Is it the Board of Directors or the shareholders — decide what kind of role you want these people to play in your enterprise.

- ✔ **Exit options:** These also need to be made clear right at the start, so you're not in for surprises later. See Chapter 16 for more info.

- ✔ **JV entry pricing:** Work out and seal a pricing strategy with your partners that ensures high profits. This process ensures that the partnership is protected and competitors are kept out.

- ✔ **Legal implications, governing laws, and arbitration:** Such implications as compliance and tax laws are best handled with an Indian law firm. Chapter 13 relates to the legal aspects of doing business in India.

- ✔ **Management of the company:** Work out details between you and your partner.

- ✔ **Mode of investment:** See what works best for you and see if it suits your partner too. It's best to get these details ironed out at the start. Chapter 9 deals with the financial aspects of doing business in India.

For a venture agreement to be valid, you and your venture partner have to pay a specified amount as stamp duty on the agreement. The agreements have to be registered either with the RBI or the SIA, depending on which authority gives clearance for the project.

The Indian government allows a JV company to conduct business by passing either ordinary or special resolutions. Ordinary resolutions are the prerogative of shareholders having 51 percent voting rights in the company, while only those with 75 percent shares and voting rights can pass special resolutions. Be sure to make up your mind as to the level of control you want in the joint venture.

The amount of money the Indian partner is willing to invest has a bearing on this level of control, because those who hold the purse strings call the shots. Keep this in mind, because some companies fail when they believe that just a foothold in an Indian JV does the trick. For more details on seeking a partner and vetting his credentials, take a look at Chapter 6.

Foreign-owned company

A foreign business entity can set up a subsidiary company and establish a presence in India through three options:

- ✓ **A wholly-owned subsidiary:** Incorporating an Indian company with 100 percent foreign equity means you've set up a wholly-owned subsidiary.

- ✓ **A listed company:** You can incorporate a joint venture company with an Indian partner and/or with the Indian public and get to work as a listed company. A listed company can access funding more easily than an unlisted one. The distinctions are now blurring because new rules permit mutual funds to invest in unlisted companies. I suggest you keep in touch with Indian finance laws and brainstorm with your Indian auditor or consultant before deciding one way or another.

- ✓ **An unlisted company:** You can incorporate a joint venture company with an Indian partner but don't need to list it — in other words, you function as an unlisted company. A number of venture capital companies have made a beeline for India and are investing in unlisted companies. They wait for three to five years and then go for an Initial Public Offering — list the company — and sell their stake. They're currently looking at returns of around 30 percent per annum on their investment.

As compared to other entry methods like liaison or branch offices (see the sections "Liaison/representative office" and "Branch office" earlier in this chapter), a subsidiary company provides the maximum level of flexibility for conducting business in India. And both public and private companies can be formed by registering the memorandum and articles of association with the Registrar of Companies in the state where the company's headquarters is to be located.

Some drawbacks do exist, however, including the need for compliance with certain procedures of incorporation and cumbersome exit procedures that require enormous amounts of paperwork. For more info, check out `http://ezinearticles.com/?id=507492`.

Business process outsourcing

Business process outsourcing (BPO) provides an opportunity for your business to have some of the basic functions contracted out for a fraction of the cost. The scope of BPO options includes such areas as internal finance and administration, back office procedures, customer care, and human resource management.

The most popular types of outsourcing are

- **Direct outsourcing:** A foreign company enters into an agreement with an Indian company to take over some aspect or aspects of its work, leaving it free to cope with core areas.

- **Indirect outsourcing:** A foreign company enters into an agreement with another, which then farms out the work to an overseas firm.

- **Build own transfer:** A foreign company ties up with an Indian one to set up a development center and operate it for a pre-determined period and then transfer it.

- **Captive outsourcing:** Foreign companies set up their own establishments here because of cost and other advantages

If you want to use BPO, you have to follow a few steps to get you there. Take a look at the steps below to get the basic concept of a BPO plan:

1. **Request a proposal.**

   Study every aspect of the process you want outsourced and prepare a comprehensive document, based on which you hope to attract the right partners. Make sure you present your requirements and terms clearly, or you'll have to plow through a lot of utterly unsuitable stuff.

2. **Sign a memorandum of understanding (MOU).**

   This stage is preliminary and one where you show your initial interest in firming up a business relationship.

3. **Start agreement negotiations.**

   Clearly put forward the role you expect the Indian firm to play and negotiate terms and conditions. If necessary, talk to others who've been there and done it, so you have a rough idea of what's fair and what's not.

4. **Get an outsourcing agreement.**

   The contract should cover such aspects as duration, scope, deliverables, confidentiality, and termination. See Chapter 13 for more insights into contracts in general.

5. **Review service provided.**

   See if it meets your requirements. Pinpoint areas where improvement or fine tuning are required. Take steps to see that loopholes are plugged. Talk to your Indian collaborators, iron out the problems. If necessary, fly key team members to your home establishment or vice versa, to provide hands-on experience.

6. **Take a call.**

   Either renew the deal or terminate it. Chances are you won't need to think of the latter option.

The above steps are just an outline to pique your interest. Check out Chapter 6 for more information on BPO.

Other modes of entry

You have a number of other options that you may want to consider as you make a plan for starting up your business in India. These options include the following:

- ✔ **Indian companies shopping for overseas investors:** More and more, Indian businesses are going abroad for M&A candidates; if you're open to investment, this may be a viable alternative capital.

- ✔ **Foreign companies setting up distribution arrangements with Indian firms:** Because the Indian market is so vast and leveraging the market as a whole may be difficult for a new entrant, distribution or agency arrangements are popular options. Local market knowledge and marketing are extremely appealing benefits, as are the related low costs.

- ✔ **Foreign businesses franchising in India:** The setting up of franchises in India has become popular in recent years, especially in the hospitality, retail, and computer education industries.

- ✔ **Foreign businesses selling directly to Indian consumers:** Foreign companies can directly sell goods to end users in India. To make such sales, setting up any legal entities in India isn't necessary.

Although laws and procedures have been simplified to promote investment, I suggest that you hire a legal firm before signing any checks for Indian investments. For a moderate fee, a local lawyer can quickly make the language in application forms more understandable, and he can advise you on the recent changes to laws or policies. More importantly, a local legal firm can define all the incentives offered by state governments and build these into the investment decision both financially and legally.

Apart from wholly-owned and run Indian legal/consulting firms, some internationally known names also operate in India such as Ernst & Young, McKinsey, and A.T. Kearney. Overseas companies should ask existing lawyers to name a suitable legal/consulting firm in India. Transfer of legal advice and opinions between the parent company and its Indian counterpart can then be as smooth as Indian silk!

Putting Your Plan into Action

For a cut-and-dried list of the steps (laid out by the World Bank) you need to take to get your Indian business ball rolling with any of the entry routes described previously in this chapter, refer to the following steps:

1. I presume you've chosen a name for your company. You need to make it official by getting it approved by the Registrar of Companies (ROC). You have to submit the name, along with the Memorandum of Association and Articles of Association to the ROC. Keep your fingers, toes, and eyes crossed while the ROC goes through the papers. After the ROC gives you the go ahead, get the documents printed.

2. The next stop is the Superintendent of Stamps or an authorized bank. Purpose of the visit? To get the Memorandum of Association and Articles of Association stamped.

3. Back to the ROC, taking with you the duly stamped papers. And don't forget the registration fees. In return, you get a certificate of incorporation. For more info on registration fees, check out www.doingbusiness. org/ExploreTopics/StartingBusiness/Details.aspx? economyid=89.

4. Have a company rubber stamp made.

5. Now you need to get a PAN. No, don't start digging through your cookware. You're not going to cook anything. You need a Permanent Account Number (PAN) for tax registration, and to get one you have to go to the nearest Unit Trust of India (UTI) office.

6. Visit the Assessing Office of the Income Tax Department to get yourself a Tax Account Number so your income tax can be withheld at source (an important tax in India — more details in Chapter 9).

7. Next comes registration. Register your business under the Mumbai Shops and Establishments Act, 1948.

8. Register for Value Added Tax (VAT) (for more on this, turn to Chapter 9) with the Sales Tax Officer of the ward in which your company is located.

9. Register for the professional tax.

10. Tired? Well, you're almost there. Visit the Employees' Provident Fund Organization and register there.

11. Register with the Employees' State Insurance Corporation for medical insurance. Whew! You're done!

The route may seem tortuous to you, but it shouldn't actually take you very long or make your wallet significantly lighter. The whole process should be completed in about five weeks and cost about $530 according to present estimates.

Before your new project can start functioning, and depending on the nature of your business, you also need approvals and clearances from various Indian authorities such as the Pollution Control Board, Inspector of Factories, Electricity Board and Municipal Corporation.

For up-to-date information, you can visit these government Web sites:

- **Department of Industrial Policy & Promotion:** www.dipp.nic.in
- **Department of Commerce:** www.commerce.nic.in
- **Directorate General of Foreign Trade:** http://dgft.delhi.nic.in
- **Ministry of Environment of Forests:** www.envfor.nic.in
- **Ministry of Small Scale Industries:** www.ssi.nic.in
- **Reserve Bank of India:** www.rbi.org.in
- **Ministry of Finance:** www.finmin.nic.in
- **Ministry of Corporate Affairs:** www.mca.gov.in
- **Investment Commission of India:** www.investmentcommission.in/policies_and_laws.htm

Chapter 6

Doing Business from Abroad: The Long Distance Relationship

. . . .

In This Chapter

▶ Turning to India for sourcing

▶ Understanding the Indian business process outsourcing boom

▶ Keeping in contact with Indian business colleagues from overseas

▶ Identifying challenges and how to cope with them

. . . .

*I*ndia's workforce and strong manufacturing base make it a major economic attraction for the West. Many Western businesses choose India for a variety of tasks and processes, from sourcing to outsourcing and everything in between. In recent years, technology has added a new dimension. Have you ever used the Internet to buy anything with a credit card? If you have, chances are you've used a business process that India developed, and your long distance relationship began. But you want to expand on that relationship as you tap India for your business needs.

This chapter helps you better understand India's ability to trade and also presents today's options for doing business in and with the country without having to leave your home, office, or comfort zone. I offer information on the most promising possibilities for leveraging India's strengths and provide you with ways to negotiate the pitfalls and ensure the success of your "virtual" relationships while you do business from overseas.

Sourcing from India

It's hard for some to believe that sourcing from thousands of miles away on the other side of the globe can help increase profitability, but for a variety of reasons, that can be just the case. In this section, I explore the possibilities for sourcing in India and help you get started on the right track.

India can be an attractive option for sourcing because it offers a multitude of choices and value for your money. India's varied raw materials and skilled and intelligent workforce are two of its most attractive features (and with the dismantling of many governmental controls and the presence of big-ticket multinationals, the volumes and variety have increased). Add to this India's lowered costs — sourcing from India can improve your bottom line — and take advantage of India's infrastructure in the form of ports and airports, and you won't need to look any further.

Looking at India's sources

India has a vast manufacturing base that churns out a variety of items from aircraft and chemicals to machinery and food products. The "hot list" of products that the West looks to India to provide is growing every day. India's ever-growing resources include some of the following:

- Automobile ancillaries
- Electronic goods
- Readymade garments and textiles
- Software
- Specialty chemicals
- Tea

And if you're interested in getting in on the other end of the transaction — manufacturing products in India — take a look at Chapter 12.

Finding the right supplier

Locating potential suppliers in India used to depend heavily on trade fairs, where overseas companies met with a variety of potential suppliers as well as the relevant trade missions or consulates. Interaction with Indian chambers of commerce and industry trade organizations were also very important (see Chapter 8 for more information on those groups).

These methods for finding suppliers are still around, but their role has been diminished with the advent of dramatic improvements in all forms of communication — especially the Internet. Today, many Web sites exist to fulfill your quest for finding a supplier. Here are a few sites to browse:

✔ www.indiamart.com

✔ www.exportersindia.com

✔ www.trade-india.com

In a hot economy like India, no single source is likely to be current or complete and some of the best vendors are so busy that they don't need to list themselves widely. So explore several options because some methods are still better than others.

Calling upon a consultant to find a supplier is often your best option. I explain the details in Chapter 7.

Finding a supplier on your own

Finding suppliers on your own is very difficult, if not impossible. One expatriate business I worked with needed to get a gloves supplier for their factory workers, and they had a hard time from the very beginning: They couldn't find an appropriate local trading company, and after some frustration they eventually sought references from the local people they hired. Some of the Indians on their staff had worked for manufacturing companies, and the engineering team provided a list of potential suppliers. The business then selected a supplier through the regular process of RFPs, interviews, and customer reference checks. You're better off not trying to find suppliers on your own. Rely on local resources to guide you.

Take Nokia for example: Through an extensive review process, Nokia found an excellent supplier for the cafeteria in their factory. First they selected local and global partners and sent out requests for proposals (RFP). The RFPs allowed Nokia to assess the potential suppliers' business models, financial stability, and processes. Based on that information, they narrowed their choices down to three. They then ran customer reference checks, and after that, the managers actually visited each potential supplier, checking the cleanliness of their kitchens and even personally tried out the food!

Using a matchmaking company to find a supplier

A matchmaking company is a service that can help you find suppliers. India isn't as well networked as other Asian countries with regard to matchmaking companies. Instead, experienced foreign businesspeople often use their own contacts. They sometimes cite concerns that with matchmaking companies they felt they had no control on supplier selection. They are also aware that although corruption is being reduced in India, it still exists and were wary of the objectivity of certain recommendations even though they hadn't seen any evidence of wrongdoing. Matchmaker companies on whom you do reference checks from other satisfied customers do the trick. Sometimes your relocation company who helps you settle down can point you in the right direction too.

Building the India network

It is a good idea to have a network among Indian business and social contacts. Business organizations are useful as you interact with well-established Indians who guide you by word of mouth. Your own Indian staff can also be invaluable in making recommendations.

Networking isn't a distinct service as such, just the process of leveraging your contacts to get what you want.

Inspecting your supplier

After your potential suppliers list has been whittled down to a few choices, you need to interact with the suppliers to make sure they're solid and up to the task.

Uncover all the details about your proposed suppliers. You may even want to hire an audit firm to carry out this task. The inspection is conducted with the cooperation of the supplier and should cover the following items:

- ✔ Bankers and auditors
- ✔ Compliance with environmental laws
- ✔ Current list of clients/suppliers
- ✔ Factory details (capacity, technology, workforce, testing facility, and so on)
- ✔ Office locations and facilities
- ✔ Ownership
- ✔ Shipping or transportation company used
- ✔ Volumes imported or exported

Covering these bases gives you an excellent idea of the size and business style of the supplier and also provides you with counter checkpoints. For example, an overseas bank can ask for a confidential credit worthiness check with your supplier's bank in India.

The Indian concept of time is pretty elastic. Also, by nature, Indians find it difficult to say "no," even if they know that you're asking for the moon. So make sure your Indian suppliers understand all the implications of what you require, agree with your schedule and fully appreciate the importance of adhering to it. I include more useful details in Chapter 16.

Importing and exporting data

Raw data on imports and exports is readily available in India. Every item of import and export is meticulously fed into the Indian Customs computer system. The data includes item descriptions, exporters, importers, country of origin, tonnage, value, and date of import or export. You can get your hands on that data by contacting the relevant government authorities (www.commerce.nic.in/eidb/Default.asp) and also from various business publications.

Check out these magazines:

✔ *Business Today:* www.business-today.com

✔ *Business Week:* www.indiabusinessweek.com

✔ *Businessworld:* www.businessworld.in

✔ *Dataquest:* www.dqindia.com

✔ *Domain B:* www.domain-b.com

✔ *India Today:* www.india-today.com

✔ *Outlook Money:* www.outlookmoney.com

Take a look inside these newspapers:

✔ *The Business Line:* www.epaper.thehindubusinessline.com

✔ *Economic Times:* www.economictimes.indiatimes.com

✔ *Financial Express:* www.financialexpress.com

✔ *The Hindu:* www.thehindu.com

✔ *Indian Express:* www.indianexpress.com

✔ *Times of India:* www.timesofindia.indiatimes.com

Comprehending Business Process Outsourcing

In addition to India's massive amount of trade in the inflow and outflow of goods, it also enjoys a significant volume of trade in the services sector. India has developed a global reputation as a center for *business process outsourcing* (BPO) in recent years. Sometimes referred to as "back office for the world," India provides an opportunity for your business to have a range of its basic functions done for a fraction of the cost. The word is rapidly being replaced by status elevating ones such as "knowledge partnerships."

Many Western businesses have already recognized the potential for BPO in India. They saw that they could easily farm out their non-core (yet critical) business functions to Indian firms, allowing them to focus more on core activities while increasing profitability. Now a dazzling variety of companies all over the world rely on Indian BPO.

The following areas are some of the most common in Indian BPO:

- ✔ Computer programming
- ✔ Customer care and technical support
- ✔ Data entry/Processing/Conversion services
- ✔ Human resources and administration
- ✔ Insurance processing
- ✔ Legal services
- ✔ Market research analysis
- ✔ Medical transcription
- ✔ Remote network maintenance and monitoring
- ✔ Telemarketing
- ✔ Typesetting and publishing
- ✔ Web-based training

With all the buzz surrounding the growth of BPO in India, you need to understand why India is such fertile ground for BPO and how you can capitalize on the opportunities. In this section, I fill you in on those details and reveal a few potential problems to overcome to help make your transition to Indian BPO a smooth one.

Planning your outsourcing strategy

The boom in BPO that India has experienced in recent years has created some well-worn paths, and India now has hundreds of BPO companies. But you still want to explore your options and decide which BPO solution is best for your business' needs.

The rate at which a company outsources to India is really a function of their comfort level about the process and how keen they are to leverage the business advantages that Indian outsourcing has to offer.

If you would like to test the waters before jumping right in, though, consider outsourcing a function that isn't critical so the financial benefits and process efficiencies accrue quickly. That approach may also embolden the company to follow up by outsourcing the critical functions as well. After successfully outsourcing one function, other functions may be transitioned much faster.

The length of time needed to get a BPO up and running in India depends on various factors:

- ✔ **Location:** If you choose a BPO unit in a city with easy availability of expertise and infrastructure, your operation can function sooner than if you opt for one in a less-developed area.

- ✔ **The process being outsourced:** The outsourcing strategy depends on which activities/areas are being outsourced. If generic, well-understood areas are outsourced, the transitioning can be smooth and fast. For example, if the "help-desk" activity is being outsourced to a call center, the transition can be accomplished within four to six weeks. If a process that is specific to your organization is being outsourced, it would be advisable to outsource one function at a time. (Even in accounting, the software platform and accounting guidelines for your organization may be unique.)

- ✔ **State government policies:** The governments of various Indian states are vying with each other to woo investments and many offer concessions. Some have single window-clearance facilities that offer faster clearance of paperwork than others. So check out this aspect when you're researching prospective collaborations.

You must be prepared to invest time in training the BPO resources on the specific standards, conventions, and processes that are required. You may need to budget for up to 12 weeks for completion of the transitioning process (after identification of the BPO entity). In general, a small operation in a simple process should be active in about three months.

The value of business process outsourcing becomes really attractive only by rapidly scaling up in India. Outsourcing a small-scale operation may not be worth the management effort and investment. In fact, the project could follow a "hockey stick" model of profitability, where it goes through a negative cash flow and loss in the initial period, and can break even over a span of 12 to 18 months of steady-state operation.

You can find plenty of information on BPO in India, and the setup process (including approximate costs for the major components in starting an operation in India) is readily available from reputed sources, such as the National Association of Software and Service Companies or NASSCOM (www.nasscom.in) and other industry analysts at the following Web sites:

- ✔ www.dqindia.com
- ✔ www.expresscomputeronline.com
- ✔ www.idcindia.com/about/about.htm

Finding and evaluating potential partners

If this is the first time you're dipping your toe into India's BPO waters, you may want to go through a local expert. Several firms specialize in matchmaking (see "Using a matchmaking company to find a supplier" earlier in the chapter) and call themselves "third party intermediaries." They can offer help with anything from drafting the RFP to vendor qualification and selection and finally getting the operation started in India. Service providers today even take on the responsibility of setting up the infrastructure in India and obtaining all the statutory clearances — for a fee, of course.

But if you've already been introduced to India and have a presence through any affiliate industries, there's obviously a cost advantage to the do-it-yourself model, even if it's applied to some parts of the entire process. Most established BPO companies in India provide you a reference list of customers and you could make inquiries with them. Areas that would be important for evaluation include the following:

- ✔ The management team in the BPO
- ✔ Internal processes, documentation, quality standards, and certification
- ✔ Staff strength and their ability to upgrade their output and performance levels and to increase the size of their teams and infrastructure to meet growing business needs (called *scaling up*)
- ✔ Infrastructure (power backup and communications)
- ✔ Service/quality level assurances
- ✔ Funding options

Putting together a contract

Just as in any other business deal, getting a solid contract in place for a BPO engagement is important so the responsibilities of the service provider are agreed on, and service level agreements and consequences for non-compliance are clearly specified. The most important aspect in a BPO contract is delivery. Therefore, service-levels are very important. Most BPO contracts have a separate Service Level Agreement (SLA) that defines the acceptable quality/service levels in terms of quantity, time and other parameters, performance metrics and their availability to your organization, problem escalation and resolution procedures, and remedies for non-performance.

A new breed of lawyers is associated with the IT/BPO industries and is able to provide the required legal services. Most international law firms have forged associations with Indian legal firms who provide similar services.

Getting your BPO management act together

To manage your BPO operations in India, set up a BPO liaison cell in your organization. The person in charge must understand the Indian culture and business practices. This cell should be able to provide — on a daily or periodic review basis process — clarifications and other information that the BPO firm requires. All BPO operations require some time and attention of the top management in your organization to make them successful, especially during the initial stages.

You may also want to put together a detailed communication plan that includes written processes that can be thoroughly discussed and explained when dealing across time zones. Your plan should emphasize the frequency and structure of reports and contingency planning for unforeseen holidays, work shutdowns, power interruptions, and broken communication channels.

Watching out for bumps in the BPO road

Setting up with BPO in India has a tremendous upside, and the majority of foreign companies who make the effort are pleased with the results. But problems do arise, and it's best to know about them before you begin depending on an Indian BPO company for your important back office functions.

The following sections highlight some of the problems that you may encounter.

A shortage of skills

One problem that you may encounter is an anticipated skills shortage. Yes, this is true at certain levels, particularly the middle management and senior leadership levels, but the media has been overemphasizing this problem. The surest indicator of an impending skills shortage would be your chosen BPO firm's recruiting lead time, average salaries, and attrition levels. Keeping in close contact with the BPO firm provides plenty of advance warning if any type of skills shortage stands a chance of affecting your business. Ask the firm about their attrition levels, recruitment, and human resources policies.

The skills shortage, if it comes in the next five to ten years, is likely to impact only English-speaking, voice-based processes. The Indian government has already initiated proactive English-focused education guidelines to prevent such a shortage from occurring. Back-end (non voice-based) transaction processing is unlikely to have a skills shortage in the foreseeable future because there's a huge reservoir of three-year degree graduates that's yet to be significantly tapped in the BPO sector. The numbers of such graduates (who primarily fuel the BPO sector) that come out of universities every year is also much higher than the four-year degree professionals.

Cost increases and management investment

Indian BPO firms are chasing talented, skilled employees. Annual increases in salary costs help to secure top-notch workers and therefore BPO firms may look for increases in their billing rates. Remember that you can always link these increases to service level performances.

You need to invest in some management staff to liaison with your BPO firm in India. The management team of the foreign company is ultimately responsible to its board/shareholders for the success of the BPO in India. It needs to monitor and exercise close control of the daily operations in the Indian company.

The problem of overpromising

At times, like companies everywhere, Indian BPO companies agree to do more than they can deliver, so develop a good sense of what can and can't be accomplished in a given time frame with your BPO. Coaching them on "underpromise and overdeliver" is a role you may have to play.

Scam artists

Because this industry is growing, many unsavory entrants and fly-by-night operations are also setting up shop. Many of these firms assume that promises of low prices alone secure business for them. Watch out for these firms. Don't scrimp on the process and take time to identify the right BPO entity for your needs.

Staying in Touch with Your Indian Business Family

Conducting business with a group of foreign colleagues in an unfamiliar setting when you're sitting right there with them can be tough, but when you're oceans and time zones away, the challenges can pile up and confusion can set in. However, with a little forethought, planning, and some understanding of the Indian psyche, you can operate a couple of continents away as effectively as you could if you were just across the hallway.

Keeping the lines of communication open

Communicating with your colleagues in India is a critical way to make certain that everyone is on the same page and to avoid unnecessary problems. The distance can make things tricky, but if you can keep a few communication keys in mind, you'll have it made.

When working on long-distance project management with an Indian company, spell out important technical details you require in simple English without any local slang. It's also a good idea to repeat the details often and emphasize how crucial they are to success. It's worth the extra care to make sure that everyone involved is absolutely clear.

E-mail, phone, and conferencing

As you expect, most communication is taken care of via e-mail. Some companies are, however, encouraging more telephone contact (including video conferencing) to try and personalize things. Quality Web and video conferencing facilities can make communication with your Indian business colleagues a much easier undertaking and help to build more productive relationships.

Indians are usually willing to accommodate the time difference, but calling them in the wee hours of the morning won't be very efficient for business. Communicate with your Indian colleagues and set up times to talk by using either traditional telephones, Internet telephony, or perhaps even an online instant messaging program. (Indians don't mind working long hours, and most of them work half days on Saturdays. Finding a good time for a telephone call should be a breeze!) This ritual helps build confidence and provides an opportunity for on-the-spot problem solving. Besides, after you get used to this one-on-one interaction, reading between the lines, or words, as the case may be, becomes easier to preempt trouble.

Holidays

Keep in mind that Indian holidays can be much different than what you're used to in the West. If you don't plan your communication around these days, you could end up tearing out your hair in frustration trying to reach your Indian colleagues while they're out of the office celebrating a holiday. You can read up on holidays associated with religious festivals in Chapter 15.

An excellent tool for overcoming the problem of holiday confusion is the good old calendar. Get yourself an Indian calendar and plot out holidays (keeping in mind that they can vary from state to state) a year in advance with your colleagues. Believe me; this simple step does wonders for your scheduling, not to mention your hair.

Tackling logistical considerations

Logistics are critical, and they're doubly important when you can't be present on the business site. To successfully do business in India from overseas, consider the following logistical considerations:

✔ Study the transportation connections to major cities (rail, road, and air travel).

✔ Look up distances from important geographical markets and to relevant ports.

✔ Confirm that the telecommunications infrastructure is up to snuff. Inquire about the availability of new telephone connections using a manual or automatic exchange, long distance capabilities, mobile options, broadband capacity, and so on.

✔ If you need a warehouse facility, make sure adequate space is available.

✔ Find out distances to the offices of government agencies like excise, sales tax, labor, factory inspection, and pollution control.

✔ Check the location of industry-assisting agencies like the State Financial Corporation and Industrial Infrastructure Corporation.

Adjusting for Indian tendencies

India has a dizzying population made up of over a billion unique individuals, but it's safe to say that many Indians share certain personality traits in common. Knowing about these traits won't instantly familiarize you with a billion Indians, but it may help you identify some characteristics that can make communicating with your overseas colleagues difficult and allow you to sidestep problems.

In this section I share with you some common Indian personality traits and how they can create obstacles to doing business. And mostly importantly, I explain how you can hurdle these communication barriers with grace.

Making the management structure clear

Indians work best when they are clear about the managerial hierarchy under which they need to function. You need to make sure that any relevant management structures are explained in detail, so your Indian colleagues know who's the boss, and where the buck stops. It's also very helpful to clearly define goals and schedules and install an overall management monitoring system.

Indians are known to be accused of poor process discipline, and by and large may work without a really structured management framework of monitoring and control as the West knows it. Before you and your long-distance colleagues plunge into work, provide training in these areas so it matches your expectations.

Sharing information

Sharing information also encourages and motivates Indians to think of the future from an insider's point of view, and to visualize possible changes that could impact the business — things that may never occur to you as a non-Indian. Your Indian colleagues and partners appreciate you being upfront and will be much more willing to contribute and do their best to ensure the venture's success.

Indian partners may unthinkingly and innocently pass on information that you shared to competitors, so when you share information make it crystal clear what's confidential and what's not.

On the whole, Indians are a more emotional lot than other groups. This emotionalism can cross business barriers, and although it may seem unorthodox, you can use it to your advantage. Ask about the families of your Indian colleagues and partners, and remember their birthdays and anniversaries. You may even consider sending a small gift to build relations with an effective work force (I explore the ins and outs of gift giving in Chapter 15).

Avoiding Potential Pitfalls

Conducting business from around the globe presents a set of challenges and concerns, and your dealings in India are no exception. Certain aspects of doing business in the West that you take for granted may not be guaranteed in India, and questions that you're not accustomed to asking need to be addressed. For example, have you made certain that you're not involved (directly or indirectly) with child labor? Are hazardous materials being used improperly?

This section sheds some light on the potential problems that you can face while managing your Indian business dealings from afar.

Make personal visits

You can operate your business without having a physical presence in India and be content with what you can achieve sitting continents away. But getting up close and personal may be even better. If it's possible make the trip to India to see for yourself the way your business is being run. It's hard for you to get a feel for your Indian business — no matter how large or small — without first-hand experience. See for yourself the setup and the people, make face-to-face assessments, and ensure that things are headed in the right direction.

Ideally, you should have a small team from your Western office in the Indian office initially, at least until the business is stable and running smoothly. Even for a tried-and-true process, a representative should visit the Indian operation periodically to conduct quality audits and proactively address other process improvement issues.

By the same token, your Indian business colleagues also need to meet you to see for themselves that you're just as human as they are and also to appreciate the differences that are going to impact your work together (for example attitudes toward punctuality and deadlines).

If you travel to India to have a look at your partner's facilities, make sure that the safety rules and regulations are being obeyed. Otherwise your product may be blacklisted. The textile, carpet, construction, and fireworks industries have been offenders in the past.

If you really can't make a personal visit, you can always use the services of an international neutral inspection agency. There are national and international agencies that work to see that international labor standards are maintained. India has its own laws regarding employment conditions and has ratified the major global human rights treaties, and works with national and global voluntary organizations to ensure that sweatshops find it difficult to survive. The Export Inspection Council of India can be contacted at www.eicindia.org/eic/ournetwork_list.htm.

Avoid the Indian sweatshop

For many years, India faced the harsh reality that businesses employed women and children in difficult working conditions. Today India has numerous laws to ensure fair labor and business practices, including minimum age and wage requirements.

Make sure you and your partner are following these regulations. Breaking child labor rules can attract a prison term of three months to two years with or without a fine of between Rs 10,000 to Rs 20,000 (Rs is short for rupees — Indian currency).

The industry of child labor

Child labor was extensively used in two major industries: fireworks in Tamil Nadu and carpets in Kashmir. The glass bangle industry and quarries also employed a lot of children. These tiny laborers worked in unhealthy and even dangerous environments — ill-ventilated places for long hours, handled hazardous chemicals, and no primary education. (These are now by and large things of the past.) They pretty much sacrificed their childhood to contribute to their family's income. But laws are being stringently enforced now and the government works in tandem with non-governmental organizations to either remove children from factories altogether or at least offer them safer environments and shorter hours of work, coupled with the chance of achieving basic education as a kind of temporary relief measure.

If you're utilizing a production facility, make a detailed inspection of the factory and follow procedures and rules with regard to labor and conditions of work. Study these policies in detail and question your Indian partner to satisfy yourself that no rules are being broken. I include information on some of these issues in Chapter 12.

Adhere to regulations and securing licenses

You wouldn't dream of violating rules and regulations at your business back home, right, so why would you run the risk of doing it with your Indian business venture? Violating rules — whether they be labor, environmental, or safety related — has serious repercussions, not only for your organization as a business entity but also for the community as a whole.

To avoid this mistake, make sure you have up-to-date information on the rules and regulations that affect your company's presence in India, and require that proof of the Indian operation's adherence to those rules be given to you periodically.

For example, if your business is in any position to cause environmental damage in India, you need to abide by a number of anti-pollution laws. These regulations were put in place after many serious accidents began to affect India's environment. Arrange a joint meeting with your Indian partners and the local pollution control board to make sure that you're following the relevant rules, and see to it that they're followed in the future.

You may also have to secure various licenses for your business operations in India. To ease this process, hire a reliable advisor to be on site in India who can guide you through the paperwork and red tape. You can also refer to the information provided by organizations like the Federation of Indian Chambers of Commerce and Industry (FICCI) and NASSCOM for additional details on the framework. I provide more information on these important groups in Chapter 8.

Involve a legal firm

Because India's states are each unique, you need good legal counsel in the state where you plan to do business.

Working with attorneys in Singapore or even New Delhi is often not good enough because they won't necessarily have the local legal knowledge you need. Think regionally or locally. For example, if you need to use external temporary labor to complete a project deadline in Chennai, you need to find local lawyers who're knowledgeable in Tamil Nadu labor laws.

Talk to your lawyers. Talk to Indian lawyers who've worked with other foreign businesspeople. Talk directly to other foreign businesspeople and their employees. Talk to policymakers. You have a lot of talking to do, but the legal snares you can avoid (such as running into employment laws, investment rules, termination guidelines, and contractual problems) can make all the talking well worth your time.

Chapter 7

Building Your Team India

I once heard of an incredibly powerful line in a company's balance sheet. It said, "The best assets of this company have not been listed in this balance sheet. They are the 3,000 people who work here, and their value is priceless."

This idea is true all over the world. Your most important assets are your employees, and this concept is especially true for your business as you start up in India. The people you hire make your business successful, and your growth depends on the investments you make in time and resources.

The people of India are special. They're intelligent, quietly observant, and can be shy and outspoken at the same time. If you figure out how to harness the power of the Indian employee, you can be off and running in your journey toward Indian business success.

In this chapter, I explore the possibilities for your Indian team. I let you know how to assemble and keep that team, and I fill you in on a few important employment issues that help keep your ship running smoothly with a happy, productive crew.

Valuing Education: It's the Indian Way!

Indian children are sent to school at a very early age in comparison to their Western counterparts, and the school curricula are intense. Most educated Indian children know at least two languages (one is English), and many go on to pursue higher studies in technical and non-technical institutions.

The Indian preoccupation with knowledge has been passed down through the generations, and it is still a driving force in the population today. The pool from which you find your key employees is a well-educated one, and, perhaps more importantly, full of Indians who want to continue to grow and develop.

Indians have always rated education and the pursuit of knowledge very high, and the results are undeniable. The number system was developed in India, as was the concept of zero. Algebra, trigonometry, and calculus started in India. Where was the world's first university located? You guessed it. Back in 700 B.C. the first-ever university was founded in Takshila. It taught over 60 subjects, and more than 10,000 students passed through its doors. I devote an entire chapter to one of Takshila's most illustrious students later in this book, so check out Chapter 19.

The Indian educational system is getting better all the time. Elementary education is now required in India, and more availability of qualified people has brought in more job opportunities, and with it, improved lifestyles. The improvements in urban India are spilling over to rural areas too. These results in India's cities have been outstanding.

The rural areas are more of a struggle to cover all in these locales, but a National Policy on Education is committed to imparting basic education to all the country's people.

University education is seen as the route to employment, and more and more students are flocking to colleges to get technical degrees. The students who graduate from India's professional colleges are very bright and can compete with the best in the world. Familiarity with or fluency in English is an added asset, too. Good engineering or medical colleges are difficult to get into because they demand very high grades to attract the crème de la crème.

Several top technical institutes in India are worth your attention. You should know the names because they're equivalent to the Ivy League universities of the United States, and their graduates are all but guaranteed to have successful careers. A few of those institutes are as follows:

✔ Indian Institutes of Technology (IITs) in Delhi, Kanpur, Kharagpur, Mumbai, Chennai, Guwahati, and Roorkee

✔ Indian Institute of Science in Bangalore

✔ Birla Institute of Technology and Science (BITS) in Pilani, Rajasthan, Goa, and one soon to be ready in Hyderabad

✔ Veermata Jijabai Technological Institute (VJTI) in Mumbai

✔ National Institute of Design (NID) in Ahmedabad

✔ Sir J.J. School of Art in Mumbai

- Indian Institutes of Management (IIMs) in Ahmedabad, Bangalore, Indore, Kolkata, Kozhikode, and Lucknow

- Jamnalal Bajaj Institute of Management Studies (JBIMS) in Mumbai

- XLRI (formerly known as the Xavier Labour Relations Institute) in Jamshedpur (near Kolkata)

Indian academicians are also among the world's best. Foreign universities often invite them to come teach for a semester. Leading professors and even Indian Administrative Services (IAS) bureaucrats take sabbaticals to teach in American universities like Columbia and Harvard.

Indians reserve the term *school* for primary and secondary education, up to 12th grade. After that, students attend colleges and it's derogatory to say that they go to school. Americans use the term to describe various educational and academic levels, so be aware of the difference!

Finding the Right Indian Employees

India offers a vast pool of quality manpower, but finding talent to suit your specific needs can be a little difficult if you don't know where and how to look. Indians may be technically qualified for a position, but they may not have the particular skills that foreign business executives seek. They may also be used to very different work practices than those prevalent in the West. And even if you find people with the technical skills you require, you may need to explore whether they fit in with the work culture you want to build for your business in India.

Thanks to the booming economy on the one hand, and the struggle to provide training (see Chapter 12 for more information on that) on the other, you may find a serious shortage of skilled persons in some segments, while others are bursting at the seams with job seekers.

You may also discover that finding Indians to suit your requirements at the top levels is hard. Competitors in sectors like IT, marketing, and retailing snatch up experienced professionals, and the employee turnover in these fields is quite high. Always be watching out for attrition and have a forward hire plan with people waiting on the bench to complete deadline driven projects.

If you want to find the best candidates for the jobs you offer, consider adopting a number of different strategies. In this section, I detail those strategies and help you decide which ones make sense for your business.

Holding teachers in high regard: The Gurukul system

You've probably heard the word "guru" at some point, but did you know that the word's origin is Indian? It means one who removes the darkness of ignorance by shedding the light of knowledge (literally gu = darkness, ru = remove). Put simply, it's another word for a great teacher.

Gurus have had an important role in India through the centuries. In ancient India, the Gurus were certainly revered. They lived frugal lives and taught the sons of kings and rulers. These children stayed on campus, as it were, with the Gurus, for about 12 years and took in all that the Guru had to teach them in various educational disciplines. Students shared their masters'

simple lifestyles and served them and their families. The guru legacy has been preserved through the generations, and even now teachers are highly respected in India.

From the teaching field came two of India's greatest presidents: Dr. S. Radhakrishnan (India's first president) and the country's current president, Dr. A. P. J. Abdul Kalam. Dr. Kalam, a scientist, says his first love is teaching, and he wants to return to it after he completes his term as head of state. Clearly, Indian teachers are held in high regard, and their students (your future employees) are bright and engaged as a result.

Conducting on-campus interviews

Interviewing potential new employees on college and university campuses is a very popular recruitment strategy in India. The process is simple:

1. **Start by evaluating various institutions according to the quality of education offered and the grading systems they employ.**

   Make sure you focus on the most appropriate campuses. Try the schools listed in "Valuing Education: It's the Indian Way!" earlier in this chapter.

2. **Go to the institutions that offer the kind of qualifications you're looking for in your prospective staff.**

3. **Conduct interviews on campus on a pre-arranged date.**

   Most colleges have all the facilities you need to hold interviews and discussions. The advantages are that you save a lot of time and money, and you're sure to see bona fide credentials.

Here are some key ideas to remember when recruiting on college campuses:

✔ Keep an eye out for popular recruitment drives at colleges and universities and make a note of the campuses that other successful companies are visiting. Then follow the leaders.

✔ Many universities have a professor or a small cluster of professors who double as placement officers. They organize placement programs for graduates and invite companies to give presentations, conduct interviews, and recruit on campus. Stay in touch with these key contacts and use them to keep your company's name buzzing in the campus air.

Contact the colleges you're interested in and they can direct you to the right people. A forum of placement officers also exists who are student counselors from each university. The Ministry of Indian Education in each state can supply you a list of these people.

✔ Build an *employer brand* that catches the imagination of the students. At most well-known business schools in India, the students decide the sequence in which companies visit the campus. A good pre-placement presentation that clearly highlights the significant aspects of your company and what the company offers in terms of work environment, job content, opportunities to grow and develop, compensation, and career advancement opportunities are important factors in determining when your company gets invited.

✔ Build up a relationship with the institute and its students through summer internships. Former interns can be valuable ambassadors for your company when they return to college after the summer.

✔ A new company would also do well to gain visibility by organizing and sponsoring campus events.

Hire graduates from the celebrated Indian Institutes of Technology (IITs) and Indian Institutes of Management (IIMs), but the second level universities are also doing very well, and may just have that perfect candidate you're looking for. Anna University in Chennai, University of Roorkee, Jawaharlal Nehru University, and University of Mumbai are some good examples. Keep your hiring options open.

Innovative use of language

Although many Indians are talented English speakers, you still run into unfamiliar phrases and what can seem like odd uses of the language. Take for example this hopeful job applicant's response to an advertisement for an open position: "Dear Madam, in response to your above, please find attached my below . . . "

Depending on their home regions and where they went to school, Indians have regional accents and use alternative terminology and idioms. One phrase that usually befuddles is *doing the needful.* This phrase means doing whatever is required to fulfill a request. If you're interviewing a prospective Indian employee and you comment she needs additional training before getting the job, you may hear that candidate say "I'll do the needful and get back to you." It sounds odd, but rest assured, the job gets done!

Placing advertisements and holding walk-in interviews

Cleverly designed advertisements in the media specifically targeted to catch the eye of potential recruits can work wonders when you're trying to find quality employees. India's national and regional newspapers and business magazines are all good places to advertise openings.

But be warned that an ad in such a paper may leave you snowed under with résumés. One recent ad for 300 vacancies produced 10,000 applicants!

You may also consider setting up walk-in interviews in conjunction with the advertisement. You can hold meetings at business centers, your office, or a hotel if you expect many candidates to show up. Walk-in interviews are a good way to conduct multilevel interviews. *Multilevel interviews* use combinations of written tests, psychometric analysis, and spoken skills. An Indian engineer may not speak well but could excel in the other key areas. His lack of eye contact, unfocused answers, and inability to toot his own horn may not be reasons for you to toss his résumé in the "reject" file, because his position may not require those traits. These interviews can definitely weed out the less promising candidates, though, and take a more and more refined look at the available talent with certain specified skill sets.

If you decide to hold walk-in interviews that you advertised in a major media outlet, ask an Indian colleague to sit in with you in the interviews so she can help you decide good from bad and also help you bridge any communication gaps.

Using placement agencies

When you're aiming to fill positions that require particular skills, placement agencies can be extremely useful. Placement agencies cover multiple locations so you can hire in different cities. They specialize in compiling extensive files filled with résumés from skilled Indians and matching those candidates with the skills you require in a particular open position. In doing so, they can save you a great deal of time and trouble.

In addition to improving the efficiency of your hiring process, placement services can give you access to a better candidate pool within an industry. If a good placement agency approaches a person of a high profile, that person takes the opportunity much more seriously because he knows that the agency has been considering résumés from all over India and even the world.

You can choose from a variety of placement agencies. Whether you go with an international or Indian firm is a matter of what's most convenient for you — both options have very attractive firms. Check out these firms:

- ✔ **Egon Zehnder International:** An international firm specializing in assessing and recruiting business leaders. Check them out at `www.egonzehnder.com`.

- ✔ **Stanton Chase International:** An international firm that provides global executive search consulting services. Visit their site at `www.stantonchase.com`.

- ✔ **ABC International Placement Service:** An Indian placement agency that's one of the widespread and leading sources for Indian and overseas job opportunities. Go online to `www.abchr.org/index.html`.

- ✔ **Ma Foi Management Consultants Limited:** An Indian agency that focuses on recruitment and human resources (HR) services. Visit the Web at `www.mafoi.com`.

One European car company recently used a placement agency to hire all its recruits for a start-up operation. The company used the agency in conjunction with media advertisements and got the agency to list the positions on the company's behalf and take care of the subsequent sifting through résumés, interviews, and testing. By the time the candidates were ready to meet the car company's hiring panel, the remaining choices were the best of the best.

Check the payment structures for placement agencies before you retain their services. For senior-level recruitments, some agencies insist on a non-refundable retainer fee. Assess the company's modus operandi, and make sure that it does all of the pre-screening legwork and doesn't just pass on the résumés it receives to you.

Participating in job fairs

If you keep your eyes on the newspapers you can find advertisements for job fairs, which are becoming more and more common in metropolitan areas of India. They may be function- or industry-specific, and some are even open to all employers and candidates.

If you want to capitalize on the growing popularity of job fairs, all you need to do to get set up is to communicate your interest by using the contact information provided in advertisements for job fairs (all the big fairs are advertised well in advance in the media). You can also visit `www.timesjobs.com/timesJobWebApp/tj/JobFairs/jobfairs.jsp` for a listing. After you're at the fair, make sure that you create an attractive booth with posters that announce your company's mission and policies to potential candidates who're milling around at the fair.

To make sure things run smoothly and ensure that you don't waste valuable time banging up against the language barrier, be sure to take along some of your key Indian personnel there to help you assess and recruit candidates.

Tapping the recruitment power of the Internet

In the West, employment Web sites are becoming increasingly popular for both job-seekers and companies looking to advertise for open positions. The same trend is happening in India. Well-educated, Indian, job-seekers are Web surfers who seek out and find the career opportunities you post online. Web sites are a particularly useful way to find junior- to mid-level staff. (One French company I know filled more than 70 positions using the Web.)

To take advantage of this efficient, cost-effective way to find recruits, advertise your openings on major employment Web sites:

- ✔ www.monster.com
- ✔ www.jobsahead.com
- ✔ www.naukri.com (*naukri* means *job* in the Hindi language)

These portals offer you a wide choice and are also very easy on the wallet. In addition to listing the jobs you have open, look into what it takes to get your company on the sites' preferred employers list.

It sounds like a no-brainer, but be sure to also advertise open positions on *your* company's Web site. If you want to go a step further, advertise your Web site on popular Indian television stations like Star TV, which drives potential job-seekers to your home on the Web.

Seeking non-resident Indian hires

Many non-resident Indians (NRIs) — Indians who've moved away from the country to pursue education or the attractive salaries of Western jobs — are looking for a reason to come home, and a job opening in your company could be just the reason they need.

Big NRI fish in small ponds

NRIs are often homesick and looking for good situations that allow them to move home to India to be with family and again immerse themselves in the familiar Indian culture. If you manage to hire an NRI to work for (or head up) your Indian office, you may often find that she's an exemplary employee.

I know a customer-service hospitality company that grew from small to big to enormous in a very short time behind the outstanding work of a COO of Indian origin. He had been a medium-size fish in a big pond overseas in the IT industry, and when he moved back to India to help grow his employer's company, he found himself to be a big fish in a medium-size pond. He enjoyed far more job satisfaction, and as a result, he was able to grow the company exponentially, implementing Western best practices yet understanding his local India team. He made a lateral move monetarily, but traded the fast paced life of the West for quality time with his family, which was the reason the company was able to attract him despite the fact it was smaller than his previous employer.

NRIs join your company for the right reasons, stay on board, and work hard to meet and exceed business targets.

This scenario is a win-win situation: the NRI can come home to his cultural roots and you gain an employee who's highly qualified, experienced in the Western ways of doing business, and also able to provide leverage in India with superior communication skills.

The best way to reach NRIs with your job postings is to list the available positions on employment Web sites that cater to NRIs. Also be sure to advertise through your home and other overseas offices, so that any NRIs living in those areas are likely to spot the listings. Word of mouth also works, so spread the word around your company, and ask your employees if they know any NRIs who may be interested in a job. Indian newspapers overseas are also a good place to advertise for NRIs. Try out www.indiawest.com or www.indiaabroad.com.

Recently, many Indian candidates have been fudging their academic and professional backgrounds in an effort to gain an advantage in the job market. Hire an agency to perform reference checks and verify credentials on job candidates for you (for a fee, of course). I recommend starting at recruiting companies for recommendations of good agencies.

Retaining Your Team through Various Compensation

After you've assembled your Indian team for your business, you need to focus next on how to keep that team together. Because the economy is booming and the job market is jumping, you may find that demand pulling your Indian employees away. Your terrific new team could disintegrate as fast as you put it together!

To retain and build on your Indian team, you have to make sure various bases are covered. Compensation packages are important and include so much more than money. When trying to retain employees, you need to think of the entire job experience. For example, an NRI may take a position in your company because he's looking for an enjoyable, challenging work environment in his home country. If you throw money at him but don't foster the right type of company culture, you could lose a key employee. You need to compensate your employees appropriately and offer an interesting, challenging work atmosphere that allows employees avenues for career growth.

Compensation options

You may have heard that salaries in India are only a fraction of what the West pays. True. But labor costs in India are rising, especially in high-growth industries like IT, so you need to keep your Indian employees happy with their pay. Salaries rise with increasing demand for experienced workers, but India is still much less expensive than the West. Junior- and mid-level professionals in particular are still being paid substantially less than their counterparts in the West, though the quality of their work is often comparable.

Experience and quality of education are key factors in determining pay rate. Indian employees who graduated from the IITs and IIMs (see "Valuing Education: It's the Indian Way!" earlier in the chapter) command higher wages than their contemporaries who went to less renowned colleges.

Pay rates do vary from industry to industry and from job to job. After you reach the highest levels of the top companies doing business in India, the salaries begin to resemble those for senior executives in the West.

Although salaries continue to spiral upward, more and more companies are changing from the older Indian way of automatic 10 percent pay increases per year to linking salary increase to performance.

From your company's point of view, regularly rewarding employees based on performance makes excellent business sense. However, the performance appraisal system needs to be objective and, more importantly, transparent. Without transparency, the system can cause a lot of heartache and eventually prove to be counterproductive in India. People take the scores and comments personally unless you take the time to explain the reason behind the markings.

Typical Indian compensation packages are made up of various components. These elements are described in the following sections.

Basic salary

The basic salary of an employee in India usually accounts for between only 40 and 50 percent of the total compensation package, partly because there have traditionally been tax advantages to receiving other perks. But this is changing now as the tax structure adapts with the introduction of fringe benefits taxes, which tax travel, company cars, and business promotion expenses. You have to either offer employees some flexibility or figure out what works best for you.

Fringe benefits

Although they're beginning to be taxed more regularly, fringe benefits are still attractive. Indian labor laws outline mandatory retirement and long service benefits, death and disability benefits, and medical care benefits. Your employees may also be eligible for the following benefits:

- **Provident funds:** Compulsory, contributory funds that are set up with post-retirement interests in mind.

- **Gratuity:** This sum of money is a legal entitlement of any employee as part of retirement benefits and linked to years of service.

- **Medical/Accident insurance:** Medical allowances may come in a variety of forms. Companies may reimburse expenditures incurred by the employee for his and his family's medical treatment, pay a fixed allowance for routine check-ups, or sign up for a group medical insurance policy.

- **Leave:** See the section "Leave and Holidays" for more info.

  All companies with ten or more employees must also provide paid maternity leave to all female employees who've completed 80 days of continuous service in the twelve months preceding her expected delivery date.

- **Profit-sharing bonus:** When the company makes money, expect to share the wealth.

Most companies also provide their senior executives the following benefits:

- Superannuation/pension
- Housing (covered later in this section)
- Company car
- Personal loans for housing, cars, and so on
- Life insurance protection for dependants

Fringe benefits for employees can be costly, so be sure to keep an eye on how the perks affect your bottom line. Also, pursue legal advice when drawing up a salary package. If you have an HR department they can advise you on all issues; otherwise, your auditor or lawyer can help with salary particulars.

Allowances for your employees may cover a variety of other costs:

- Appliances
- Children's education
- Commuting
- Dearness (cost of living)
- Furniture
- Leave travel fare (LTF)
- Professional education
- Transportation
- Travel
- Utilities
- Work clothing

For your non-Indian employees, you may want to consider additional benefits:

- Travel back home twice a year
- International school fees for employees' children (fees for these schools are substantially higher than local schools in India)
- A living allowance for spouses and children living back home
- A driver and car

A driver and a car are a necessity for senior managers to perform optimally. Indian traffic is crazy, and commute times are increasing with city expansions. A driver and car allows the manager to sit in the back of the car finishing up his phone and e-mail business from his wireless device while the chauffeur drives. Two cars and two drivers for the manager's spouse and kids are also attractive perks, although not must-haves.

Employment laws are regularly amended; employers need to be aware of the latest changes. To stay on top of the game, read your newspapers (changes are given ample coverage in the media) or speak with a consultant.

Leave and holidays

Be prepared to be generous with leave because it's very important to Indians. Twenty days of leave a year is normal for all employees who are covered by employment regulations, and sometimes employees choose to take that amount in a big chunk. Employees may also want to take leave during school and college holidays because families use those times to visit with extended family members in their native states.

Public holidays and festival seasons are also tricky situations to manage, especially if they come close to weekends. You may suddenly find a lot of empty cubicles when you come to work just after or before a weekend that follows holidays. Indians usually plan so that by taking just one day's leave, they can have a string of days off.

Your best bet is to plan a rotating roster or a block closure if your business can afford it as some companies do. That procedure allows your employees to be off at the same time, and customers know this policy in advance so there aren't any unpleasant surprises.

Housing benefits

Housing-related benefits can be extremely significant in India. Employers often reimburse a portion of an employee's rent in the form of house rent allowance (HRA), a portion of which isn't subject to income tax.

Almost without exception, all middle- and senior-level managers expect the company to provide them accommodation. In a congested city like Mumbai, where housing has been a perennial headache, this can be a substantial expense for a foreign company setting up shop in India for the first time. In Mumbai, an ordinary three-bedroom apartment of about 1,200 square feet in a good suburb costs between $190,000 to $290,000 (USD) for an outright purchase. Monthly rentals in the same area range between $2,200 to $7,000 (USD). Given the high cost of office rentals in Mumbai, setting up becomes a costly exercise. It's little wonder that other cities like Chennai, New Delhi, and Bangalore are extremely attractive on this front.

Termination packages

Before liberalization in India, joining a company and ending up retiring from it many years later was common practice. Pink slips were unheard of. As corporate India raises the bar, however, this practice has changed. Performance dictates the future, and securing a job at a particular company doesn't mean that an employee can settle in for the long haul. Downsizing was once an unfamiliar concept, but it's now a fact of life.

As termination has become more and more common, severance payments have surfaced and are now part of the Indian HR landscape. Voluntary retirement schemes are often drawn up for employees working for companies struggling through hard times. IT employees, however, are more often laid off with severance packages.

Common compensation packages

You have many options for compensation and benefits for your Indian employees. There are a few packages that are especially prominent among foreign companies setting up in India for the first time. One common mid-level package includes the following:

- ✔ Twelve percent of the gross annual salary of the employee is contributed to a provident fund
- ✔ Car allowance (with or without a driver)
- ✔ Medical insurance for the employee and his immediate family
- ✔ A contribution for housing rental depending on the location

In addition to these attractive benefits, an annual bonus and a soft loan for housing may also be offered, without commitment and dependent on both personal achievement and the performance of the company. An annual bonus is given on completion of year one.

If you want help setting up benefit packages for employees working in your new Indian venture, check out these specialists:

- ✔ **Hewitt Associates LLC:** www.hewittassociates.com
- ✔ **William Mercer:** www.mercerhr.com

Instilling Loyalty in Your Team

A company's HR department didn't use to be incredibly important, but now they've become a critical department that's charged with the task of motivating, improving, and retaining staff. Increasing company loyalty is extremely important, and it often helps to have an Indian HR manager working with any Western personnel in that department so that the employee lifecycle is well understood and addressed at various stages.

Your HR department — whether that's you or a staff of fifty — needs to make your company as attractive as possible. In this section, I let you know what it takes to hang on to and motivate your new Indian team.

Developing your company culture

After you present the bigger picture of who you are as a company and what you hope to achieve, you next have to inspire your team and develop a sense of unity and company culture. Here are a few pointers:

- ✔ Make sure your company's culture comes through in your vision statement and mission statement.

- ✔ Display your vision and mission statements prominently in the workplace — employees can have a constant reminder of what they're trying to accomplish as part of a team of dedicated individuals.

- ✔ Give your staff members cross-cultural training so they understand the similarities between your culture and theirs and can figure out how to adapt to differences. Sue Fox's book, *Business Etiquette For Dummies* (Wiley), is a good reference book to have in your library for your Indian staff. If you check out www.globalindian.com, you get e-learning solutions especially for Indians to understand working in intercultural situations.

- ✔ Indians have the software of their minds programmed to looking up to their bosses and superiors, so inspire them and lead the way.

Some companies offer gyms, free cafeterias, and sporting areas to enhance the working environment and contribute to their company culture. These additions help employees feel like they aren't missing out on life when they're working hard. If you have the resources, consider offering some of these outstanding workplace opportunities.

Recognizing the importance of family

Indians have extremely strong family values. The centuries old joint-family system has given way to the nuclear family system in many cases, but family ties remain strong. Most young Indians attach a good deal of importance to taking care of aged parents. This responsibility sometimes influences their career decisions and job choices, so keep track of family compulsions while recruiting people and planning their career movements.

Here are a few examples you may need to consider:

- A professional with dependent parents may not want to move out of a particular city because the older people wouldn't want to do so.
- Another employee may not want to pull his children out of schools they've been used to and enter them in new ones at a critical time in their educational career, say when they're within a year of facing Board Examinations.
- In instances where both partners are employed, one may resist a transfer if it places the spouse's career in jeopardy.
- One person I know has steadfastly refused to take postings out of a particular city because his child, with a congenital disability, was under the care of a particular doctor with whom he was comfortable, and he didn't want to risk a change.

Employers generally consult their staff on their willingness to accept other postings. At the time of annual appraisals, this question regularly comes up, whether or not a transfer is being contemplated. This way, employers can keep track of the employees' commitments and openness to change to avoid trouble.

Offering training opportunities

Training sessions have become more prevalent in India in recent years because businesses understand the benefit of holding several sessions to increase retention. Training can also develop loyalty among your employees because it can continually improving your staff's skills. This scenario is particularly true of the IT field, which is constantly developing.

Keep in mind that many Indian workers have had no exposure to the international style of working, and training sessions — both in-house and external — can help them improve in that area and also help you develop a more adept staff.

When you hold a series of training sessions for your employees, be sure to ask for their feedback, so you know what worked and what didn't. It also helps to consider making the sessions as attractive as possible. A training module out of town or at a plush hotel that your employees may not normally visit can be a terrific way to keep them excited and engaged.

Also remember that even though a training session's meaningfulness is obvious to you, it may not be so clear to your Indian employees. You may need to convince them of the importance of a specific training session. You run into this more if you wait until employees have settled into their positions before bringing up the idea of training sessions.

For Indians, training abroad is highly valued, because it offers exposure to the best practices and facilities in the world. If you can swing it, offer training opportunities in your home country or at your company's headquarters. Syndi Seid of www.advancedetiquette.com is a good resource for U.S.-based training in life skills. Participation in company-wide training, seminars, and conferences inspire your Indian employees to a higher level of performance, and it just may up your retention levels.

Understanding Staffing Specifics in India

In addition to the sweeping topics of building and retaining an Indian team, there are also several smaller concerns with which you need to secure and make the most of your staff. You need to understand Indians culturally, socially, and personally. If you know what makes them tick, what values they live by, and what motivates them, you can better understand your employees and connect with them.

In this section, I offer a few staffing notes, so you can understand how to develop your team and make your employees into global Indians.

India's performance fixation

Performance evaluations and affirmations of exceptional performance are very important to Indians. Most Indians are used to assessment programs in which performance is thoroughly dissected, analyzed, and graded.

As a Westerner, you may be inclined to play things down when evaluating an Indian employee's performance, giving an outstanding employee, say, a 2 on a scale of 1 to 5 (where 1 is the top score). But that may demotivate your Indian employees, and as a result, they may worry about how their prestige is diminished in the eyes of their colleagues, friends, and family. Put simply, they take it hard. They may even try to argue the score or grading system with you.

When evaluating the performance of your employees, if particular team members have performed on an extremely high level, tell them that and rate them high. These ratings earn you a perennially hard worker. Performance evaluations should be very specific and subcategories should be clearly linked with examples to allow the employee clarity.

Nontraditional working arrangements

As India's economy has grown and changed in recent years, the idea of the standard, set-in-stone workday has diminished. As in Western countries, nontraditional working schemes are now very much a part of the work environment in India.

Working from home

Until very recently, the flexibility of working from home wasn't an option for Indians. But after the country threw open its economic doors to the world, many Indians have come to realize that this option is viable in some sectors.

Many companies offer work-from-home options, but only to those who've proved themselves competent and diligent. Women particularly benefit from this option, because it allows them to balance the demands of home and career.

If you do choose to offer work-from-home options when recruiting, be sure to have checks and balances in place to ensure good performance from those employees and specify the pay structures from the beginning.

Freelancing

With an increasing demand for qualifications and experience, more and more people with special skills are leaving the confines of regular employment and offering their talents to multiple takers. Many placement agencies have specialists on file whose services can be purchased for specific projects or in particular situations. Call them advisors, troubleshooters, or just freelancers — they use their specific skills to cater to your needs, and the outcome is usually a happy one. This avenue is certainly one you may want to explore.

People skills

In India, business and personal lives aren't really separated. So you may have to vary your people skills to suit specific occasions. For instance, in the West, you may not know the first thing about the private life of a very valued secretary, but in India you're not only asked probing questions about your family, your background, your likes and dislikes, but also you're expected to ask about your colleagues' kids, their hobbies, and possibly even their dogs. If you don't, you may be considered standoffish and condescending.

If you're not aware of the friendly interest Indians take in other people's lives, you may think they're downright nosy. Don't take that stance. Realize that their interest in your life is genuine and good-natured, and offer them as much information as you feel comfortable with.

I know an Italian couple who carry on a long-distance business relationship with India by using the Internet. Apart from the normal, work-related communications you may expect, the Italians get to hear of their staff's little problems and life issues. They hear of setbacks in relationships and the loneliness of life in a big city after being used to the close family ties of village life. They even serve as a shoulder to cry on from thousands of miles away! The Italians know that their Indian colleagues are accustomed to that kind of relationship, and so they've taken it all in stride. They embrace their roles as mentor *and* boss, and the relationship has been very successful.

Trade unionism

Trade unionism is a movement that unites workers under common banners to secure maximum benefits. Individual organizations have unions, with elected leaders, who speak for them with the management, negotiate terms, and champion the cause of even individual employees. These unions may tie up with other unions in the same industry. For example, individual banks, like the State Bank of India, the Indian Bank, and so on, have their own unions, but they also come under umbrella unions covering banks as a whole. Taking the process a step further, unions in various industries are members of larger, nation-wide trade union organizations, which wield a lot of power. These unions organize protests, including strikes, to focus on issues and win rights.

Just as Communist China is now welcoming industry, so are the Communists in India. They've figured out how to stifle their natural antipathy toward businessmen and look instead at prosperity for the people. Both West Bengal and Kerala are now actively wooing industrialists, and going out of their way to prove that, contrary to earlier trends, conditions are no longer unsuitable for businesses. Of course, the going isn't always smooth — there are still protests and Cassandras who spit fire and brimstone and harangue anyone who listens about the dangers of capitalism. But by and large, the industrial climate has improved in both these regions, and you could have the early bird advantage if you choose to take up the invitations of the state governments. If you want to know more about this aspect of doing business in India, turn to Chapter 13.

Groupism in the workplace

India is a mix of a startling number of cultures, but for the most part, this doesn't affect the workplace. You can expect a certain amount of groupism among employees with a similar background, just as you may expect a New Yorker to hit it off with another New Yorker in the same office.

On the whole, the country is professional enough to lay aside its ethnic and religious differences when it comes to work. However, if you're aware of ethnic preferences and strengths, you may be able to leverage them to your advantage. For instance, some communities are traditionally made up of businesspeople, and others are known for their financial wisdom. Others still are used to managing a multifaceted enterprise, like farming, and are used to delegating responsibility. For more information on these major business castes and communities, take a look at Chapter 3.

Using Consultants in India

Using consultants for your business needs is a very good option in India, because they know the ropes much better than you, at least initially. Consultants can help you with the whole slew of business needs, covering areas like recruitment, working out pay packages, training, changing management, and business strategy as a whole.

A good consultant can tell you what to do and what *not* to do, offer solutions when you hit roadblocks, and point you in the right direction when you don't know which way to turn. All are invaluable assets when you're playing on someone else's turf. In this section, I explain how to find a consultant and how to manage him.

History of trade unionism

Kerala, the southernmost Indian state, was the first in the world to have an elected Communist government. The leftist parties, primarily the CPI and the CPI-M, play a leading role in the country's politics. They're currently the ruling party in two states, and also offer support to the central government. Trade unionism is an accepted part of the business scene in India, though the disruptive nature of the concept has by and large worn off.

There was a time when industrialists and businessmen studiously shunned both West Bengal and Kerala because they were infamous for labor unrest. Strikes or *bandhs* were the order of the day there, and businesses lived on the edge, never knowing when a seemingly trivial incident would erupt into a major, statewide issue, involving various unions across a number of industries. Protests would flare up, and in the best-case scenario, traffic became snarled as processionists bearing red flags and shouting slogans wound their leisurely way across the main roads, attended by a few bored police personnel. In the worst-case scenario, a peaceful afternoon could turn ugly within seconds, with rioting, arson, and looting.

Finding an appropriate consultant

Find the most appropriate consultant for your business needs is critical. For starters, try your country's embassy. Embassies have lists of consultants they provide on request, depending on your business's necessities.

Another good way to find the right person is to ask those folks who've traveled the road before you. Look for a major company in your area of interest, which has an establishment in a city you're interested in, and ask them for advice. Here are a few options:

- ✔ Cairn Energy in Delhi
- ✔ IBM in Bangalore
- ✔ Ford or Nokia in Chennai
- ✔ Google in Hyderabad
- ✔ Caterpillar or World Bank in Mumbai

Talk to the successful businesses that sound the most interesting to and relevant for you. Most companies are willing to give you insights into the type of person you need to look for and share contact information. You can't go wrong if you choose this method.

While selecting a consultant in India, keep in mind a few pointers:

- ✔ Make sure he understands perfectly what your requirements are in various fields. If you aren't completely clear up front, you may not find out that you aren't being given what you expect until it's too late.

- ✔ Investigate your consultant's credentials, and ask for his experience in the fields where you require his services. Follow up on referrals, and do plenty of research into your potential consultant's previous experience.

- ✔ If you're looking for guidance regarding business strategy, ask the consultant for her success stories.

- ✔ You can test your consultant with a situation to see what ideas and possibilities spring to her mind.

Managing your consultant

Managing expectation is the most crucial aspect of doing business in India. After you've hired someone, telling them your needs, taking stock of the services every once in awhile, and tweaking it to exactly what you need are all required. Therefore, spend time managing the consultant you hire.

Most consultants take on multiple assignments, so ensure that a confidentiality agreement is signed, or you may find that your interests are being compromised.

Contact the American Chamber of Commerce in India (Amcham India: www.amchamindia.com) and equivalents from other countries, which have branches in the major Indian cities, to explore specifics such as cost. These organizations maintain valuable databases that you can access. After you get a rough idea about the remuneration rates and other details, contact the consultant you've zeroed in on, and, all other criteria being equal, fix a scheme of payment and figures that are acceptable to you both.

Put everything down in writing — in triplicate, if necessary — and have all the copies duly signed, so everyone knows where they stand.

Chapter 8

Dealing with the Powers That Be

. . . .

. . . .

*O*ne of the biggest challenges for a foreigner seeking to do business in India is figuring out the ropes of India's government and dealing with its bureaucracy. India has a system that actually works rather well, although many aspects of it may seem unique and new to you.

Relationships with the appropriate government officials are very important, as is the knowledge of how to go about procuring information from the government. You also need to develop a basic knowledge of India's legal framework and build your business connections through industrial relations. I cover all of these bases in this chapter, and provide you with insight on how to interact with the powers that be.

The Nuts and Bolts of the World's Largest Democracy

In what can only be described as a modern political miracle, the seventh largest and second most populous country in the world (with over a billion people), a land that features countless languages and religions, is actually a working democracy. In terms of population size, India is the largest democracy in the world. The framework and fundamental workings of India's government are essential knowledge for anyone interested in doing business in the country, and I cover those basics for you in this section.

The levels of government

India's federal government is known as the central or union government. The central governing system is based on a *bicameral* or *double-house system* of parliament made up of two houses:

- ✔ **The lower house:** Known as the Lok Sabha, this house is made up of elected representatives of the people sent from every part of the country, each one representing one constituency. The Council of Ministers is collectively responsible to the Lok Sabha.

- ✔ **The upper house:** Known as the House of Elders or the Rajya Sabha, this house is made up of members either elected by State Assemblies — the counterparts of the Lok Sabha at the state level in the federal system, or nominated by the President.

The Prime Minister, himself a member of the Lok Sabha, draws his council of Ministers from the same lower house, though sometimes even a Rajya Sabha member gets a Ministerial berth, on condition that he stands for election and wins a Lok Sabha seat within six months. The Parliament as a whole passes bills to which the President gives his approval, and they become law.

Much like the U.S. federal system the country is subdivided into states, with each state being managed or politically administered by its state government. (India got the technique of divide and rule from the British and has suitably Indianized it.) The states are roughly demarcated along linguistic lines, and they keep dividing and subdividing — three were added as recently as a couple of years ago! What started out as 14 states has now reached 28. (I explore the features of India's states further in Chapter 3.)

In addition to India's 28 states, it also contains seven union territories, which are specific areas that weren't put within the borders of neighboring states. Union territories are administered by the central government. They have aspirations of greatness: they want to earn state status, which the central government can grant as it deems fit. Many union territories have tax structures and other rules which may mean special benefits for your business, depending on your area of operation. Consult with your Indian contacts for details.

If you want to make a success of your business in India you need to talk with the central state governments in the state where you've chosen to locate your business.

The branches of the Indian central government

The Indian central government is made up of three essential foundation blocks: the legislature, the executive, and the judiciary. In this section I present you with a brief summary of each.

The legislature

In the Indian capital of New Delhi, the Indian Parliament comprises two Houses:

- **Lok Sabha:** This level is the Lower House or the People's House or the House of Commons — call it what you will. The members of the Lok Sabha have been duly elected by the people of a particular constituency.

- **Rajya Sabha:** This house is the Upper House or the States Council or the House of Lords. The Rajya Sabha consists of eminent Indians elected by members of the Assemblies of states and union territories, along with 12 members nominated exclusively by the President of India. (The Assemblies are the state-level versions of the Parliament at the Centre).

The executive

The leader of the party, who wins the majority in an election by convention, becomes the Prime Minister. The real executive power is vested with the Prime Minister, not the President, who's more of a figurehead. Indian presidents are chosen by an electoral college comprising members of the two Houses of Parliament as well as state legislatures. All bills passed by Parliament have to have the President's approval before they're made law, but Indian presidents only very rarely exercise their option of withholding consent to a bill.

The Prime Minister puts together a Council of Ministers commonly referred to as the Union Cabinet, who then assumes the executive responsibility of running the country under specific portfolios, such as Finance, Defense, Foreign Affairs, and Social Welfare.

India borrowed the Prime Minister concept from the British. Indian Prime Ministers hold at least one key portfolio and serve as head of government for all practical purposes. The Prime Minister appoints Ministers in the Union Cabinet and allocates portfolios.

The judicial

Given the political system and structure, India's founding fathers realized the need for an independent judicial system and enshrined this in the Indian constitution. Essentially, what this means is that nobody in India, including the President and the Prime Minister, is above the law.

The Judiciary is independent of Parliament. At the top is the Supreme Court — an integrated system with a single judicial hierarchy. The Supreme Court, located at New Delhi, has a Chief Justice and other judges. The judiciary guards the Constitution of India.

Each state also has High Courts as well as lower courts. The course of justice winds its way upward, step by step, with the Supreme Court being the final authority. Turn to Chapter 13 for more information on legal issues.

The importance of religious unity

India is a rich tapestry of religions, cultures, ethnic groups, and political convictions. Many times, these distinctions overlap, and over the years Indians have become tolerant and assertive at the same time. Indians live in a contextual and consensual mode and that's what makes it work for them. Indians mix and mingle, and though often the threads that make up the country pull in different directions, they come together during critical times to form the force that's India.

In recent years, there have been shining examples in the leaders of India that enjoy religious diversity. India has seen a Catholic-born woman (Sonia Gandhi) stepping aside, even when her party had majority, so that an adherent of the minority Indian religion Sikhism (Dr. Manmohan Singh) could be sworn in as Prime Minister by a Muslim President (Dr. A. P. J. Abdul Kalam) to rule a nation which is 82 percent Hindu.

India's state and local governments

The governmental procedures at the state level more or less mirror the central government (see "The branches of the Indian central government" earlier in this chapter). The leader of a state's majority party becomes the Chief Minister of the state. At the state level, the House of Representatives is called the Legislative Assembly. Most states have just one house, but a few states also have an upper house or Legislative Council. The Chief Minister appoints a council of Ministers, which is referred to as the State Cabinet. These Ministers are responsible for managing the affairs of the State.

Indian state governments are basically autonomous, and further down the government structure you find the local bodies, commonly called the Municipal Corporations, and the *Panchayats,* which govern at the city, town, and village level. All are comprised of representatives elected by the people.

The division of power between central and state

The central government of India is responsible for the country's overall administration, including macro reforms and policy changes. Different legislative powers of the state and central governments are clearly spelled out to avoid any conflicts. But that's not to say that trouble never breaks out. Like any ordinary family unit, India also has its spats about rights (and wrongs), but it usually settles them amicably.

Inevitably, areas overlap and become potential areas of conflict. To contain such situations, three lists exist that define the legislative powers of the state and central governments.

These three lists are

- ✔ **The Central List:** Provides a division of powers and describes where the government has legislative authority. Parliament has the exclusive right to frame laws on matters of defense, foreign affairs, currency, income and service tax, customs and excise duty, railways, shipping, posts and telegraphs, and so on.

- ✔ **The State List:** Provides a division of powers and describes where the government has legislative authority. The State List includes items like public order, police, public health, communications, agriculture, lotteries, taxes on entertainment and wealth, sales tax, VAT (value-added tax), and octroi (tax levied on goods brought into certain cities).

- ✔ **The Concurrent List:** Outlines conditions under which the central government can make laws in consultation with the state governments. The Concurrent List includes areas such as electricity, newspapers, criminal law, marriage and divorce, stamp duties, trade unions, and price controls.

The voting system

India has universal franchise (meaning that all can vote regardless of caste, race, and gender) with the voting age starting at 18 years old. The election process in India is a source of wonder to the rest of the world. The country is divided into a large number of constituencies, and each sends representatives to the central and state governments to participate in running the country.

Voting is done by secret ballot. Indians are on the whole responsible citizens, and long, winding lines can be seen outside polling booths on election day. For such a vast, culturally and religiously diverse country, elections are conducted fairly smoothly. The country is divided into constituencies on the basis of population, and these in turn into wards, each with a booth. Eligible voters can choose from among various candidates. Their votes are recorded by electronic voting machines. These votes are counted, and the candidate who has the majority wins. Elections are a marathon exercise, given the size and diversity of the country, in terms of terrain, climate, and population.

Indians aren't predictable in the way they vote; they do truly show that they speak their mind when they choose. The Indian public has proved its political astuteness over and over again, catching the world and its own incumbent governments by surprise and proving experts and exit polls way off the mark. All too often surveys conducted outside polling booths, from a random sampling of people leaving after casting their votes, have shown that the votes swing one way or another, but when the results actually come out, these polls are totally wrong. Pre-poll surveys have also given incumbent governments or opposition parties hope, which has subsequently proved entirely unfounded.

India's political parties

India has a dizzying array of political parties — far too many to describe. But you should be aware of a few important parties that currently play a prominent role in the Indian government.

Read the Indian newspapers and watch the Indian news channels to keep up to date with emerging political developments in the central and state governments. These developments can have major implications for you and your business, whether you have a physical presence in India or are doing business from abroad. The fortunes of a particular political party may well affect your own!

The big national players

One very important political party is the Congress (I). It began as the Indian National Congress (INC) in the pre-Independence era but underwent a few changes over the years. The Congress (I), along with the Bharatiya Janata Party (BJP), are two of the main political entities at the national level.

Standing almost shoulder-to-shoulder with them in importance are the Leftist parties — the Communist Party of India (CPI) and the Communist Party of India–Marxist (CPI-M). These have a distinct presence at the state level, and in fact, the Left rules in the States of Kerala and West Bengal.

After India secured its independence, the INC held an overwhelming majority in the Indian political scenario. However, this situation has changed somewhat and in the last few elections a number of political parties have come to the forefront. Some have had enough success to rule on their own, but in the absence of a clear majority, coalition governments have been the norm for a while now.

Coalition governments are alliances of political parties that share what's called a common minimum programme (CMP) — a set of basic common objectives. India arrived at this system through trial and error, but it seems to work well, given the multiplicity of parties in the country. The coalition currently in power is the United Progressive Alliance (UPA). The Congress (I) is the major constituent of this alliance, and India's present Prime Minister, Dr. Manmohan Singh, belongs to this party. He has chosen his Cabinet Ministers from the Congress (I) and other members of the UPA.

In the current coalition, the Leftist parties also provide a "support from outside" element. They vote with the government on important issues after a consensus has been reached, which ensures that important bills aren't voted down in Parliament by strong opposition parties merely on political considerations.

Regional parties

The parties at the regional level include the Dravida Munnetra Kazhagam (DMK) and the All India Dravida Munnetra Kazhagam (AIADMK) in the State of Tamil Nadu. These parties wield enough clout at the state level to come to power independently, and their supporters play a deciding role in sending members to the Parliament at Delhi. In fact, the DMK is currently a key constituent of the UPA.

Party affiliation

Under the constitution, an Indian citizen doesn't have to be affiliated with any political party to run for a general election. In reality, an individual with absolutely no political backing can run for election. These individuals are called *Independents*.

Independents are wooed by political parties that aim to bring the independents into their fold and help to establish a majority. They often call the shots in elected governments, and sometimes withdraw support abruptly, leaving the hapless government hanging. That situation is followed by a tortuous process of conciliation and bargaining, which sometimes succeeds and sometimes doesn't.

Understanding India's Legal System

By and large, the Indian legal system has been modeled on English Law, which makes it far easier for Westerners to understand than the legal systems of other Asian countries. This applies to civil, criminal, and economic laws.

While it is true that the Indian legal system — especially the judicial system — is overworked and sometimes suffers from inordinately delayed verdicts, the fact remains that the law and standard procedures are respected. The delays have become a focus of some concern and various measures are being thought of and implemented to make the system work more efficiently. Regardless of the speed of the system, you need to understand certain features of the law in India, and this section contains that useful information.

India is a land of diverse religions and each has codes of conduct applicable to it. So adherents to each religion have a set of personal laws to conform to. As far as criminal offenses are concerned, the most important rules are those set out in the Indian Penal Code and the Code of Criminal Procedure. Infringement of Intellectual Property Rights, violation of environment and human rights norms, and non-payment of fines are all punishable offenses. Chapter 13 deals with law in more detail.

Indian economic law

When doing business in India, it is important to realize the existence of some essential economic laws. These include laws framed as early as 1872 (which are still applicable) as well as those framed just a few years ago.

The basics

Broadly speaking 20 essential economic laws exist with which you need to be familiar. They form the overall legal framework of the Indian business environment. I've listed them chronologically:

- **The Indian Contract Act (1872):** Established the framework within which contracts can be executed and enforced.

- **Negotiable Instruments Act (1881):** Set rules for promissory notes, bills of exchange and checks.

- **Workmen's Compensation Act (1923):** Set the compensation to be paid by employers to injured workers.

- **Sale of Goods Act (1930):** A mercantile law that complemented the Contract Act (see above).

- **Payment of Wages Act (1936):** Established a minimum monthly salary for industrial and factory workers.

- **Industrial Disputes Act (1947):** Provided for the investigation and settlement of industrial disputes.

- **Minimum Wages Act (1948):** Fixed minimum pay rates for certain jobs.

- **Factories Act (1948):** Regulated labor in factories.

- **Employees Provident Fund and Miscellaneous Provisions Act (1952):** Established provident funds, family pensions, and other monetary benefits for factory employees.

- **Maternity Benefits Act (1961):** Regulated post-childbirth time off for female employees.

- **Payment of Bonus Act (1965):** Regulated bonus payments to be made to certain categories of employees on the basis of production, profit, or productivity.

- **Monopolies and restrictive Trade Practices Act (1969):** Established rules to prevent unfair concentrations of economic power.

- **Indian Patents Act (1970):** Set rules for patent protection in India.

- **Payment of Gratuity Act (1972):** Provided for payment of gratuities to Indian employees in certain industries.

- **Copyright Act (1975):** Helped establish copyright protection in India.

- ✔ **Arbitration and Conciliation Act (1996):** Set up to govern arbitration issues. You can read more about this in Chapter 13.
- ✔ **Geographical Indications of Goods Act (1999):** Provided legal protection for goods originated in a particular area or region within India (examples include Darjeeling tea and Basmati rice).
- ✔ **Trademarks Act (1999):** Helped establish trademark protection in India.
- ✔ **Designs Act (2000):** Helped establish protection of designs.
- ✔ **Competition Act (2002):** Provided for the establishment of a commission that promotes competition, protects consumers and ensures freedom of trade.

In addition to the above acts, you need to take note of Indian Company Law, which gives details of how to function as a corporate entity in India.

By and large, the economic legal system provides a fair, equitable and transparent working framework for both the employer and the employee. The Indian Contract Act and the Negotiable Instruments Act are both considered top of the legal charts. These have helped in administering complex contracts in a changing Indian business environment and facilitating smooth flow of monetary transactions. A fair understanding of at least these two laws is essential for doing business in India.

Find books that elaborate on and explain the details of the Indian Contract Act and the Negotiable Instruments Act. Treat them like twin Bibles while doing business in India. You can ask your Indian contacts to get copies for you, or you can just browse some online book stores.

Some problems

India's economic laws aren't easy to read. Contradictions abound. General problems may relate to infringement of environment norms or employment rules. The expatriate businessman has to tread carefully and consult with Indian law firms to ensure that he doesn't break any rules.

For example, Article 301 of the Constitution of India says that "Freedom of trade, commerce, and intercourse — subject to the other provisions of this Part, trade, commerce, and intercourse throughout the territory of India — shall be free." But then, Article 304 is about "restrictions on trade, commerce, and intercourse among States," which may be interpreted as being in the public interest. According to this, a state is allowed to impose any tax on goods imported from other states or union territories to which similar goods manufactured or produced in that state are subject, taking care not to discriminate between imported goods and those manufactured or produced in the state itself. I talk about the taxation system in a little more detail in Chapter 9.

Make a thorough study of the Indian economic laws — both central and state — before you firm up your business plan. See "The levels of government" earlier in this chapter.

Legal help

While the basic economic legal framework remains unchanged, the liberalization of the economy has brought with it numerous changes that certainly impact your bottom line.

Most companies have realized the value of retaining a local chartered accountancy firm (this is separate from auditors and financial advisors) whose specific mandate is to keep tabs on all economic law changes announced by both the state and central governments. The firm not only provides updates on new regulations brought in by the governments but also gives a brief summary of the impact of the regulations on the company.

Rules change with bewildering frequency in India, where the economy is still opening up. Especially in promising fields like Special Economic Zones (SEZs), these changes may or may not be publicized or trumpeted. At times, only the head of the concerned government department may be notified. So make sure to have an Indian contact who can keep you updated on developments. He can network with the heads of departments to get you the information, but you should do some networking yourself now and again. Personal contact with the regulatory authorities can help keep you in the loop, and you can often build on the progress that your Indian contacts have made.

Exploring Industrial Relations

As your business grows and develops in India, you should socialize with other businesses. These relationship are important because you can glean a ton of info on your competition and meet potential suppliers and network. A company doing business in India should actively socialize on the following three fronts:

- ✓ **The industry forum level (for example, Chambers of Commerce or Federations of Indian Industry):** The advantages to belonging to these forums include getting to know the players, getting a better feel for the market's intricacies, and belonging to a group that can unite and make representation to the government when changes or solutions are required. You can also access veritable treasure troves of data that can be quite useful for research purposes. Socializing at this level is easy, because fellow industry members welcome new entrants, and overseas companies are attractive because they open up reciprocal foreign business avenues for local companies in the same industry. Read all about The Associated Chambers of Commerce and Industries of India at www.assocham.org.

> ✔ **State Government Industries Ministry:** Socializing at the state level is also easy because states are always looking for a fresh investment that generates new employment and wealth. State governments have a lot of leeway in granting industrial licenses, leases, land, and so on.

> ✔ **Central Government Ministry pertaining to the industry:** From an overall macro point of view, the Central Government Ministry concerned with your area of interest has a role to play. Especially in an era where the Indian economy is opening up, having a business influence in the right place in New Delhi can be quite useful.

Consider cultivating beneficial industrial relations with numerous specific groups. I devote the rest of this section to describing a few of the particularly strong examples.

My advice to you is to cultivate these major chambers of commerce in India, and if you're eligible, take memberships in them. These circles can lead you to the right contacts and help lobby for changes that may affect not only your business prospects but also India's long-term interests.

Federation of Indian Chambers of Commerce and Industry

The Federation of Indian Chambers of Commerce and Industry (FICCI) dates back to the days of British rule. It was set up in 1927 at the suggestion of Mahatma Gandhi, and it is the oldest, largest apex body of Indian business and a rallying point for Indian enterprise. FICCI numbers more than 1,500 corporations across the country among its members, not to mention more than 500 chambers of commerce and business associations. It is the direct and indirect voice for more than 250,000 business units of all sizes and types.

Headquartered in the heart of New Delhi, the FICCI has world-class infrastructure and its executive committee is made up of industry leaders including key innovators, wealth creators, and employment providers. The FICCI is a body that constantly interacts with the government on economic issues, works toward promoting global trade and investment, and acts as an international business forum, offering information and guidance to investors from abroad. It also has a vast database that consists of important contacts and details about the companies registered with it.

FICCI has links to the World Trade Organization (WTO), the United Nations Industrial Development Organization (UNIDO), International Labour Organization (ILO), the World Bank, the General Agreement on Tariffs and Trade (GATT), and other important organizations. It also has Joint Business Councils with various other nations. These strengths allow it to help both Indian businessmen succeed abroad and overseas businessmen succeed in India. Explore the FICCI further at www.ficci.com.

Confederation of Indian Industry

The Confederation of Indian Industry (CII) is an organization of the industries, by the industries, to borrow a phrase. It's non-governmental and non-profit, and it aims to promote the growth of industry in India by working with various industries and the government.

The CII works in a consultative capacity to improve the business atmosphere in the country and efficiency. The government considers its views when framing policy and putting in place measures for resource mobilization. The CII holds a national conference each year, bringing together representatives of different sectors — academia, government, and industry, for example — to debate on national development issues.

The CII also works toward harmonious relationships between the central and state governments, vital to expanding business opportunities in the country as a whole. For more on central and state governments, see "The levels of government" earlier in this chapter.

The CII has over 5,800 direct members from both the private and public sectors, while its indirect membership runs to about 95,000. It offers a range of specialized services and global linkages, which can be very useful to you as a foreign businessperson trying to get started in India. The CII also has branch offices in various countries — the United Kingdom (UK), Australia, the United States (U.S.), France, and Japan (to name a few). For more information, check out the CII's Web site at www.cii.com.

The Confederation of Indian Industry (CII) has a special council for multinational companies. This body holds a briefing for about 500 organizations and arranges discussions with key government officials. That should be reason enough for you to make your business known to the CII.

One of the major goals toward CII is the institution of a single window clearance system for investment projects. This system greatly reduces the confusing paperwork for you as an overseas investor, and India's attraction as an investment destination will automatically soar.

National Association of Software and Service Companies

The National Association of Software and Service Companies (NASSCOM) is for the IT software and services industry in India what the CII and FICCI are on a grander industrial scale. This association is a not-for-profit body, but membership is limited to those folks who're involved in software development, services, and IT-driven business process outsourcing.

NASSCOM's aim is to make India a top global source for software and services, and to this end it is pushing quality in both management and product standards. You can read more about them at www.nasscom.org.

NASSCOM's members include international organizations based in the U.S., the UK, the European Union, Japan, and China. The group is a member of the Asian-Oceanian Computing Industry Organization (ASOCIO), a group of computing industry associations from the Asian-Oceanian Region, and a founding member of the World Information Technology and Services Alliances (WITSA).

Another organization to check out is www.tie.org. Headquartered in the U.S. with Indian chapters, the Indo-US entrepreneur can be a useful networking and best practices sharing forum for mostly IT firms.

Networking and Navigating the Indian Government

As you set out on your business path in India, you're going to need to work with various levels of the Indian government to get things done. Securing approvals, working within regulations, and acquiring specific information all require that you play ball with Indian government officials. To succeed, you need to know the key players and be familiar with the details of the playing field. I explain both in this section and highlight a few other important rules of the game.

Getting to know Indian government officials

The political administrative system in India has been modeled on the British system and therefore has two key components: the ministers and the civil servants, called *babus*. You need to understand the importance and roles of both to work with the government efficiently.

Being a minister

In India, you don't have to have any minimum qualifications or skills to be a Minister in the central or state cabinets. The only essential criterion is the ability to get the people to vote.

Becoming a civil servant

To become a member of the civil service in India, a person has to pass a stiff competitive examination at the post-graduate level. He or she then becomes a member of that elite force called the Indian Administrative Service (IAS). (Irreverent Indians say that the acronym can stand for other things, including Invisible After Sunset!)

The successful civil services candidates are also absorbed in specialized categories like the Indian Railway Service (IRS) and the Indian Police Service (IPS), while the creamiest layer — the folks who score the highest — get a chance to join the Indian Foreign Service (IFS) or the diplomatic corps.

While ministers may come and go, the civil servants remain as the true mandarins of power in New Delhi and in the state capitals. The vitality of your business depends on establishing contact and remaining in touch with them. Mixing it up with the industrial federations described earlier in this chapter helps you start the networking process.

The civil service has a strict code of ethics in terms of seniority and rank that you need to understand if you want to do business with the government. For more information on how the civil service operates, visit www.civilservice india.com and http://ias.nic.in or ask your Indian contacts and colleagues for details on who's currently in power and how to contact individuals.

Building the right government contacts

Of course, you don't need to go to the ministry level or the secretary level each and every time you need to get something done. It's good to have contacts at various levels and encourage others in your organization to cultivate relationships with their peers in government offices. Tackle each issue at the appropriate stage, and pursue it at higher levels as necessary. Approach the highest rungs only when all else fails. You can also leave it to your Indian contacts to establish links with the lower levels of authority while you focus on the power centers.

But at the basis of your contacts are the ministers and the bureaucrats (or civil servants). I cover their influence in the next sections.

Ministers

Apart from the few major ministers I mentioned earlier in this chapter (see "The branches of the Indian central government"), a range of others exists both small and large, including a minister of fisheries, education, information, home affairs, and social welfare. These ministers are chosen from the House of Commons.

The ministries of finance, power, environment, and industries are among the right Ministries to know. Your standing in the business world is definitely higher if you can drop the names of a secretary or two in any of these ministries. And if you manage to get the ear of the minister himself (or herself), get set to watch your competitor turn an interesting shade of green!

Cultivate relationships in multiple ministries and discover the art of working simultaneously with several of them. At least one foreign businessperson I know came to India to do business and left the country quite adept at getting his way with the powers that be. The trick is to concurrently work on building relations and smoothing issues with a variety of government officials.

Civil servants

The term *civil servant* may sound like it implies a position of weakness or submission, but that isn't the case here. Civil servants in India are prestigious. They refer to themselves as government servants, and they are often called IAS officers, which stands for Indian Administrative Services.

To earn this lofty post, candidates must pass a stiff round of exams followed by a grueling interview, and only the best and most brilliant minds make it. IAS officers are extremely powerful and are in fact masters in the halls of power.

High-ranking IAS officers are grouped as secretaries; the real power centers in the civil service cadre have these titles. The pecking order (in descending order) is as follows:

- Chief Secretary
- Secretary
- Joint Secretary
- Additional Secretary
- Deputy Secretary

Each ministry, under a minister, normally has these five officials. More often than not, a sixth official, referred to as a director or financial advisor, is thrown in the mix.

It's at the offices of these secretaries that many international corporate games are plotted and won. Surprisingly, even today not enough importance has been given by overseas corporations to these powerful government officials.

As high scholastic skills are needed to be a Secretary or IAS officers, getting to know them comes with a bonus — they can be excellent intellectual company. They also network very effectively, so don't be disheartened if you know only an IAS officer in a ministry not connected to your industry. Leverage that person and he can connect you to his colleagues in a different area.

Ministers come and go with each government, and IAS officers fairly typically stay on to advise each one. These bureaucrats answer queries for ministers in parliament, help strategize and even aid them in speech writing. But it isn't uncommon for IAS officers to take a sabbatical and fly off to teach for a semester or two at an Ivy League school, as they are the sought-after intellectuals of India.

Putting India's Right To Information Act to good use

Discovering the best methods for procuring information from the Indian government makes life much easier for you as you set up and grow your business. Luckily for you, there's been a recently legislative development that has greatly simplified the process — the Right To Information (RTI) Act.

The RTI Act was passed by Parliament in June 2005 and went into effect in October of that year. It superseded the Official Secrets Act and other special laws that had until then guarded government information in independent India.

Put simply, the act gives all Indians the right to ask for information from any public body, which, in turn, is required to respond within 30 days. As a foreigner, you may not be able to take advantage of the act directly, but you can always get your Indian contacts to submit information requests on your behalf. And you (or your Indian contacts) don't even have to say why you need the requested information — you just have to provide your contact details.

The RTI Act empowers Indians to

- ✔ Request any information (defined as any material in any form, including records, documents, memos, e-mails, opinions, advices, press releases, contracts, reports, papers, models, data material held in any electronic form, and information relating to any private body that can be accessed by a public authority under any other law for the time being in force)

✔ Make and take copies of documents

✔ Inspect documents

✔ Inspect the progress of works

✔ Take samples of materials used at worksites

Information sought via the RTI Act is provided by designated Public Information Officers (PIOs) or Assistant Public Information Officers (APIOs). For more information on how to seek information, visit www.rtiindia.org. And the information doesn't come free. Fees are involved, and each department is different. Don't worry; they won't set your bank balance back too much. The rules of payment vary from state to state, and so do the application formats.

The RTI Act leaves the state of Jammu and Kashmir out of its purview. If you're particularly keen on getting some info out of that state, don't throw this law in the faces of the officials there. They'll throw it right back at you.

The *Right* stuff

The Right To Information Act has proven to be a tremendous help in clearing Indian business hurdles. To understand the scope of its impact, consider this hypothetical situation.

Suppose you need a no-objection certificate from the Pollution Control Board of a particular state. You've properly applied for it and worn out a couple of pairs of shoes "following up" the progress of your application. Despite your efforts, all you've been able to extract from the deadpan clerk in the board office is "It's being processed, sir." Before the RTI Act was passed, I would've advised you to invest in a third pair of shoes and be prepared for some of your financial planning to go out the window. But the RTI Act provides you with a course of action.

To speed the process along, you can have an Indian partner or contact file an application for information with the appropriate department and request a day-by-day report on the certification's progress and the names and designations of the officers through whose hands it has passed. You can also ask what action has been taken against these indivduals for not processing your application and demand to know when the certificate may be expected.

Chances are you'll have your certificate before your favorite shoe store can find that third pair of shoes in your size.

The RTI Act is a major deterrant to corruption. And yes, there's corruption in India, but the situation is improving, thanks in part to the RTI Act. According to the 2006 findings of Transparency International (a Berlin-based global organization that fights corruption), India is among the countries to have significantly improved its ratings (corruption has decreased) from the previous year.

Some corollaries exist to the RTI Act. For example, information that's deemed crucial to India's sovereignty and security of strategic scientific or economic interest, or disclosure which constitutes breach of privilege of legislatures can't be procured. You also can't get information, including commercial confidence, trade secrets, or intellectual property, that can harm the competitive position of a third party, unless the authorities are satisfied that larger public interest is served by disclosing this information. Many other restrictions exist as well, so to get the full scoop visit www.rtiindia.org.

Make a copy of any RTI Act applications your business submits and keep them on file for your records.

Chapter 9

Counting Your Rupees and Paise

• •

In This Chapter

▶ Getting familiar with Indian money

▶ Taking a look at India's banking structure

▶ Financing your business in India

▶ Comprehending India's tax system

▶ Familiarizing yourself with audit and compliance issues

• •

Money and the movement of money are two of the most important aspects of doing business in any setting. India is no exception. If you're going to be successful with your fledgling business venture in India, you need to be familiar with the country's currency and how it can work for you *and* against you. Many of the elements of currency and finance in India are the same as you've seen in other parts of the world, but some differences can be a pain in your neck (and your wallet) if you don't grasp them early in your endeavors.

In this chapter, I explore India's money and how it moves through the country's economy. I also examine a few financing options, and touch on India's current system of taxation. Finally, I impart a bit of wisdom on audit and compliance concerns, which may help you avoid some major headaches as you get your start in India.

Understanding Indian Money

Money has been a part of Indian culture for centuries. Coins were minted there as early as the sixth century B.C. *Lakshmi,* the Hindu goddess of wealth, is held in special reverence, and many businesses display a picture of Lakshmi with gold coins cascading from her hand.

You need to be familiar with the ins and outs of modern Indian money in order to do business at even the most basic of levels in the country. In this section, I explain the details of Indian currency and shed light on the Indian system of counting.

Rupees and paise

Indians count their money in rupees (Rs for short — always placed as an abbreviation before the numbers) and paise. The rupee is abbreviated as *INR* in foreign currency exchange contexts. It's divided into one hundred equal parts, each called a Paisa (much like dollars and cents). One hundred paise (plural of paisa) equals one rupee, and these two forms of currency are the country's only legal tender. Physically speaking, the money is made of paper and metal. On paper, the denominations range from the one thousand-rupee note to the one-rupee note, though the latter is a rarity now and mostly a coin. Coins in circulation range from 25 paise to Rs 5. Figure 9-1 shows the 100-rupee note.

Figure 9-1:
The Indian 100-rupee note.

You may come across a five-rupee, two-rupee, or even a one-rupee note, and they're all perfectly valid legal tender. But remember that the Reserve Bank of India (RBI) has stopped printing these low-value denominations so that in the near future they fall out of circulation. This same holds true with the five-paise and one-paisa coins.

If you do come across a one-rupee or two-rupee note, you may want to hang on to it because it could increase in value as it becomes more and more rare.

All matters concerning the rupee, including the minting of coins and printing of notes, are under the authority of the RBI. The RBI is responsible for all currency management. The bank works closely with the Finance Ministry and has a major role to play in the overall monetary policies of the Indian government. Check out "Checking Out India's Banking Structure" later in this chapter for more info on the RBI.

Money talks — in 15 languages!

Because of the vast array of cultures and languages within India, the country's currency notes are adorned with 15 different languages! That is done so any Indian can determine the denomination of any note. Although the main languages are English and Hindi, the side of an Indian rupee note of any denomination lists different scripts. Those are the vernacular languages, spelling out the value of that bill. Check out Figure 9-1 for an example.

Surprisingly, India's neighbors Nepal and Bhutan, who have their own sovereign currencies, accept the Indian rupee as legal tender! However, especially in casinos of Nepal, the 500-rupee note and the 1000-rupee note aren't accepted because there have been many instances of counterfeiting. You can use notes in denominations of Rs 100 and below, instead.

Lakhs and crores

To fully grasp India's currency, you need to be familiar with the Indian system of counting. Indians don't talk in millions and billions, and certainly not in trillions and zillions. Instead, they talk in *lakhs* (sounds like the English word *lack* and originally came from Lakshmi goddess of wealth) and in *crores* (sounds like a cross between the word *crow* and *roar*).

The placement of commas makes the difference between how Indians count their money and you count yours. Commas are used as separators, but their placement is different than Western placements and may seem strange to you at first. Examining a few examples is the best way to gain a clearer understanding of how lakhs and crores work, and I provide several for you in Table 9-1.

Table 9-1	Counting your lakhs and crores	
What Indians Call It	*In Numerals*	*What Westerners Call It*
One lakh	1,00,000	One hundred thousand
Ten lakhs	10,00,000	One million
One crore	1,00,00,000	Ten million
Ten crores	10,00,00,000	One hundred million
One hundred crores	100,00,00,000	One billion

To master the lakh and crore system, it may be even simpler for you to always keep in mind that a million is equal to 10 lakhs or one hundred million is 10 crores. As you work to become fluent with these systems, remember that India isn't the only country that uses lakhs and crores. India's neighbors Pakistan, Sri Lanka, and Bangladesh also use an identical system.

Checking Out India's Banking Structure

Understanding the banking structure in India is crucial for you. You need to know how transactions are conducted. India doesn't follow the federal structure of banking common in some countries (the United States, for example). Instead, the country's structure is a bit more unified. India's banking system is complex because it consists of various levels at which the banks operate. Ranging from a gigantic entity like the State Bank of India (formerly the Imperial Bank of India) to non-banking finance companies, you find a huge spectrum. This section helps you wrap your brain around the intricacies of India's banking framework.

The Reserve Bank of India

India's central bank is the Reserve Bank of India (RBI). It came into existence in 1935. The basic function of the RBI is clearly set out in its official preamble, which states that it's the RBI's responsibility "to regulate the issue of Bank Notes and keeping of reserves with a view to securing monetary stability in India and generally to operate the currency and credit system of the country to its advantage."

The role of a central bank like the RBI can't be understated, especially in a developing economy. Apart from issuing currency, its main functions include

- Acting as the banker of the government, formulating and implementing the Indian monetary policy
- Regulating the Indian banking system, prescribing and regulating the entire banking mechanism
- Managing the Foreign Exchange Management Act (FEMA)

The RBI also monitors the flow of credit to different segments like agriculture, commercial, small-scale industries, and export, in accordance with the government's finance policies.

The State Bank of India

To fully understand nationalized banks, you need to be familiar with a bit of their history. Until 1969, the only public sector bank was the State Bank of India (SBI). That year, Indira Gandhi — the first woman prime minister of India — nationalized 14 banks. The aim was to provide and improve banking infrastructure and also facilitate cheap loans to farmers. In 1980, a few more banks were nationalized. With these nationalized banks, the government — through its watchdog the RBI — worked to control the banking structure in India to provide a stable and transparent system.

The SBI is a public sector bank that was originally known as the Imperial Bank of India, and is considered a British legacy to the country's banking system. The government is considering a proposal to transfer the RBI's share in the SBI, National Bank for Agricultural and Rural Development (NABARD), and National Housing Bank (NHB) to the central government. If you want to read more about the SBI, visit www.statebankofindia.com.

The Indian government and the RBI work out the foreign exchange control policy together, but it's the RBI that administers it and monitors capital account transactions. The RBI operates out of 22 regional offices, most of which are located in state capitals. For more information on the RBI and its many functions, check out www.rbi.org.

Other bank categories

Apart from the RBI, the banking structure in India is comprised of six other categories of banks. According to the Statistical Outline of India, the categories and number of Indian offices run by each (in parentheses) are as follows:

- Nationalized banks (35,075)
- Regional rural banks (14,760)
- The State Bank of India (13,890)
- Other scheduled commercial banks (6,320)
- Foreign banks (245)
- Non-scheduled commercial banks (25)

As you can see from the list above, the banking system is dominated by the nationalized banks. They control about 75 percent of the overall Indian banking assets. In comparison, foreign banks control 6 percent and private banks control 18 percent. The Indian government limits the role of foreign banks now, but this control is set to change beginning in 2009, when other banks will be allowed to compete with the Indian banks on a level playing field.

While nationalized banks hold the most sway, private banks are making their mark in tech-savvy India, by offering non-traditional services like Internet, cell phone, and telephone banking. ATMs are also flourishing.

The usual banking hours in India are 10 a.m. to 2 p.m. on weekdays and 10 a.m. to noon on Saturdays. Most banks have 24-hour ATMs, and money transfers through these banks are a breeze.

Non-banking finance companies

Under the umbrella of financing in India there are also family-owned banks, money lenders, and a sector made up of non-banking finance companies (NBFCs). These uniquely Indian companies are something like the thrift institutions or building societies of the West. They play an important role in providing credit to both the manufacturing and service sectors. The unorganized sector — that large portion of trade that takes place between companies unaffiliated with any representative body or group — patronizes this financial service segment the most.

Essentially, NBFCs cater to a niche market, offering tailor-made financial services. Though central and state governments are involved here (NBFCs acquire shares, bonds, securities, and so on, which the state and central governments issue), private companies are the biggest players in this core segment.

It's easier to get permission from the Reserve Bank of India to start an NBFC than it is to secure a license to open a bank. If you're interested in getting in on the action, foreign equity investments are allowed in some categories of NBFCs. You can discover additional details at www.finmin.nic.in/the_ministry/dept_eco_affairs/investment_div/fifs.htm.

Figuring Out Financing in India

When you come to the matter of funding your business in India, you can get financing from banks, specialized lending organizations, or from the capital market. Your choice depends on factors like the amount you need, the timing, and of course the interest. In this section I provide you with a few Indian financing possibilities.

In 1991, the government liberalized the number of industries that are open to foreign investment, eased approval requirements, and allowed majority foreign equity ownership. There are some restrictions and ceilings, depending on the sector and the nature of business. You can read more about options for foreign investment in Chapter 5.

As you read this section, you may realize that sourcing of funds for a foreign company in India is quite uncomplicated. Your company can adhere to its business plan and put together the best fund sourcing system for its particular situation.

Frequent changes occur in the regulations governing equity percentage permitted and the industries open to foreign participation. Companies wishing to enter the Indian market should make efforts to get the most up-to-date information before firming up business plans. Consult your financial advisors in India and stay on top of possible developments via specialized finance and business newspapers, such as the *Economic Times, Businessline,* or *Financial Express.*

Getting to know the basics: India's Foreign Exchange Management Act (FEMA)

The Foreign Exchange Management Act (FEMA) is the key act governing finance issues for a foreign company operating in India. It's a simplified regulatory system for foreign exchange deals, and as an expatriate you need to become familiar with India's regulations on holding foreign currency, its rules for owning real estate, and the intricacies of export regulations.

FEMA replaced FERA, or the Foreign Exchange Regulation Act. This name change from *regulation* to *management* illustrates the shift in the Indian government's focus. Initially the emphasis was on regulation and conservation of foreign exchange, but that has changed to facilitating trade and managing foreign exchange reserves.

FEMA looks at foreign exchange in two broad ways: capital account and current account. The act covers such subjects as capital account transactions and export of goods and services and stipulates, among other things, that foreign exchange dealings should be conducted only through authorized persons. The act applies to all residents of India and extends to their businesses outside the country too. FEMA is administered by the RBI and enforced by a specially-created Directorate of Enforcement.

For more information on FEMA, visit www.femaonline.com.

Transactions in foreign exchange can be made on current accounts (checking accounts) barring a few exceptions. The rupee is fully convertible on current accounts. If you're a foreign institutional investor (FII), you can bring in and send home money. But Indian firms and residents can't freely convert the rupee to buy land or funds overseas. And Indian companies need the RBI's permission to borrow on the international market.

Violations of the foreign exchange rules are subject to monetary penalties and even imprisonment. External commercial borrowings (ECBs) are recognized as a major source of funding in India. You can get them from banks, financial institutions, and export credit agencies. But remember that there are regulations governing these transactions, though they're nowhere as cumbersome as they were prior to liberalization.

Using banks and institutional finance

India has an extensive banking system in place that is conducive to doing international business. The banks individually are liquid and can be relied on to provide financial assistance tailor-made to the needs of many different types of businesses.

Bank funding for a company in India comes from either the public or private sector banks. Depending on the amount, the banks may want to form a consortium. Funding from the banking system is no different in India than elsewhere in the world — capital from this source is invariably used for short-term working capital purposes.

For longer-term financing, institutional financing is the norm. In India, institutional financing is provided mainly by the following:

- The Industrial Credit and Investment Corporation of India (ICICI)
- The Industrial Finance Corporation of India (IFCI)
- The Industrial Development Bank of India (IDBI)
- Unit Trust of India (UTI)

In addition, State Financial Corporations (SFCs) exist that are term loan sources funded by individual states to promote business and investment. All these are sources of debt funding and the choice of one institution over another basically depends on the available interest rates and procedural formalities to get the loan.

The National Bank for Agriculture and Rural Development (NABARD) provides funds for the less high-profile sectors — agriculture, small scale industries, and handicrafts, to name a few. It also funds rural infrastructure schemes, so explore this as a funding option if your interest lies in farming.

Playing the stock market

Since liberalization, the Indian capital market has been often described as stratospheric. There are as many as 23 stock exchanges in India. The most vibrant one is the Bombay Stock Exchange, which trades close to 3,000 companies. This market obviously is an exciting prospect for foreign companies looking to do business in India.

Players in this stock market include individuals, institutions, bankers (who manage mutual funds on behalf of their clients), and also FIIs. Investments in debt and equity by FIIs shot up from $26 billion in March 2004 to close to $40 billion by September 2005! As in the West, India has developed a bunch of merchant bankers, underwriters, portfolio managers, and issue registrars that fully facilitate equity management.

Understanding India's Tax Structure

Broadly, the tax system in India is three-tiered:

- **Central government:** This branch levies some taxes. The central government collects tax on all types of income and wealth, part of sales tax, service tax, and customs, and excise duties.

- **State government:** This level levies others. State governments collect intrastate sales taxes, entertainment and profession taxes, liquor manufacturing excises, stamp duties on transfer of property, and property taxes.

- **Local government:** They collect the third and final set of taxes. Local governments levy octroi (taxes on goods brought into some cities) and charge for public utilities like water supply and sewerage.

As with most other areas of the Indian economy, the tax system has reforms that have been recently set in motion. These reforms were intended to rationalize the tax structure, to bring more people into the tax net, and to simplify the payment procedures. Indian tax rates are moderate, with a peak tax rate of 33.6 percent (a typically bureaucratic number) for individuals and the same flat rate for corporations. You can file your tax returns online, and the introduction of the Permanent Account Number (PAN) has helped track money through the system. The government has made arrangements for non-residents and expatriates doing business in India to acquire a PAN. For more on getting a PAN, see Chapter 5.

Tax types

Two main types of taxes exist in India: direct and indirect. Direct taxes are a burden on the payee, while indirect taxes can be passed on to consumers. You need to be familiar with the nuts and bolts of both.

Direct taxes

Direct taxes are personal income taxes, taxes on corporate income, wealth taxes, gift taxes, expenditure taxes, and interest taxes. Within the realm of direct taxes in India, you certainly need to know about income tax. Your residency status in India has a bearing on the government's take on what you earn. Taxes on the business income of foreign companies aren't the same as those levied on Indian companies. India has a different set of rules for residents and non-residents:

- **Residents:** If you've spent a minimum of 182 days in India during the year in question, you're a resident for tax purposes. Broadly speaking, if you're a resident then your worldwide income is subject to taxation.

- **Nonresidents:** If you're a non-resident, the Indian government asks that you pay taxes only on the income you earn from your business dealings in India. Non-resident companies and branches of foreign companies are taxed at a rate of 40 percent, plus a 2.5 percent surcharge, and the 2 percent education tax, making the effective tax rate 41.82 percent.

Everything you earn other than from agricultural sources — there are no taxes on agricultural income — should be taken into account when calculating your income tax.

The government has earnings ceilings for income taxes. For the assessment year 2006–07, India's income tax payees — comprising a mere 3.5 percent of the billion-plus population — were divided into the following three categories:

- Those earning Rs 100,001 to 150,000 annually are subject to a 10 percent taxation of the amount exceeding Rs 100,000.

- Those earning Rs 150,001 to 250,000 annually are subject to a 20 percent taxation of the amount exceeding Rs 150,000, plus Rs 5,000.

- Those earning Rs 250,001 or more per year are subject to a 30 percent taxation of the amount exceeding Rs 250,000, plus Rs 25,000.

These rates are liable to change, so do keep track. The Union Budget for 2007–08 doesn't make large-scale changes in these figures, but the basic exemption limit for tax assessees has been upped by Rs 10,000, taking it to Rs 110,000 for men while for women it's 1.45 lakh and for senior citizens, 1.95 lakh. Keeping abreast with financial news is a must.

The vast majority of Indian residents earns less than Rs 100,000 per year and isn't required to pay income taxes. Those earning more than Rs 1 million are hit with a 10 percent surcharge, while the government's thrust on education can be seen in the 2 percent tax charged on all taxes.

If you have long-term capital gains, you attract a tax of 20 percent, but the good news is that this doesn't apply to gains from listed securities, provided you've been holding them for over a year.

If you've paid excess tax, you can always claim a refund, provided you fill in the appropriate form within the specified time limit. It may take a while to get back to you, but it will come eventually. And all claims for Tax Deducted at Source (TDS), which is the term for withheld taxes, must be supported by proper documents.

For more info on refunds check out www.incometaxdelhi.nic.in/taxsys/ refund.htm and www.incometaxtn.gov.in/pro_display.jsp?file= refu_01_01_01.htm&smid=32&mmid=5.

The income of the previous year is taken into account while calculating tax to be paid in any one year. The financial year is from April 1 to March 31 in India. The Web site www.incometaxindia.gov.in provides a great deal of additional information. You also need to find out about Corporate Tax, which includes the Minimum Alternate Tax that hinges on book profits, Excise and Customs Duties, and Capital Gains tax.

Indirect taxes

The indirect taxes include service tax and value-added tax (VAT). VAT is a relatively new system that aims to have all states charging a uniform rate for the same product. It has been implemented in most Indian states. VAT is intended to ultimately replace the different rates of sales tax levied by the various states and will mop up revenue for the government from the value addition that a product gains at various stages.

Octroi entry tax (a tax levied on movement of goods into some cities), stamp duties, and property taxes are other examples of taxation in India. Octroi has been dispensed within states implementing VAT. Import duties and excise duties (tax on production) are the other kinds of indirect taxes.

At present indirect tax comes to 12.24 percent including the education tax, but remember that rates change every now and then. Get set up with an Indian tax consultant to help you wade through the details. For a comprehensive listing of finance and tax consultants, visit www.eindiabusiness.com/ indian-service-providers/tax-planners-practitioners-agents- consultants-indian-service-providers.html.

Ask your tax consultant to explain transfer pricing, which relates to the pricing of goods and services sold from a parent company to a foreign subsidiary.

In trying to facilitate fair calculation of profits and tax, India introduced Transfer Pricing laws. Under these laws, the pricing of goods or services sold by one company to another in the same group is to be determined by using arms length price (the price that would be charged in the transaction if it had been entered into by unrelated parties in similar conditions). For details, see www.incometaxindia.gov.in/transferpricing.asp. Make sure you have all the necessary documentation.

The challenges of a changing tax structure

In keeping with India's constantly changing economy, the tax regime in the country is evolving. The structure presents a few concerns:

✔ Pricing uncertainties are one effect of the changing tax structure. VAT, which is optional for states, adds to the complication. Some states jumped on the bandwagon at the introductory stage while others adopted a watch-and-wait policy. When the tax regime changes, implications vary. In Tamil Nadu, for example, where VAT was introduced from January 1, 2007, there's some confusion. Previously, a company with many branches could transport products for sale between states and pay only one sales tax. Now that VAT has been introduced, that company is required to pay an entry tax as well as the VAT. This is why a tax consultant is imperative to your project's success in India.

✔ Duties, which don't always keep pace with changing technology, are another problem area in the evolving tax regime. For instance, anesthesia ventilators attract a small tax, but complex anesthesia machines are taxed over five times more. Improved technology has made simple anesthesia ventilators a thing of the past — they now come with many more features. Healthcare companies say these can't be classified as "anesthesia machines." Customs authorities disagree; in their book, the new pieces of equipment aren't ventilators.

✔ You may find that a product you're marketing has to be pulled off the shelves for a while in a particular state because of these tax variations. It takes time to work out the implications and re-price. That sort of confusion is just a side effect of liberalization and progress, and the setback should only be temporary.

There's a good deal of chopping and changing going on, and with every annual budget presented by the central government's Union Finance Minister and his counterparts in the various states, rates and focus could change. The

Indian central government's budget is usually presented on the last working day in February, and the business community waits with bated breath for its release. The salaried class also pays close attention, hoping for tax relief.

Brian, a businessman from Australia, was surprised by the complications of the tax structure in India. His Indian partner warned him about tax issues, and he factored in the cost of hiring a professional tax consultant. This cost turned out to be very low, compared to the benefits of having access to sophisticated tax know-how. The professional was able to interpret loopholes and keep the business working within the confines of the law. Brian ended up saving 20 percent on his overall project figures in the first year alone. Corporate tax laws are complex and cumbersome, and Brian advises all foreign companies to use the services of a tax specialist familiar with the Indian tax structure.

Tax concessions

Opportunities do exist within India's tax regime to reduce the depth to which the Indian government reaches into your business's pockets. These opportunities include a variety of rebates, deductions, and other breaks that your business can qualify for.

Consult an Indian tax professional to make sure you're taking full advantage of your business's tax situation, but in this section I help familiarize you with some of the basics.

A sampling of tax break opportunities

Tax breaks are available for a variety of businesses, and projects set up in specified underdeveloped areas are eligible for tax holidays. You or your Indian colleagues should research the possibilities and consult with your Indian tax professional, but a few examples are as follows:

- ✔ 100 percent export-oriented projects are exempt from taxation (under certain conditions).
- ✔ Soft loans and concessional credits are available to specified industries.
- ✔ Industrial undertakings in free trade and export-processing zones are given tax holidays for specific periods.

Rules differ from state to state and from time to time. Keep abreast of developments from media reports, your tax consultant, and your contacts at the Free Trade and EPZs.

Some other concessions are also available in these special zones. For example, the government grants indirect tax incentives to exporters — they aren't required to pay excise duty or sales tax (VAT) on their goods. A number of other zones offer tax concessions:

- Industrial Parks
- Electronic Hardware Technology Parks
- Software Technology Park Units
- Special Economic Zones (SEZs offer many advantages. See the next section.)

Tax breaks at Special Economic Zones

To promote economic growth in specific areas throughout India, the Indian government has put in place several Special Economic Zones (SEZs), which offer businesses a number of benefits — including tax breaks — if they set up shop within a zone.

Chapter 5 highlights the basics of some SEZs, the details are included in the following sections.

Understanding SEZ jargon

Here's some SEZ jargon to bone up on:

- **DC (Development Commissioner):** DCs are powerful government officials and are normally appointed for four-year terms. Every SEZ has one. One DC can be responsible for one or more SEZs.
- **BoA (Board of Approval):** This group is a government body established for the clearance of new SEZs.
- **Developer:** This group can be a company, group of companies, or government bodies that develop the infrastructure and the land inside the SEZ. (You'll probably set up a unit within an SEZ, so you're not a Developer.)
- **DTA (Domestic Tariff Area):** The DTA is all the territory that's outside the SEZ and within India.

Choosing an SEZ

To choose an SEZ, first identify your needs and then determine an appropriate location. SEZs are being set up all over India (Chapter 5 includes a listing). Some locales are near international ports or airports, some are in areas where labor is cheap, and some are in areas where a specially skilled workforce is available. Shortlist two or three, evaluate them with regard to the other criteria important to your business's location, and then make your choice.

Making SEZs work for you

Most SEZs are product-specific and only certain industries are allowed to operate there and qualify for the tax concessions. For example, some SEZs are devoted to textiles, others to gems, and still others to the automotive industry. In other areas only non-polluting industries are allowed. On the other hand, multi-product SEZ exist where all production activities are permitted and eligible for concessions.

Because the idea is to woo investors, things have been made particularly easy for all types of investors, foreigners included. You have a single window clearance facility available for government procedures, and no limits are set as far as value addition and minimum export quantity.

SEZs work toward promoting exports via tax concessions, and offer breaks with both direct and indirect taxes. The advantages with direct taxes are particularly strong:

- ✔ Absolutely no taxes are due for the first five years of operation.

- ✔ Fifty percent of earnings are exempt for the two years after the first five.

- ✔ As a bonus, you get to carry forward your losses. As far as the indirect taxes go, you don't have to pay any type of duty on raw materials or capital goods for your SEZ unit, whether you import these or get them locally, but you have to use them within five years.

Though the aim is to promote exports, you can also sell your products in the DTA, after paying the applicable taxes.

Adjusting to SEZ changes

The rules on concessions may change as SEZ is still a promising field in India, and issues are being ironed out when they crop up. Study the SEZ ACT 2005 and the SEZ Rules 2006 for more information.

The Development Commissioners of the various SEZs are aware of all the latest changes in rules, some of which may not even be published as gazette notifications. If you build a good rapport with the DCs and they're clear about what you need, they can tell you if and how new rules may affect your prospects. Don't hurry into any decisions.

You may find the uncertainties worrying at times, and you may get the feeling that while you're cooling your heels waiting for permissions, facilities are being used by Indian companies to take advantage of the concessions under a thin veil of foreign collaborations. According to experienced foreign business-people, these situations are part of the game, but a small price to pay for the advantages SEZs have to offer. For more information on those advantages, you can visit www.sezindia.nic.in.

Double taxation policies

Knowing the details of the double taxation agreement between India and your country could help in minimizing your tax liability and in reducing the incidence of withholding taxes in India. India has signed comprehensive double-taxation avoidance deals with many countries. There are area-specific agreements too, relating to aircraft profits, shipping profits, and so on. Most of these agreements grant relief from double taxation by the credit method or by a combination of the credit and exemption methods.

The goal of India's double taxation policies are to find a fair way of taxing income in terms of source and place of residence. Very broadly, these treaties ensure that you don't have to pay tax for the same income twice — once in India where it's generated and again in your own country. The existence of double taxation treaties is a major "pro" factor when potential investors weigh the comparative options of locating their units in various places. India's treaties encourage the flow of trade and technology.

India's most favorable tax treaty is with Mauritius, and so a good portion of foreign investment in India is routed through Mauritius. Companies based in Mauritius that invest in shares of Indian companies are exempt from capital gains taxes in India.

Dealing With Audit and Compliance Issues

In India all incorporated entities need to get their books audited by an Indian chartered accountant and need to file annual returns with the Registrar of Companies. Audit is also compulsory under the Income Tax Act if your sales exceed Rs 4 million. Companies having foreign investment would also need to file periodical returns with the Reserve Bank.

In the following sections, you get the run down on the process of filing taxes in India — it's not really as complex as it seems to be at first. You also get a peek at the auditing process — what it's about in general, and the documents required.

Filing your taxes

Here are the basics of what you need to know for tax filing:

- India's fiscal year (April 1 through March 31) is the accounting year for all companies.

- ✔ Taxes on income in one fiscal year are usually paid in the next fiscal year (apart from TDS and advance tax — the income tax that's computed and paid in advance as three installments for the year), which is known as the "assessment" year.

- ✔ Companies must file a final return by October 31st of the assessment year. This return states income, expenses, taxes paid, and taxes due for the preceding tax year.

- ✔ Returns for non-corporate taxpayers who need to have their accounts audited are due on October 31st.

- ✔ All others assessed for income tax must submit returns by July 31st.

India's tax filing deadlines are mandatory, but the authorities extend them in some years to encourage compliance. These extensions are widely advertised in newspapers, and a good tax consultant can also keep you updated.

Companies must make prepayments (advance payments) of income tax liabilities during the accounting year. These prepayments are due on the following dates:

- ✔ June 15th (15 percent of total tax payable)

- ✔ September 15th (30 percent)

- ✔ December 15th (30 percent)

- ✔ March 15th (25 percent)

Don't postpone your payments or you could be hit with fines or even legal action! If tax authorities can prove you've fudged accounts to conceal income, you could be fined one hundred to three hundred percent of the tax evaded. Overpaid amounts are refunded after the filing of final tax returns.

Getting audited: It's required

Audits of company accounts are required in India. Companies prepare their financial statements according to the provisions of the Companies Act, 1956. These financial statements must be audited by chartered accountants (CPAs in the West) and an audit report has to be submitted to company members.

Annual reports circulated to members are generally comprised of the following:

- ✔ Director's report

- ✔ Auditor's report

- ✔ Balance sheet

- ✔ Profit and loss account

The central government may ask some companies to submit a cost audit of accounts, which is the process of verifying cost accounts or records and checking whether the previously prepared cost accounting plan has been carried out. The object is to ensure that costs per unit are kept at reasonable limits. This submission has to be completed by a cost auditor who should be a cost accountant under the Cost and Works Accountants Act, 1959.

The Income Tax Act, 1961 requires a tax audit to be conducted by a chartered accountant for taxpayers whose businesses make sales worth over Rs 4 million a year or gross more than Rs 1 million from a profession. Again, audit reports should be issued by a chartered accountant in order to claim tax incentives, tax holidays, and/or benefits.

You could, of course, file your own tax returns, after making a thorough study of all the relevant rules and regulations. But I strongly recommend that you engage Indian professionals to guide you in tax and audit matters. Nobody knows how to leverage the Indian laws like a capable Indian auditor.

Part III
Going About Your Business in India

The 5th Wave   By Rich Tennant

"This concept was a big hit in Nome. I wonder why it failed here in New Delhi."

In this part . . .

Make your product here, sell it, settle differences, and enjoy your time here all over a cup of nice Darjeeling brew. After all, your business venture should be about enjoying the nonbusiness side of India as well, right?

This part explains all aspects of manufacturing and sale, but it also covers the fun side of India and how to enjoy your time in the country. You also discover some legal issues and how to avoid them.

Chapter 10

Enjoying Your Stay in India

. . . .

In This Chapter

▶ Planning for your trip to India

▶ Dealing with culture shock

▶ Finding a place to live

▶ Managing everyday life

▶ Getting socially involved

. . . .

Mark Twain once said, "India is the cradle of the human race, the birthplace of human speech, the mother of history, grandmother of legend, and great grand mother of tradition. Our most valuable and most instructive materials in the history of man are treasured up in India." As you can imagine, most foreigners truly enjoy their time in India, and the chances that you'll feel the same way can be greatly increased if you're fully prepared for your Indian experience.

The focus of this chapter is to inform you of a few things to know for your visit and help you handle the daily life and cultural shock of being in a foreign country.

Whatever your experiences in India, one thing is for certain: You'll eventually return home or move on to your next assignment with a wealth of stories to share with family and friends. India can entice you and win you over with her charm. You can look forward to a great deal of hospitality and interest in you and your life.

Preparing for Your Visit

To make your visit smooth and in the true spirit of peacefulness which is at the heart of India, this section shows you how to get your visas and paperwork in order to minimize any hassles before you travel to India.

Obtaining visas and residential status

Securing the appropriate documentation is an important task, and you should be prepared to complete a vast array of application forms — work permits, visas, and resident's permits. Your company may be responsible for handling most of this very involved and complex process on your behalf.

But should you handle the process yourself, you need to first submit a visa application form, your passport with the necessary minimum validity, two identical copies of passport-sized photographs, the application fee and various supporting documents (see three letters mentioned below) to the proper government official. For more details, I suggest you contact the nearest Indian embassy.

Securing a visa

There are various types of visas based on your role in India:

✔ **Business trips:** For your business trip, you need the Business or B Visa. This document is valid for six months (or for a year or more, with multiple entries), but the duration of stay on each visit is restricted.

✔ **Employees:** Employment visas are different. Employees relocating to India should apply for one at the Indian Embassy in their home location. Various documents are to be submitted, and the Embassy can guide you in this respect.

If you're taking up a job with an Indian or an India-based firm, you usually need to present three letters:

- The contract or offer letter

- A letter from your employer stating why you're needed to do a job that an Indian can't do

- A letter from the employer agreeing to bear all expenses should you need to be sent home for any reason at any time

Spouses and dependants travel on the X Visa. There are also Tourist Visas, Student Visas, Missionary Visas, Journalist Visas, Transit Visas, and so on. Go to www.indianembassy.org/consular/visa_guide.htm or http://pubweb.fdbl.com/ihp8/global/media85.nsf/public-country-briefs/india?opendocument for more information on visas and visiting India.

Don't go to India with a Business visa or any other type of visa in the hope of changing your status after you're there. It's nearly impossible to change your status and you may have to return to your home country first.

Getting a passport

You need to obtain a passport from your own home country for any international travel. Indian visas require a minimum six month to a year validity remaining on your passport. Check with the Indian embassy in your country.

Obtaining a Residence Permit

Anyone intending to stay in India for more than 180 days needs to have a Residence Permit, and the paperwork is essential for foreigners who want to set up a personal bank account in the local currency. To get this important document, register with the Foreign Regional Registration Office (FRRO) at the city where you'll be living within two weeks of coming to live in India. Children below 16 years of age also need to be registered.

Use this proof of residency when settling hotel bills or getting quotes for domestic air travel prices — you can insist on being quoted in rupees instead of U.S. dollars, which constitutes substantial cost savings.

The following documents are needed for obtaining the permit:

- **International Service Employee Contract Letter:** An appointment letter from your company that includes remuneration details
- **Secondment letter:** Issued by your home country organization, stating that you've been sent to work in its Indian branch
- **Employment visa:** Must be of multiple entry status
- **An "X visa" with multiple entry status:** Necessary if your children or spouse accompany you while you're in India
- **A visa validity of three to five years:** Validity is necessary to avoid concerns or issues on trips
- **A welcome letter from the Indian counterpart:** Shows that the Indian entity is expecting you and looks forward to your arrival (make sure that you receive this in your homeland before departing for India)

Booking your flights to India

Using a travel agent in your city who has done bookings to India and knows of all the various options and routing is a good way to go. There are many Indian travel companies on the Web nowadays such as `www.travelguru.com`. Other well established Indian travel companies include Thomas Cook and Cox and Kings.

When you begin the process of booking your flights to India, don't be surprised if you aren't able to find direct flights. You may have to arrive through Frankfurt, Germany or Singapore, for example.

You can get a direct flight, for instance through Bangalore, but do explore the option of flights that come by other routes. This option can save you money and you may get better flight dates and times.

Making health and hygiene preparations

Indians live with more than one billion people, and the more people around the greater risk for a host of viruses. Because reduction of bacteria and viruses is much more advanced in developed countries, when you travel to India, you need to consider a few concerns about the hygiene.

On the good side, Indians are more relaxed and less paranoid about germs, which may stress you out. But the Indian approach is really the only way to live in the tropics. Take precautions but try not to be too anxious about germs; otherwise, you waste most of your time worrying. Conversely, some preventable exposure occurs due to this lack of concern. Either way, take a few measures to stay healthy in India.

Exposure to some new germs is unavoidable when you travel to a foreign country. Check with your family doctor before you leave to get the scoop on necessary immunizations and preventative drugs. Table 10-1 contains some useful immunization details.

Table 10-1	Recommended Immunizations for Visiting India
Immunization/Disease	*What You Need to Know*
Childhood vaccines	Newborns and children living in India require the same number of protective immunizations as those living in other countries. Clinics and private doctors can provide the vaccines for diphtheria, whooping cough, tetanus, measles, mumps, and polio.
Cholera	Some people prefer to get a cholera vaccine, but careful personal hygiene and cautious food and water consumption are considered to be more effective in preventing cholera than the currently available vaccine.

Immunization/Disease	*What You Need to Know*
Hepatitis A	Common in the Asia Pacific region. Originates from contaminated water, ice, shellfish, fruits, and vegetables. The Gamma globulin shot administered every six months provides passive protection against Type A viral hepatitis. A new vaccination that lasts up to five years is now available; it alleviates the need for frequent Gamma shots.
Hepatitis B	Transmitted by body fluids and dirty needles. Injections consist of a recombinant vaccine given three times over a six-month period. Vaccination is effective for 13 years.
Japanese Encephalitis	Transmitted by mosquitoes, it occurs mainly in the rainy and early dry season. Three injections of inactivated virus taken over a one month period are recommended.
Malaria	A mosquito-borne disease that's caused by a parasite. Some doctors recommend weekly doses of chloroquine, while others discourage its long-term use. There are many new antimalarial drugs that are better than chloroquine. Chloroquine is considered safe for pregnant and nursing mothers, babies, and young children. It is available in liquid form for babies in India. Some foreigners in India do take the weekly dosage of chloroquine, while others prefer to go without it.
Meningitis	Commonly seen in overpopulated areas, with intermittent epidemics in northern India. Meningitis transmitted by inhalation of airborne droplets via the upper respiratory tract. A single dose injection is recommended.
Polio	Most citizens of Western countries have already received polio vaccinations, but if for some reason you haven't been vaccinated, it's wise to do so before visiting India.
Rabies	Pre-exposure rabies immunization isn't routinely recommended. Post exposure rabies vaccine and human rabies immune globulin are available at all medical facilities.

(continued)

Table 10-1 *(continued)*

Immunization/Disease	What You Need to Know
Small Pox	As of March 1980, no country reported any cases of small pox and immunization is no longer required, except for a few African countries. Because the risk of vaccine-related illness is now greater than the risk of contracting small pox, check with a doctor before being immunized.
Tetanus	A cut on a piece of metal or even a fall on a mud tennis court in India could expose you to tetanus, because these courts have a thin film of cow dung to hold the ground together! So tetanus shots are wise. A booster shot is recommended before visiting India.
Typhoid Fever	Prevalent in India. Four vaccine capsules taken every other day are effective for 5 years.
Yellow Fever	A single primary or booster dose of yellow fever vaccine is valid for ten years. Immunization is currently required for travel to tropical Africa, Central and South America, and to India.

Observing a few health dos and don'ts

Keep in mind a few other health and hygiene tips:

- Don't drink tap water anywhere in India because it leads to diarrhea. Bottled water is readily available in most places and can usually be home-delivered.

- Don't eat uncooked foods like salads, cold cuts, custards, and ice-cream because they can cause diarrhea. Only eat these items from reputable sources.

- If you're stricken with diarrhea despite your best efforts, drink fluids in small quantities at frequent intervals and contact your doctor.

- Avoid heat-related ailments. Apply sunscreens, wear a hat, and wear appropriate clothing during your stay in India.

  Drink plenty of fluids, especially bottled water and rehydrating electrolyte drinks to keep yourself in good health since this heat and humidity could tire anyone unused to it.

India has excellent medical facilities and highly qualified doctors and surgeons. With proper precautions (including meticulous attention to cleanliness, particularly hand washing), your stay in India should be a healthy one. Many foreigners who've lived in India for a while can vouch that, with adequate precautions, no serious illness will occur.

Carrying the essentials

Staying healthy in India is a lot easier if you bring along a number of essential health and hygiene items when entering the country. Those items include the following:

- ✔ Copies of your medical and dental records and copies of a recent chest x-ray in case of a run-in with tuberculosis

- ✔ Copies of your children's immunization records (if they're joining you in India)

- ✔ A sufficient quantity of any special medication you or members of your family need. Many medications are available in India but may have a different name. Bring copies of prescriptions, so varying drug names don't pose a problem

- ✔ A record of your family's blood group and Rh classification (blood type information)

- ✔ An extra pair of glasses or contact lenses and a copy of your vision prescription

- ✔ A basic first aid kit

- ✔ Health insurance information, including coverage for medical evacuations, which are usually routed to Singapore

Getting Your Feet Wet in India

When you come to India, prepare for your senses to be assaulted. I tell all my clients that, especially if they're visiting the country for the first time. Nothing you've heard about India quite matches up to the reality. And don't think "I have been to Mexico, so I know how it will be." Nothing prepares you for India, except India itself. The crowds, the heat, the apparent chaos, the dirt, the traffic, the stunning contrasts — everything is an attack on your senses. But after the initial shock and with an understanding of the contradictions and the unwritten codes of Indian life, you can start to truly enjoy one of the most fascinating countries in the world.

Recounting an initial Indian encounter

India is a unique country, one that can be quite shocking for some Westerners. Your first encounter with Indian culture will almost certainly be a memorable one, and I've heard numerous stories about the initial shock that foreigners describe when seeing India for the first time. One of my favorite descriptions is from Sue Price, a Canadian:

"Life happens all around you — people living everywhere, worshipping, doing business, and sleeping in the streets. Cows, sacred to Hindus, wander freely about the streets. Hindu temples dot the streets and alleys, filled with images of innumerable gods, ornately decorated with vibrant colors and gold leaf, redolent of sandalwood incense. Strangely attired *sadhus* or holy men roam the streets, their faces daubed with colored, holy ash. Women rustle past in their bright, flowing saris. Cattle-drawn carts rumble through the streets bearing piles of fruits and vegetables. Spicy odors waft strong and pungent. All this goes on while my chauffeur drives me and my kids in a Toyota with our windows rolled up and the cool air conditioner blowing. I can't believe I am in a major city."

Culture shock often affects spouses and dependents more than foreign businesspeople doing business in India. If your family is joining you in the country, keep this fact in mind and pay attention to their feelings and emotions. You may have an office to go to and plenty of work to keep you occupied all day, but your family will face the strain of adapting to day-to-day life in a truly foreign environment.

So what can you do to get over culture shock as soon as possible? Here are a few suggestions:

- ✔ Get to know the people of India.

- ✔ Talk to your new Indian colleagues, co-workers, and friends to find out why and how they do things.

- ✔ Immerse yourself in the culture.

- ✔ Join in on Indian activities — try attending a religious ceremony, wedding, housewarming party or work-related activity.

- ✔ Laugh and see the funny side of the culture gap. A sense of humor can be your best coping mechanism.

In hopes of easing your early days in India and lessening the culture shock, I offer a number of tips in this section for you to consider.

Arriving at the airport

Your first steps in India are most likely going to be in an airport. Your experience in the airport undoubtedly serves as an interesting, lively entry into the country. Knowing what to expect helps you keep your wits in what can sometimes prove to be a hectic setting.

Noticing people everywhere

Even if your flight has been a long one, be prepared for a surge of humanity after you land. India's population crossed the billion mark in 2004, and to your inexperienced eyes, it may seem that a good chunk of that population is waiting outside the airport. But don't be alarmed — that mass of people is perfectly normal at an Indian airport. Indian relatives and friends are notorious for showing up in droves to greet their loved ones when they come back to the country. The occasion can cause quite a crowd, and it can be a strain on the incoming passenger.

Also at the airport, expect enormous quantities of cabin baggage and piles of check-in luggage to complicate your path to the immigration counters. And be prepared to wait in long, winding lines, although they never seem to take as long as you think. Take heart in the fact that Indian airports are used to handling huge amounts of travelers, so even though it seems like a lot to you, for them it's just another day.

Considering hang-ups with customs

Indian Customs won't usually bother you unless you're carrying excessive amounts of electronics, gold, weapons, or pornographic material, which is banned in India. Widespread availability of imported items in India is increasing all the time, although it can be costly. If there's anything in particular that you can't live without, make sure you bring an ample supply. However, if you keep an open mind there's usually a suitable local alternative.

Check out what's allowed and what's not at www.cbec.gov.in before you pack your bags.

If possible, have someone waiting for you at the airport in India and keep a cell phone number handy in case of emergencies or delays.

Catching a ride at the airport

If you don't have someone to pick you up at the airport, rest assured that you can find suitable ground transportation for a good price. Use the pre-paid taxi counters. Rates are pre-set and standardized (and if the shock is still hitting you and you leave your luggage in the truck, your driver can be tracked down later). Cabs are plentiful and you shouldn't have a problem finding one that can take you where you need to go.

After you're outside the airport in India, the noise, heat, and sheer emotional power of India hits you all at once. One foreign businessman told me that there's really no "easing" into India. It's more like trial by fire!

Understanding Indian currency

India's currency system is based on units called rupees and paise. The country also counts in a different way than what you may be used to, using a system with *lakhs* and *crores* instead of millions and billions. You can find all of the details in Chapter 9.

All major credit cards are accepted in India, and negotiating your financial transactions is quite easy this way. Do carry at least some cash on you though, especially if you're traveling to a new place, make sure you have a minimum of Rs 5,000. And don't worry; carrying currency is far safer here than in the West because muggings are practically unknown in most places in India.

Traveler's checks aren't particularly useful in India. You may have a hard time finding a place to cash them. If you want to use traveler's checks, go to a bank or one of the few authorized money changers to do so.

Finding a hotel room

You need somewhere to stay while you're in India, and many Westerners choose to stay in hotels while they're in the country. India has many hotels that meet or exceed international standards in all its major cities and even in some Tier 1 cities. (You can read more about the tier system for India's cities in Chapter 5.) Tier 2 cities are catching up, too, and many have good options for accommodation. Several global hotel chains operate in India, so you won't be without options. But note that hotels do fill up quickly, so advance booking is a must.

Your company, an experienced Indian travel agent, or even an Indian contact such as a relocation agency or India destination service provider can help you find corporate discounts and advice on locations. Currently the situation in most big cities is a shortage of rooms in best hotels, so it bears repeating that you book in advance.

Hotel staff are usually very welcoming and go out of their way to make you feel comfortable. One foreign client of mine told me that when she and her husband were on a look-see trip to India they were amazed at the hotel staff's enthusiasm in keeping their young son Nicholas occupied. The restaurant manager amused him with his keys, the waiters entertained him between trips to tables, and he was allowed to generally romp around. "What a wonderful country, where children can be children," my client remarked.

The concept of service apartments (fully furnished, move-in-ready apartments that often feature maid service) is catching on and is a viable option if you don't intend to put down even shallow roots.

Settling In for a Longer Stay

A one- to two-year contract where a company sends employees to start up a business in India is becoming common these days. If you find yourself in this position, you may need hand holding and more detailed advice from a relocation company to help you in the city of your choice.

In this section, I provide tips on finding a home, hooking up your basic utilities, and getting medical care. Be warned that adjusting to life in India may take some time, but living in India can be a great experience if you have an open mind and the will to simply get used to a different lifestyle. Things aren't going to be like "back home," so you may as well jump in with both feet into this adventure. If you do, you can enjoy an amazing overseas stint.

Finding a place to call home

If you're going to be in India for a while, look into long-term accommodations. Your home is your castle, temporary or otherwise, and you can feel settled if you get into the right home. Renting or buying property is the question. In India, renting is often the only option because buying property for foreigners requires special permissions from the Reserve Bank of India.

Renting an apartment

Many foreign businesspeople choose to rent apartments. Ask your Indian contacts and co-workers, or other expatriates, for the name of a good broker or firm that can help you find a suitable apartment. Look for one who's used to working with foreigners. They are more familiar with your needs and better able to negotiate prices.

After you've located an apartment you like, negotiate a lease. Most landlords aren't too keen on putting everything down in black and white, but rest assured that they do what they say they're going to do, whether it's in writing or not. So vagueness in your lease shouldn't be of too much concern.

A good relationship with your landlord is very important. Expect him to be warm and welcoming but to not take it well if you start complaining about many minor problems. It's often easier to just get a repair company to attend to small problems, and that route can be fairly cheap. If you insist on whining about minor issues, you may be asked to leave the property soon after you've settled in. The patience of some Indian landlords can be very slim.

Residential units and office buildings that are for rent in India often don't offer some of the amenities that are taken for granted in the West. For example, don't expect well-equipped kitchens. But these are points that can be negotiated, and after you have a lease agreement, landlords will typically invest in adding features to and cleaning up the property.

You may also find that some buildings don't look great on the outside, and that first impression can be pretty negative. Keep an open mind though. The inside could be newly renovated and acceptable. That's just another example of how you need to measure things differently in India and let go of the idea that your life will be exactly like it was at home.

Buying a home

Expatriates don't typically buy homes in India due to the permissions and the difficulty in repatriating the funds. Only the returning non-resident Indian (often an American of Indian origin) may end up buying his home. If you get this permission, then buying a home requires the help of a realty agent and a well-established lawyer. The fees you pay both, which could be 2 to 3 percent of sale value, will be money well spent. They take you from home search to registration of the property at a local government office, which can all be quite time consuming.

Real estate isn't a licensed trade in India and anyone from a milkman to a watchman can become an agent if he chooses to. Ask for referrals from your Indian and expatriate acquaintances to find reputable help.

Dealing with utilities

Common utilities like electricity and water can be an adventure in India. Power outages are still quite common and frustrating. You may consider investing in a small generator or inverter so that at least part of your power supply can still run if there's an outage.

Water comes from different sources: wells, pipelines from the city's reservoir, and from bore wells. Keeping track of these different sources and keeping the taps running is a difficult task for the Indian government. One house in India usually has both a government supply through pipes and a well for back-up when the government supply runs dry, which does happen. Insist on opening the taps to make sure the faucets are working.

Many households without good water buy large tanker-loads from private suppliers and use them to fill overhead or underground tanks that can be used to supply the house.

Disposing garbage isn't something anyone takes the time to explain to you in advance, so watch what others do and follow suit. Sometimes the garbage collection truck comes and sometimes it doesn't. There's usually a common dumpster on the street where garbage is collected.

Getting medical care

Falling ill in a foreign country isn't a very appealing thought, but you can take comfort in the fact that medicine is advanced in India, and healthcare is a booming business in the country. The standards of hygiene are improving, and treatment costs less in India than in the West. The quality of care is so high and the cost so low that many people actually travel to India for their healthcare needs: Medical tourism is a booming area of growth in the country! While Western doctors may do hip replacements, Indian doctors are intelligent enough to do hip resurfacing, which is gentler and lasts longer. Add to these factors excellent bedside manners and giving you their time, and you can understand why some people prefer to be treated in India.

Dealing with medical emergencies isn't a problem in India because adequate ambulance services and competent hospital emergency wings exist. Twenty-four-hour pharmacies are located in all Indian cities, and as soon as you move into your home you should familiarize yourself with the closest one. Home delivery of your prescriptions may be available, too.

Doctors in India are known for their caring manner with patients. Medical relationships are often for a lifetime in India, and doctors can become part of a family. Nurses are caring, but like in other countries they can vary a lot in their bedside manner. They administer drugs and injections without a spoken word of explanation (ask them to explain and they will), and at the same time they want to hear everything about your family, and they'll settle down with you for a nice chat. Obliging them is a good way to earn some extra attentive care.

Tips for medical emergencies

Some of the foreign businesspeople I've worked with have had medical emergencies while in India, and they have some suggestions for how to handle the situation:

✔ Keep a sample of your own blood in a blood bank for an emergency. Having your own blood on hand reduces the need for doctors to find a match if you need a transfusion.

✔ Make sure your cell phone is always charged and ready to go in case of an emergency.

✔ If you don't drive, find out where you can find a reliable cab at any time of day or night.

✔ Keep cash in various denominations on hand because you never know when you may need to make on-the-spot cash payments.

✔ Have a back-up arrangement with someone you trust, to see that you have what you need (including plenty of bottled water) in case you're faced with the need to stay in the hospital for an extended period.

Navigating Everyday Life in India

Navigating your way through day-to-day life in India depends heavily on two crucial areas: your ability to build and maintain personal relationships and the realization that you have to assert yourself. Establish a healthy rapport with the Indians who play a role in your daily life by respecting your staff and colleagues and make it clear that you value the help they offer.

Work to develop your Indian friendships because there may be a time that you need to call on a friend for help. These times may include borrowing help or running to the hospital. (Indian hospitals require that a friend or relative is with you before you can be admitted.)

The second area is recognizing when you need to assert yourself. Some folks from the West are taught to be modest, but certain situations in India may require some bullish behavior. Hospitals in India are one example. Indian hospitals can, at times, seem overwhelmed with patients, and if you're not assertive enough to push ahead to the front of a line (assuming your ailment or emergency warrants that behavior), you could spend quite a lot of time waiting for care. Don't be scared to tell the management of the hospital what's wrong with you, and who you are, so that they can better serve you. Don't be shy. This is how things work in India!

One of my foreign clients had a small accident that required him to go to a well-known hospital for a precautionary x-ray. At the front desk he was directed to counter 4, and after he stood in line there for 20 minutes he reached the front of the line only to be told that he needed to go to the casualty department first. He followed the directions but couldn't find the correct place. Just as he was getting all hot and bothered, a well-dressed young man who was clearly a hospital employee came up and asked if he could help. Remembering some advice I'd given him, my client said, "Allow me to introduce myself. I'm Robert Blank, Vice President of Human Resources at Blank, Inc., and my doctor thinks I may have broken a bone in my foot." In a flash he was in a wheelchair on his way to the casualty department, had all of his forms filled out for him, and was told that his payments had been taken care of. You can take an important lesson from his tactic: Assert yourself, and you may be amazed at the results!

Developing relationships and asserting yourself both come in handy in several areas of Indian life. The following sections detail the Indian life you have to navigate each day.

Dealing with transportation in India

You have a ton of options when it comes to travel: road, air, rail, bus, and foot. Each has its own advantages, depending on where you are, where you want to go, and how much you'd like to spend to get there!

Car traffic

Car traffic in India is chaotic. Seat belts are a fairly new phenomenon and just beginning to be taken seriously. You may see six people on a motorbike, loaded up with all their worldly goods. Or you may see an autorickshaw (a three-wheeled motor car) stacked with people like the inside of circus car. Indian drivers seem to have their own code — they come close to crashing and then swerve at the last second. The cars motor away intact, although the heart rates of the passengers may take a while to cool down!

It can be hair-raising at times, but the truth is that traffic in India isn't any more dangerous than it is in other lively parts of the world. If you want to drive yourself in India, all you need is an international driving license and an iron will.

But many foreign companies don't have auto insurance coverage in India and don't want their foreign staff or families driving. The alternative is to hire a driver, which is a common choice.

Air travel within India

Work in India requires you to often travel to different cities. For government permissions, Delhi may be a destination; for sales meetings, Mumbai or Chennai may be the place to go to; for comparing figures with other Information Technology companies, you may need to go to Bangalore. For your family too, a weekend trip to another Indian city is the best way to get a real feel of India.

Flights between cities in India are easy to find because many domestic airlines offer competitive fares to all major cities and most larger towns. While you may be flying a lot for business, you need to know a few pointers of flying the friendly skies:

- ✔ Do expect flight delays. Often the airlines strike and rarely give much notice.

- ✔ Foreigners are charged more for the same seats on the same flights than Indian passengers. To avoid being charged more, obtain a Residence Permit.

- ✔ When flying within India, call the airline or the airport before you leave home to check on late departures. Take a book along to read and stay patient.

Riding the rails

A quick overnight train trip close by is the best way to taste the flavor of different parts of India. So keep an open mind to traveling by train. India's railway network is extensive, and it seems to cover every part of the country. Air-conditioned, upper class compartments are clean and make train travel comfortable. Food is often served on these trips and is part of the ticket fare, but carry your own in case you're concerned about spoilage. Bottled water, fresh fruits, and biscuits are plentiful at most stations and in some cases even your pantry car, so you won't go hungry. For more detailed information on rail travel in India, check out www.indianrail.gov.in.

Taking the bus

If you're so inclined, although I personally don't recommend it, you can hop a luxury, air-conditioned bus to travel between major cities in India. You can also take a basic government bus, but choosing that method of travel is unwise unless you have loads of patience and a strong stomach. It's dusty, crowded, often delayed, and can carry exposure to illnesses of other travelers. A good travel agent can find you a seat on a luxury bus even at short notice, and that is all you should try.

"Please adjust a little"

The chaotic nature of traffic in India usually leaves quite an impression on Westerners, particularly Americans. The breakneck speeds, near collisions, and convoluted roadways can be a major departure from what you're used to back home. One of my American clients was amazed by the traffic in India, and he even picked up a handy phrase while stuck in a traffic jam.

"In Bangalore, which is the Silicon Valley of India, the traffic has gone somewhat berserk. The bottlenecks and jams are endless and the pollution is unbelievable in this once-upon-a-garden city. I enjoy my time here and find it very cosmopolitan. The pubs, restaurants, stores,

housing, golf course, and gardens are all a delight. But driving is completely crazy. The other day, when I was coming back from work after a long hard day, I was on the arterial MG Road for 40 minutes with no forward movement at all. A little Bangalorean on a mini scooter came weaving through from the back of the line. When there was just a little less space than what he needed to inch his way through, he would simply say, "*Solpa adjust madi,*" which means *please adjust a little*, and the surrounding cars actually tried to get out of the way so he could pass! I told myself that I had to remember that phrase: "Solpa adjust madi!"

As an alternative to the bus, consider hiring an air-conditioned or ordinary taxi instead. It's a quicker choice. Do be sure before departing that the car agency is reputable. Ask other expatriates or other companies who they use. State explicitly that you want a driver who's had a break. Some drivers are known to do multiple shifts to make more money, which does nothing for their wakefulness behind the wheel.

Hitting the trails on foot

Travel by foot is a rarity in India. Of course people do trek in the mountains up north or in cool hill stations in the south. But most cities in India aren't walking cities. Bangalore has pollution; Mumbai is overcrowded, and so on. But a walking tour to capture the essence of a small area is fine to do and such guide led walks are available in all cities. You should really only walk for exercise when you have established that an area is safe and common for this activity.

Using the telephone in India

It's nearly impossible to do business in India (or anywhere, for that matter) without spending time on the telephone. Talking on the phone in India can be challenging for Westerners because Indians have a different phone manner than what you're used to and you don't have the benefit of seeing gestures and facial expressions when having a phone conversation.

Common telephone frustrations

One of the biggest telephone annoyances used to be the inconsistency of telephone connections, but those are now much more reliable in India.

So here are a few things to keep this in mind:

- ✔ If you hear silence on the other end of the line, the Indian you're talking to is probably either thinking or pausing. There's no need to say, "Hello?"

- ✔ Westerners also have trouble with Indian accents on the telephone, but remember that your accent sounds as strange to them as theirs does to you!

- ✔ Indians' English language skills are different than yours. English may not be their first language, so don't be surprised if you have to repeat yourself or break your sentences down into more manageable pieces.

- ✔ If you call an Indian office or government department that's not well versed in handling calls from foreigners, you're more likely to hear half sentences or questions like "Calling from?"(which means "Which company are you calling from or who shall I say is calling?"). Do your best to bury your frustration and refrain from answering: "I'm calling from my telephone!"

- ✔ When speaking on the phone with an Indian colleague or partner, take good notes. Note taking helps you focus on the content of the call, and you can keep a good record of the conversation so that you can take appropriate actions after hanging up.

Cell phone annoyances

No one seems to have cell phone courtesy these days. This problem is more so in India because the phones are too much of a status symbol (the more the calls, the more important the recipient is presumed to be). Lack of etiquette is part of the problem, too. So be prepared to hear different ring tones (including lilting Bollywood melodies) sounding off all around you, even during the middle of an important meeting.

If you're the one calling the shots at a meeting, establish telephone decorum early on. Specify that mobile phones are to be switched off for meetings and important functions. And most Indians don't keep their cell phone voices down, which can be quite distracting in an open-plan office. So if you encourage phones to be off, you won't have this problem.

An open call for frustration

Many Westerners find the differences in India's phone etiquette maddening. It takes some time to get used to the subtle nuances of conducting a phone conversation in India, but if you're patient you can get used to it. Resist the urge to hang up angrily, as in the following example:

Indian Employee: "I want to ask you now, what is your good name?"

Caller: "Which do you mean? I think all my names are good!"

Indian Employee: "No, I mean your name for taking down the details."

Caller: "Why didn't you say so in the first place? Do you need my first name or last name?"

Indian Employee: "You can give first last or last first."

Caller: "What?"

Indian Employee: "Your latest name used please, sir."

Caller: "Just call me Jim."

Indian Employee: "Okay Jim, sir. So your name is Jim only?"

Caller: "Yes, Jim McNeill."

Indian Employee: "Can you spell that out?"

Caller: "M-c-N-e-i-l-l"

Indian Employee: "Mc and then M like monkey, E like elephant, I like ink, L like lion?"

Caller: "I don't know what this is about elephants and lions. It is N as in navy, E as in echo, I as in India and L as in Lima."

Indian Employee: "Thank you. Can I have your mail ID now?"

Caller: "You mean my e-mail address?"

Indian Employee: "Yes, please."

Caller: "Get on with it, please, this problem is costing me all kinds of money! We can't wait until the cows come home."

Indian Employee: "Cows? Come where, Mr. Jim?"

Caller: "Oh never mind!" (He angrily hangs up the phone.)

In India, people relay telephone numbers in a pattern that may seem strange to you. Cell phone numbers are given in two five-digit parts. The first five are the phone company's string, and the second five comprise your personal number. For land lines, it's common to say "2-43-42-double four-6." The same number read by another Indian could be "2434-24-46." The "double" numbers can be very confusing!

Living with the crowds in India

You should have plenty of room in your living space in India, and you probably have room to stretch out at your office. But after you leave the spacious confines of either and enter public spaces in India, the crowds take some getting used to. Shopping on the weekends can be nerve-racking at the best of times, and during festival seasons public spaces can get really packed. There's no shame in spending some time at home during the busiest times and then getting out later to enjoy the festivities after the crowds have died down a bit.

If you're faced with a situation that requires you to stand in a line, consider taking a book along for entertainment. And be prepared to experience more body contact and less personal space than you're used to in the West. After all, more than a billion Indians have to stand somewhere! If you leave a respectable gap, someone may butt right in, blissfully unaware of your need for space!

Giving Back to India

When you do business with a country as giving as India, it's also important that you figure out ways to give back. You may think that you're doing a nice job giving back to India simply by doing business there and enriching the economy, but India may touch your heart, and then you'll want to discover ways to give more. Check out the following sections for ways to give.

Taking part in corporate social responsibility

There are many non-government organizations (NGOs) to go to as a starting point for your corporate social responsibility. Corporate Social Responsibility (CSR) is a new concept for many companies in India, and this is where foreigners can have a huge effect. It needs to move from "event-based" actions — such as the recent tsunami relief efforts — to regular corporate philanthropic and issue-based action. HIV, AIDS, fresh water supply, and education are all areas that could really use corporate assistance and attention in India.

Some impressive strides have been made by companies looking to promote green and environmentally friendly initiatives in India. The Western standards in these areas are far more advanced than those in India, and most Indian companies flout standards without hesitation. On environmental issues, India needs deep awareness programs, and widespread funding. Physical infrastructure is very poor, and if you're interested in promoting more sustainable practices that's an area on which you could focus. If you give back to India in return for all of the opportunity the country offers you, your standing in the economic community will improve by leaps and bounds. And ultimately, that's good for business.

It's hard to say goodbye

You came to India, you got over your culture shock, and now it's time to say goodbye. It can be hard to say goodbye! India grows on you, and you may find it difficult getting used to being home again. Remember that you're not alone, and your Indian friends may jump at the chance to host you for a visit or speak with you on the phone about the good times you spent while in India. That's what friends are for, after all!

An executive in a top automobile company that set up its factory in India told me that when she left, she knew that living in India was the experience of a lifetime and that she wouldn't have traded it for anything. After a two-and-a-half-year stay in the country, she felt satisfied with her contribution to her company's project and was overwhelmingly pleased that she took the opportunity to live in India. Don't be surprised if you feel the same way!

When Nokia launched their massive factory in India, they were looking to give away four hundred cell phones to a worthy cause instead of giving the phones away to guests at their launch, which would normally have been the procedure. But initially they had a hard time finding a worthy cause because they didn't know where to look. My firm helped to manage the launch, and we helped them find a group of ophthalmic surgeons who were providing free care for the blind in India. Nokia agreed that those efforts were certainly worthy of some help, so they offered the phones to some of the blind patients and they're now enjoying communicating freely on their new cell phones!

Giving alms

While living in India, you encounter beggars and panhandlers. You may find them at traffic signals, outside places of worship, or sitting at street corners. You can either choose to ignore them, don't make eye contact, or wave them away while politely making the Indian namaste gesture (see Chapter 15 for more info). However, be prepared for some beggars to be persistent; they will, however, not be abusive or show any signs of aggression usually, so please don't be afraid.

If you want to give to these folks, carry some small change with you so you're prepared to give the amount of your choice. (It can help to make the decision to set aside a certain amount for this purpose each day.)

If you offer regular donations to the same beggars, they may eventually feel that you're required to give them your money. It's a difficult situation, because the need is seemingly endless. You may find it more rewarding to get involved with a local official charity that helps to serve the basic needs of the underprivileged.

Tipping your Indian service workers

Many foreigners have questions about tipping in India, and I'm always happy to help with answers because tipping is nice in any culture. Here are a few guidelines:

- ✔ An *average* tip would be about Rs 50. That amount is used for valets, doormen, drivers, or the man who carries your groceries to your car.

- ✔ A *good* tip would be Rs 100–200, given for room service at a hotel, an excellent driver, a porter, or a barber.

- ✔ A really *excellent* tip would be around Rs 500, given maybe to a taxi driver whose services you've used for a week, or the domestic staff when you've been a houseguest, or to your maid who's recently had a baby.

- ✔ Tips for servers in a restaurant are typically 10 percent of the bill.

Chapter 11

Making the Sale

*P*op quiz: How many teenagers will there be in India by 2015?

    a. A couple of million

    b. 550 million

    c. None (India is close to discovering how to get rid of teens completely)

The correct answer is 550 million! For a very long time in the future, India is going to continue to have a workforce and consumers too! The increase in spending power among Indians starting now is causing many foreign companies to sit up and take notice. Demand in practically every sector of business is soaring, and the government is helping the trend by liberalizing what were once stringent trade laws. Indian cities vie with each other to match the living standards of the West, the middle class is buoyant, and the rural markets are ripe for the picking. It's no wonder that virtually every global company seems to be looking to make a sale in India.

Yes, prospects are good, and they're constantly getting better. But before you jump into business, you need to know some facts and get fine tuning advice to make sure both seller and consumer end up happy. In this chapter I explore the various facets of selling in India. I offer insights into the Indian consumer market and present some marketing ideas and sales strategies. Along the way, I throw in some interesting stories of success and failure and include reasons for both.

Understanding the Indian Consumer Market

The government of India is bent on opening up the economy, and already they've succeeded beyond the world's expectations. Experts predict more boom time to come, and they base their optimism on a number of factors:

- **Indian families are changing:** Young, upwardly mobile Indians are embracing nuclear families, and the old joint family system is getting rarer all the time. Older family members are continuing to work and rejecting 60 as the retirement age, allowing them to remain financially independent as long as they're healthy enough to earn a living. So in turn, households have more spending power and an increased need for a variety of products.

- **Employment rates are rising:** The number of Indians — particularly women — with jobs has been increasing. Indian women have an increasing level of income, and more and more of them are returning to work after starting families. All of this means a higher demand for consumer goods, and foreign businesses are capitalizing on the development.

- **Children are a developing consumer group:** Young Indians from newborns to teenagers are increasingly becoming pampered, and Indian parents can apparently deny them nothing. The demand for toys, children's clothes, and gadgets is growing all the time.

The Indian market is wide open, and many have already taken the plunge. In this section I describe a few tactics that are certainly worth considering as you decide how to best court Indian consumers, and I provide examples of various companies that have succeeded.

Offering international flavor

Indians are generally traditionalists, and fervently embrace the ways of their country and culture. But a growing number of Indians are willing to step outside the Indian realm and try products with a more international appeal.

Coffee has a major appeal in India. Indians thought they had coffee making and drinking down to an art, but they discovered that the West had some promising ideas. Indians have embraced such global coffee chains as Costa Coffee from the UK, Dome Coffee from Australia, and even Starbucks. The trend has been surprising. But what worked? It's simple: India's younger population grew fond of the ambience of these trendy coffee bars — not just the brews, but the experience — and got the feeling that they're citizens of the world. Success and growth for the coffee purveyors has followed.

Blending East with West

While offering Indians a global perspective with new products can sometimes yield positive results, giving your business's offerings an Indian twist or slant is a much safer bet. Indians can be pretty set in their ways when it comes to certain elements of their culture, so consider how you may "Indianize" your product to add to its value in the Indian market. It could make the difference between a bust and a blockbuster.

McDonald's illustrates how Indianization can pay off. The world's largest beef-based food chain realized their standard Western menu wouldn't work for Indians, many of whom are vegetarian and most of which don't eat beef. McDonald's changed their menu accordingly; instead of beefy double cheese-burgers you get chickpea burgers topped with mint chutney. McDonald's also has a veggie burger loaded with Indian spices (hey, a little masala never hurt anyone!) The restaurant even offers a "Maharaja Mac," made with a ground lamb patty!

You can even consider fine-tuning the Indianization of your product, aiming it at a specific region within the country. Take the latest food product offering from Maggi (a division of Nestle): delicious sambar noodles. *Sambar* is a spicy lentil and vegetable soup that's extremely popular in southern India. Maggi added the sambar flavor to their noodles and won over consumers in the southern part of the country.

The majority of products from multinational corporations that do well in India seem to incorporate Indian themes, almost trying to be more Indian than the Indians. These businesses consciously project themselves as being part of the culture of the country, aiming to dispel the notion that they're foreign and therefore perhaps not to be trusted. Beware that Indians can be very touchy about cultural imperialism.

Western food with an Indian twist, combined with world-class service, hygiene, and food quality form a recipe for a successful restaurant business in India. Keep those ingredients in mind if you're interested in that industry.

Tweaking your product to reach more of the Indian market

Because the dynamics of the Indian consumer market are very different than what you're used to, you may find that you need to make adjustments to your approach to reach a larger, more attractive market segment. Keep your business as agile as possible and be open to making changes. Customizing certain aspects of your business for India can make a big difference in your bottom line.

A fishy phone tale

The successful repositioning of cell phones has helped phone makers and service providers secure a massive (and growing) portion of the Indian market. Cell phones are popping up in some very unlikely places:

"The other day a fisherwoman in Mumbai came with her wicker basket on her door to door sales rounds. She was wearing traditional garb — a tightly tied sari, nose ring, multiple earrings, and many dots on her forehead. She was barefoot because that was the way she had lived in the village where she was born, and now she finds that footwear hampers her. She earns a dollar a day, she said. But a moment later she placed her basket over her head and reached into it with one arm to retrieve her cell phone, which had started ringing."

For example, consider cell phones — perhaps the greatest Indian sales success story of recent years. Cellular phones were introduced to India in 1994, but the phones and the service were inaccessible to most Indians at first because of sky-high charges. A cell phone was definitely a luxury item and a status symbol.

All that changed in 2002 when service providers repositioned the product with different pricing structures. Today, cell phones are as common as mosquitoes in India, and each month 1.5 million Indians join the ranks of the cell phone equipped. Carpenters, electricians, handymen, and even domestic maids — some earning less than $100 a month — have cell phone service because it helps them greatly in their work so they're reachable at all times. Because incoming calls are free, you only pay a monthly subscription of $4 and buy the $20 handset with a loan.

With the cell phone becoming a mass product, companies have found it necessary to customize the gadget even further to suit Indian needs. Some phones come with unique ring tones and color displays, and one company has rolled out products with features like a special grip and torchlight (a flashlight), targeting India's truckers! That's customization for you.

Going rural

Pursing Indian consumers in the rural markets is different than selling to urban Indians. The market drivers and logistics are different. To be successful, you have to gear your efforts accordingly. Distribution and pricing are two major pitfalls because transportation can be tricky and Indian villagers are, on the whole, much more cost-conscious than their counterparts in the cities. Rural Indians wait for spending occasions, such as annual fairs and festivals, and functions like weddings.

Going small: Sachets of success

Appropriate packaging is a prime factor for success in India. Smaller is often better, because small packages appeal to thrifty Indians and also allow them to try various products without committing to a larger purchase.

One Indian shampoo brand has had much success with the small-package concept. Chik came out with modestly priced single-use sachets (packets) of shampoo, and sales have been outstanding. Now sachets account for an astounding 70 percent of shampoo sales in India, and analysts say that the shampoo industry grew between 10 and 15 percent in volume in 2004, primarily because of small packages. Today, nearly all consumer goods are available in small packs in India, from coffee to facial creams. They cost between Rs 2 and 5.

Small packages have also helped to put a stop to bogus and counterfeit goods in India. Cheap knock-offs once flooded the market, but affordable sachets from the brand names have helped make the cheapies far less attractive for Indian consumers, who'd rather purchase a small quantity of a known product instead of a larger quantity of a bogus one.

India has some unique packaging rules that you need to consider. Your Indian contacts can provide you with details, but examples include the need for a printed Minimum Retail Price (MRP), and if yours is a food product, a color-coded circle within a square to indicate if the product is vegetarian or non-vegetarian.

Marketing Your Product in India

India is a world apart. What works in other areas of the globe may or may not work in India. To successfully market your product in the country, you have to know a little about the Indian psyche, what appeals to the Indian imagination, where Indians compromise on products and services and where they don't.

Think about these example questions: Will your product appeal to Indian housewives, many of whom enjoy comfortable lifestyles and have time to spare to listen to a sales pitch? Have you factored in India's literacy rates, especially when considering advertising and using the media to promote your business? Is your product positioned to appeal to thrifty Indians who are always on the lookout for a bargain? Read on to make your story a marketing success.

Harnessing the power of the media

India is very proud of its vibrant media, which is important for foreign firms who want to set up shop in the country to understand and embrace the role of the media here.

Life is much easier if you choose to work with an ad agency. Several national and international agencies currently operate in India, and their familiarity with the Indian market allows them to provide you with informed decisions about how to buy the right kind of ad space for your business.

The next few sections give you information on how to use the media effectively and efficiently. You need to know just where to go and what to do in order to get value for money.

Targeting specific media

Indians are spoiled with a variety of media outlets. They enjoy a dazzling array of TV stations, newspapers, magazines, and radio stations. The trick for you is choosing the most appropriate media outlets for your target audience.

For instance, if you advertise on the TV stations that are beamed into India's cities, you run the risk of missing the sizeable rural market, which doesn't have as much access to these stations as the urban areas. In the villages and remote towns, Indians watch the government's Doordarshan channel, so if you'd like your product to catch the eyes of consumers in these places, take a page out of Coca-Cola's book. When Coke started patronizing Doordarshan (or "DD" as it's commonly called), their rivals probably laughed themselves into stitches, but Coke had the last laugh when it dramatically improved its reach into rural households across the country.

Making use of non-traditional media

Television plays a major role in advertising in India, but don't let it blind you to the opportunities of non-traditional media. The non-traditional approaches are often very useful in connecting with India's many fragmented markets. Here are a few examples:

- ✔ *LG Electronics* sends employees to road shows in Indian villages where they promote LG's products using local dialects.

- ✔ *HLL (Hindustan Lever Ltd)* manufacturing soaps and other variety of goods organizes promotional programs at rural fairs.

✔ *Philips India* is into wall space. Indian villages have plenty of long walls that edge agricultural land. Philips found that not only were the owners of these walls quite happy to have them painted, but also they weren't too particular about what was painted on them. Now the boredom of long cart, truck, and train journeys in India is often relieved by reading roadside advertisements for Philips products.

Consider sponsorship to market your business. The options for sponsorship are wide open, so think about how your business can contribute to the communities of India (and reap the benefits at the same time). Here are a few ideas to get you started:

✔ Sponsor a world-class cricket match, and make your product's name known to toddlers and octogenarians alike.

✔ Partner with an organization and take a planeload of disadvantaged children on a ride in the skies to endear your business to Indian consumers.

✔ Sponsor a primary school's sports day and get the little ones telling their mommies and daddies how much they want to visit your toy store.

Jumping on the Internet bandwagon

Urban India, especially its youth, is computer savvy. Young people constitute an important chunk of India's buying power, so using the Internet as an advertisement avenue merits a close look. Urban Indians are beginning to shop online, and Internet advertising is poised to assume a major role in reaching out to customers. A recent conference I attended in Stanford University on "Persuasive Technologies" stressed the power of the Internet and mobile phones to persuade buyers. These marketing tools sure work well in India.

An example of an extremely popular use of the Internet in India is the proliferation of matrimony Web sites that allow "arranged" marriages. So a Web site like Bharat Matrimony advertises itself on Google India. On this matrimony site, a home loan company advertises to new couples who may be in the market for a new home. So think about the culture of your audience to predict how they use the Internet. Then advertise where they surf.

Using celebrity to pitch your products

Using celebrities from the entertainment and sports worlds to promote a product may seem like a uniquely Western phenomenon, but that's simply not true. Indians love their celebrities, and celebrity endorsements can have a positive effect. From Bollywood heartthrob Aamir Khan endorsing automobiles, to Indian cricket maestro Sachin Tendulkar plugging motorcycles, to Amitabh Bacchan (an ageless superstar of the Indian silver screen also known as the "Big B") voicing his love for, well, just about everything, Indian celebrities have long been tapped by the business world to attract customers and increase brand recognition. So don't look shocked when your advertising agent wants to spend a small fortune on getting a film star to plug your product. Just go with the flow, if you can find room in your budget.

If your advertising manager comes to you with a budget-busting estimate for hiring one of India's national celebrities don't lose heart. Instead, ask about a region-specific celebrity. Plenty of locally or regionally famous Indians can endorse your business in a specific area for a much more reasonable price than the national names. For example, I have an actress friend who's quite famous in Tamil Nadu. She's a sought-after brand ambassador at the regional level.

Even though Indians do generally respond well to celebrity brand ambassadors, don't assume that every relationship between a celebrity and a product is going to work. The examples are few and far between but occasionally a product and celebrity just don't gel, and Indian consumers fail to make a positive connection between the two.

One such situation came when the "Big B" and his son signed on to promote a sensible automobile. Indians were expecting the car to be extraordinary because it was endorsed by two of the country's biggest stars. In reality, the car was targeted at your run-of-the-mill Indian family. The failed message was noticed, and the car was quickly repositioned with the theme of traveling together as a family. Sales were motoring in no time.

Offering freebies and specials

When you're formulating your marketing strategy for India, remember that free product samples and special offers are very effective. Indian children are targeted most in this plan of attack. So start plastering your logo on items such as bats and balls used as giveaways during cricket season, or collectable toys that resemble the latest cartoon hits offered as freebies in packages of biscuits and other snacks. Snack food and drink makers even offer freebies — pencil kits and small dictionaries, for example — that are given away to children as they wait at the doctor's office for their annual examinations.

A variety of businesses target adult Indians, too. Products that are selling well are often packaged with a free sample of a new, related product, like a trial pack of new hair oil offered with a bottle of shampoo. Jars and other containers are always appreciated by Indian housewives and are often given away with products like coffee and tea.

If you want to do a special offer with your product, consider using a buy-one-get-one-free scheme when you introduce a new product. And capitalize on festival times because those occasions are ideal to sell items such as white goods at a discount. Rent-to-own offers with low monthly installments are also very popular.

Building a Sales Strategy and Distribution Infrastructure

To effectively sell your business's products or services to Indian consumers, you need to know which sales techniques and distribution models are best suited to serve the country's environment of economic growth and dizzying diversity. In this section I provide you with information on how to structure your sales efforts and set up your distribution network.

Responsive selling

Perhaps no other country in the world is home to such diverse groups of people, with such a mind-boggling range of ethnicities and cultures. In a country like India, responsive selling is key, and you can take a number of steps to make your sales endeavors more responsive.

Responsive selling is devising a sales strategy after building a rapport with customers and determining what they need. It's an ongoing process where persuasive tactics may have to be changed to suit changing needs.

Understanding your customers

Think long and hard about your customers and what they need to hear and see to get on board with your product. Ask yourself how your product may appear to an Indian? How it is similar to products they've seen in the past, or — maybe more importantly — how it is different? Take the answers to those questions and devise your sales strategy accordingly.

CavinKare, makers of hair care and beauty products, is a prime example of how an Indian-consumer-focused sales approach can pay off. If you're in an Indian village and you spot a traditionally-dressed youth sporting a head of startling red hair, be assured that CavinKare is responsible. To sell its hair dyes to the children of conservative Indians in rural areas, the company wisely organized live demos and offered free trials in specific areas. Indian youths now sport a variety of red-hued hair colors. Blues, yellows, and pinks haven't made it quite yet, but even the red colors have marked a clever sales victory for CavinKare.

You may forget at times how much diversity there is among Indians. But you should keep this diversity in mind and remember to not rely too much on a single sales approach, however successful it may have been in a particular place. You need to tailor not just your products but also your sales style to respond to the various groups in India. Study your target groups and cater your sales efforts to serve them.

Selling door-to-door

Door-to-door sales were once a novel concept in India. Today, wary citizens hang boards on their front gates asking salesmen to keep away.

But the door-to-door system can work because it cuts out middlemen, and an army of workers (courtesy of the country's large population) is available to you to sell a wide range of products. Many of these salespeople are under 30 years old and come from humble backgrounds. They pocket a commission-based salary, and they tirelessly cover cities — street by street and home by home — demonstrating and selling products that were unheard of earlier.

The home appliances company Eureka Forbes introduced door-to-door salesmen to the country back in 1982, starting off with vacuum cleaners. Other products followed (with varying degrees of success), and now Eureka Forbes has captured over 75 percent of the domestic water purifier appliance market. Door-to-door sales are now much more common in India, and salesmen peddle everything from fast-moving consumer goods to books.

Because this method works on a commission basis, your salespeople may be tempted to make outlandish claims about your products just to make a sale, and over time these tall tales could tarnish your business's reputation with customers. If you're planning on recruiting door-to-door salespeople, keep in mind that you need to explain your products to them very clearly, make sure that you emphasize your sales policies, and train your folks in customer service and communication skills.

Selling over the phone

Telemarketing in India is another way to market. Call center employees patiently look up telephone directories and target specific groups of customers. For example, anyone listed with the title of "Dr." gets a call on health-care products or services. Call centers are big business here in India and the popularity speaks for the effectiveness of this method. Young graduates find it an easy earning avenue, and there are even institutes that offer training. Engaging a call center to do your marketing for you should be very easy.

Selling through high-tech channels

You can even pursue high-tech sales channels in India. With the booming growth in Internet connectivity, many firms are tapping e-marketers, and now a whole range of products are sold on the net, from mobile phones to mango jelly. The computer savvy 19–35 age group is the most responsive to this approach.

If online sales don't seem promising for your business, you can always just let txt do it 4 U. Text messaging on mobile phones is a great tool for sales campaigns, especially in India, which is ranked fourth in the world in mobile phone usage. A recent text message campaign urged mobile phone users to call telephone astrologers for personalized predictions. If you can sell the future using text messaging, you can sell anything!

Selling directly

Just a few years ago, direct selling was unheard of, but recent changes in the market have created some fertile ground for direct sales, particularly in sales through product demonstrations in the home. The promise of financial independence, flexible working hours, and the fact that few professional prerequisites exist have attracted many Indians to direct sales, and many of them are women. If you're interested in direct sales for your business, personnel shouldn't be hard to find!

A wide variety of items are now sold directly in India, including home care products, cosmetics, educational products, and health drinks. The industry is growing at an average of 30 percent every year, according to the Indian Direct Selling Association. Currently 15 to 20 large direct selling companies have a national presence in India. This statistic is in addition to the over 30 small companies that have started operations and another 100 city-specific direct selling companies.

Tupperware and Amway entered India in the '90s, paving the way for direct sales in the country, and today such sales are a multi-million rupee industry. The reasons for the success of companies like Tupperware and Amway aren't a mystery. Capitalizing on the large segment of well-heeled Indian women with time on their hands, Tupperware's direct selling army has skillfully used "kitty parties" (where wealthy housewives get together for tea, conversation, and Tupperware demonstrations) to spread the word about their products.

Selling after the sale: Customer commitment

Indians like to stick to their set patterns, and this includes not only traditions but also the brands they choose. If you want to make a positive impact on Indians, work to move beyond rapport building and focus on gaining customer commitment through constant communication and post-sales service. Successful Indian brands aren't just visible because of widespread advertisements — they emphasize constant interaction and continued service to their customers.

Here's what a sales director of a confectionery company has to share:

> We made a good investment in the early stages. We hired a market survey company with a simultaneous translator and a one-way mirror to observe and listen to randomly selected groups of a wide cross-section of people before we chose the flavors of candy we were going to make in India. We quizzed them on taste, names, color of wrappings, and more, based on what they currently opted for and what they would like to see. The results were diagonally opposite in Mumbai and Chennai, but in Chennai,

Hyderabad, and Bangalore, we saw a pattern emerging. We collated all facts and used a middle path. Our individually wrapped candy now sells in India in large food stores and also in the smaller tea stalls that line the streets.

Organizing an effective distribution network

In addition to a smart, focused sales presence, you need to understand the way that distribution systems work in the subcontinent of India. Basically, there's a three-tier distribution system in operation in the country. The three tiers are distributor/stockist, wholesaler, and retailer.

This system sounds simple, but in reality the very size of the country and the multiplicity and diversity of rules in the various states have a huge impact on distribution. Your business's sales success can live or die by its distribution channels.

Within the three distribution tiers, you sometimes have additional layers like channel partnerships. These layers are very important, depending on the type of business you're in. They can cover gaps in market coverage (sales and service), smooth out logistical problems, and provide valuable information on customer/market requirements, effective pricing, competition, and inventory management.

In this section I help familiarize you with the three tiers of India's distribution system.

The distributor/stockist

Traditionally, those businesspeople wishing to import products into India for sale establish company depots or hired company stockists. Stockists were hired exclusively for individual businesses, and they passed on the business's products to the other levels of the distribution system: wholesalers and retailers, or dealers.

Many companies now use *clearing and forwarding agents* (C&FAs) as their distributors. There are two types of C&FAs: those who handle only clearing and forwarding, and those that distribute as well. The best choice for you depends on the type of product you intend to import. If the item isn't a mass product, the latter will do.

If it's a mass product — a food item, for example — you need to cover every single outlet in your target area, and a C&FA won't be up to the task. You may have to hire multiple distributors. And if you're bringing products into various states, you need local C&FAs in each because they're familiar with local taxes, interstate duties, and so on.

If you are planning on importing a mass product into India, the services of a C&FA who does distribution as well won't work because you need a very focused and comprehensive network, which a C&FA handling the products of several companies won't be able to provide. If, on the other hand, yours isn't a mass product, a C&FA who does distribution should be able to handle it for you. And in the latter case, if you're targeting various states, it's best if you have one in each because they're familiar with local laws, which may differ from place to place.

You may want to know the process of how goods are shipped:

1. **Goods are shipped from the C&FA to the stockist with trucks, while the documents for the release of the goods are sent via the bank.**

2. **The stockist receives a copy of the release document of goods shipped to him.**

   He presents that paperwork to the bank, pays the value of the invoice (for the shipped goods), and the bank gives him a goods-release document.

3. **The stockist then presents the goods-release document to the trucking company and takes delivery of the goods; which he proceeds to market.**

If you're using a C&FA and distributors, the distributors place their orders, and the C&FA invoices the quantity to the distributor and sends the stock. The distributors have their own sales structure and pay the C&FA, who in turn pays you. Ideally, distributors have their own infrastructure, including warehousing, transport, a sales force, and more. Although you may not have to worry about those things, you should put a monitoring/management team in place. These employees manage the credit with distributors, monitor the C&FA, check for visibility at point of display, and generally ensure that things are going well.

If you don't like this system, you can also use the services of a warehouse service provider. You can find a listing of these firms at www.dir.indiamart.com/ indianservices/s_wareh.html.

Stockists sometimes overbook when they feel the pressure of the quotas they must fill. The excess products find their way into the market in ways that may not suit you. Constant monitoring is the answer.

If your product is a consumer durable item (products ranging from white goods to toys to bicycles and beyond), you could set up regional hubs to supply the distributors.

Regardless of the method you choose, you have to agree on the credit and payment terms with your distributor. Options include cash payment, lines of credit, and bank guarantees. The financial terms are usually set up on a return on investment basis rather than on absolute margin. Find out from other companies doing similar business in India and negotiate the rates that are the most acceptable to all parties.

The regional distribution model is becoming quite popular in India, especially in the IT domain. Regional distributors who were once small entities have been so successful that they have sometimes been appointed the sole distributors (for that region) for some of the top IT brands in the country.

The wholesaler

The second level in the Indian distribution system consists of the wholesalers. Distributors discount products to wholesalers, who likely hold a wide variety of products, and will therefore not be affiliated with one particular company.

Be careful as you select an appropriate wholesaler. Depending on your product, you may need to take extra care to ensure that the wholesaler is set up to take proper care of your goods. Make certain that the wholesaler maintains appropriate storage conditions, and pay special attention to the facilities in relation to the area's temperature. Remember that most of India is very hot, and you don't want your products destroyed by the heat.

The retailer

The final step in the distribution system chain leads you to Indian retailers. Wholesalers sell products to retailers, who are also not affiliated with one particular company. Wholesalers are responsible for credit management with retailers and they usually supply the products that retailers order on credit and collect payment during subsequent visits.

Retailing in India

Retailing has a brilliant future in India, thanks to the upswing in the GDP (gross domestic product). More and more Indians are enjoying increased spending power. Credit cards are in the country to stay; in fact it's a status symbol to flash a wallet packed with plastic. Add to this spending power the political stability that the country has enjoyed for the last several years and the government's readiness to open up the economy, and you can see that things can only get better. India's retail scene has long been dominated by small mom and pop stores, but the tide toward larger chain retailers is beginning to turn.

The old guard of Indian retail

India's retail environment has for years been based on small, independent stores and markets. You need to understand the outlets I cover in this section if you're interested in working your way into the retail sector in India.

It's all about visibility. You can employ a marketing team that approaches these small outlets and gets them to agree to display your products. (Make sure there's something in it for them, of course.) These days, it isn't uncommon to find imported tubes of Pringles and stacks of Mars bars in a small corner that is also well stocked in chips made by the home-based-industry down the road. The same goes for local fairs. You can buy market space and get your sales team to study the market and work out an appropriate sales pitch.

The mom and pops

India's small corner and grocery shops play a prominent role in Indian retail and have for a long time. Millions of these establishments are scattered all over the country, selling a colorful medley of products ranging from soaps to stamps, with snacks and brooms and the odd coconut thrown in for good measure.

Markets and fairs

India's sprawling rural areas are home to two-thirds of the country's retail outlets. The indigenous retail industry in those areas is comprised of two elements: the *Haats* (weekly markets) and the large and very colorful *Melas* (fairs), which sell everything you need every day. In addition, annual events like cow and camel fairs trade specific items or types of livestock. These fairs are eagerly anticipated by the village folk, and they make for an extremely lively outing.

New Indian retail trends

While smaller, independent Indian retailers still dominate the sector in the country, the door is beginning to open for large chain stores and foreign retailers. The Indian government has been hesitant to open up the retail sector to foreign investors, primarily due to Leftists who have a loud voice in the coalition government. (I explore Indian coalition politics in Chapter 8.)

The Left parties aren't keen on allowing foreign investors to start up in Indian retail, although the United Progressive Alliance (UPA) government has managed to give overseas firms the right to hold up to a 51 percent stake in retail stores. Even so, Indian Trade and Industries Minister Kamal Nath cautions that the entry of foreign names must create jobs here, not take them away.

If retailing in India sounds appealing, keep an eye on future developments and work to include small Indian operations while you make your business plan. And in the meantime, there's no harm in keeping an eye open for good real estate. You don't want all the prime locations to get snatched up *before* you've made up your mind to get in on the action.

The signs of change

Signs of change in the retail sector are also coming from within India, where larger chains are making progress in lessening the market share held by mom and pop retailers. Reliance — a large Indian corporation — has recently jumped on the retailing bandwagon. It recently opened strings of convenience store outlets called Fresh, which are exact replicas of foreign supermarkets but include a distinctly Indian touch in the form of a counter which says "Puja Flowers." These are flowers used in worship in Hindu households. Reliance is firm in its stance that instead of running the local vendors out of business, it sells its products so cheap that the vendor is tempted to stock up his cart from the store.

There's a very real fear that foreign supermarket chains may run the small Indian stores out of business. You may face some resistance to your attempts to move in, so work on a strategy for handling the resentment.

Discount stores are another retail growth area in India, which isn't surprising given the Indian passion for finding a bargain. Several discount chains in Indian cities are thriving by selling their products below retail price.

The booming business process of outsourcing industry, which employs a significant chunk of the consumer population in India, should continue to grow. The industry's workforce typically work bizarre hours, and they demand round-the-clock shopping as a result. Consider how you may serve that group with 24-hour retailing.

Obstacles in Indian retail

The geographical, cultural, and socioeconomic diversity and the massive scale of India make it difficult for a single retail model to be adopted across the country. If you're interested in retailing in India, be flexible to stay in business, and heed a few obstacles as you begin your venture.

If you can't beat 'em, join 'em!

For international retail companies trying to make headway on the Indian retail scene, a big challenge is wooing away consumers from the trusted corner shop they've been doing business with for years. In fact, Southeast Asian countries proved from experience that unorganized retailers control a sizeable chunk of the retailing market, even many years after foreign direct investment (FDI) was allowed.

The mom and pop stores have also noticed that bigger players in the retail game are arriving in India all the time, and they're taking action to make a stand. Some are focusing on ways to cater to local customers' needs, and others are opting for an umbrella approach, allowing other businesses to set up shop on their premises in hopes of attracting a wider range of customers. So you have youth organizations setting up soup counters in a vegetable shop, or popcorn vendors installing their machines at the door of a general store.

Develop a strategy that allows for coexistence with the locals. Many analysts agree, suggesting that international retailing companies who can find ways to work with local Indian businesses have an edge in the market over those who decide to slog it out on their own. You can also consider cash-and-carry programs that cater to the Indian corner stores.

Getting customers into your stores

Another challenge for international retail players is creating a shopping environment that takes advantage of the increased spending power of many Indians. If you want to retail in India, think of ways to pull Indians in and encourage them to spend more time shopping and indulging their shopping impulses. Some suggestions include

- ✔ **Spice up the ambience:** Retail chains in India like MusicWorld, Barista, Pyramid, and Globus have spiced up their store ambience to promote sales. Barista, for instance, doesn't focus solely on coffee. It also features books, music, and art in its stores to appeal to the Indian coffee drinkers' intellect. It also offers wireless Internet to attract young Indians.

- ✔ **Get a great location:** Locating your store in a commercial area with entertainment options can help. IMAX theaters are proving a big draw, for example, and theaters sometimes include restaurants and food courts, so moviegoers can make an evening of it.

While the Indian government is keen on inviting FDI into the retail scene, there are some concerns that international retailers hoping to make it big in India should consider. Complex sales tax rates, octroi (a duty levied on goods entering particular cities) and excise structures, bureaucracy, inflexible labor laws, and multiple licensing requirements are a few examples. Do your homework and plan to spend some time navigating the retail red tape.

One foreign retailer discovered from experience that it's against the law in some Indian states for farmers to sell directly to retailers. Some states require that farm produce be bought and sold at government-run markets through a complex system of middlemen and farmers. There's also a confusing array of regional laws, tax rates, and customs duties to be taken into consideration when moving goods from one state to another. Investigate the state-specific regulations and speak with your Indian colleagues so that you can include the appropriate level of detail in your business plan. I include additional information in Chapter 4.

Chapter 12

Establishing a Manufacturing Presence

I have heard important people say that manufacturing is going to be the next wave of innovation in India after the outsourcing one just witnessed. India is rapidly gaining a reputation as a global manufacturing center for a wide range of products from textiles to automobiles and a lot of things in between. General Motors, Ford, Triumph International, Nokia, and Coca-Cola are only a few of the multinational companies that have built a successful manufacturing base in India.

In this chapter, I offer you a quick trip around the manufacturing scene in India. I explain the sectors that have been growing the fastest, tell you what you need to do to get started, and clue you in on a few potential obstacles. Have a look, and you can manufacture your own success in India!

Checking out India's Manufacturing Sector

Traditionally, choosing a location for a manufacturing base has often been dependent on a single factor that improves the profitability of the operation. That factor could be availability of raw material, low overhead, suitable manpower, or proximity to a captive market. India is unique in that it offers a combination of all those factors.

The Indian economy has been open to overseas business for only about a decade. Given that India was closed to foreign industry for over 50 years, the new influx of businesses from abroad hasn't been without a few manufacturing roadblocks, but overall the results have been outstanding. Many multinational corporations who've set up manufacturing operations in India have banked serious profits and are looking at different avenues of investment and expansion.

In this section, I clue you in on some of the details that make India such an attractive choice for manufacturing and also offer a look at some of the potential challenges.

Understanding the advantages

India's industrial base is both large and diverse, and it offers many advantages. The Indian population is the most important factor in its manufacturing potential. But there are other positives to consider, too. The country is rich not only in people but also in raw materials, which are critical to the foundation of a strong manufacturing base.

People power

The population explosion India experienced was once thought to be a major problem, but now it's viewed as an advantage. Many multinational corporations are looking away from China (where family planning policies have led to limitations in the available workforce) and toward India, which is bursting at the seams with people looking for jobs. Indian workers are also young — half the population is around 25 years old. India's human resources are vast, skilled, and enthusiastic.

But it's not just about quantity. There's plenty of quality as well. In the past, India's traditional strength has been in labor-intensive industries, like textiles. So strong are the traditions in this respect that whole communities have devoted themselves to such trades. But in recent times, manufacturing emphasis has shifted from labor to skills of a hardworking and trainable workforce.

India's manufacturing base is spreading out to include skilled and specialty products, including automobiles and ancillary industries, pharmaceuticals, specialty chemicals, and even hardware. Indian manufacturers have proved their worth globally by achieving an export growth of around 20 percent over the last three years.

India's manufacturing workforce also offers the following outstanding characteristics:

✔ **Low cost:** Indian wages are growing at a slower rate than in other Asian countries.

✔ **High level of software skills:** A large portion of the Indian workforce is computer savvy.

✔ **Familiarity with English:** Fluency in English is extremely common in India, so the disorganization and miscommunication caused by language barriers is considerably less than in other countries.

Raw materials

Metal and mineral production help form the backbone of any manufacturing base, and India is extremely strong in that category. The country mines four fuel minerals, 11 metallic minerals, 49 non-metallic minerals, and about 15 other minor minerals.

India produces varying amounts of the following materials:

✔ Bauxite

✔ Chromite

✔ Dolomite

✔ Ferro alloys

✔ Ferro-manganese

✔ Ferro-silicon

✔ Granite

✔ Graphite

✔ Gypsum

✔ Iron ore

✔ Lignite

✔ Limestone

✔ Manganese

✔ Mica

✔ Non-cooking coal

✔ Zinc

The Indian economy is largely agrarian, and the country enjoys surplus production in products such as coffee, tea, and pepper. There is also a substantial production of agricultural produce like rice, wheat, barley, millet, sugarcane, and a variety of dairy products.

Mining leases have just been opened up for the private sector and also for overseas companies. If you're interested in mining in India, now's the time to get in. The Indian natural resource sector could be completely remapped in the next few years with an influx of professional mining experience.

Considering the challenges

Although there have been plenty of examples of manufacturing sector success in India, challenges and hurdles still exist in setting up a profitable manufacturing unit. Given that Indian manufacturing had been completely shielded from any outside influence for close to 50 years, you may understand how there would be a few kinks to work out.

Indian industry wasn't prepared for the huge foreign business interest that was created when the economy was opened up following liberalization. The changes that needed to happen didn't always happen as quickly as necessary. Many of the problems have been ironed out, but several problematic areas remain.

Infrastructure

A lack of sufficient infrastructure has created innumerable bottlenecks in countless situations. Although the Indian government has begun to take steps to resolve it, for the next few years this area will be difficult to negotiate.

Take the Indian seaports, for example. They're buzzing with activity, and dizzying amounts of goods are imported and exported due to the presence of new international businesses. However, at times there isn't enough unloading equipment to cope with all the freight, which ends up in delays!

Power supply

Reliable, efficient sources of power have also been a limiting factor in the growth of Indian manufacturing. Each state manages its own power through the State Electricity Board, and the staffing for those entities is politically appointed, so professionalism and efficiency are lacking. There are huge unaccounted losses during power transmission, not to mention blatant theft of power. No state in India can claim 365 days of uninterrupted power supply! A number of industries rely on their own captive power generation, but that's expensive and negates some of the advantages of low cost Indian manufacturing.

Corruption

Although corruption in Indian manufacturing (and business in general) is improving, the problems still exist and plague some areas of Indian industry. While no magic solution exists to this issue, the Right To Information Act (RTI) helps root out corruption and is a step in the right direction.

India and China: Different approaches

Many Asian economies are booming, and India and China are leading the charge. Although both countries have seen explosive growth, there are many differences between the two. For example, if China wants to attract investment in a particular region, they build infrastructure: roads, railways, airports, you name it. Then they woo investors. In India, things work the other way. The investors bring in funds, and the infrastructure grows as a result.

There's no denying that China is well ahead of India in terms of infrastructure. One recent visitor to that country found Beijing and Shanghai comparable to Chicago and New York in terms of development. India has a ways to go before it can reach those standards. However, given the fact that China began its liberalization process a decade before India and also that India has had to live with the reality of cross-border terrorism for some time, the country has done exceedingly well. So well, in fact, that it may only be a matter of time before India catches up with (or even surpasses) China.

According to the RTI, anyone can file a simple questionnaire with the concerned authority and that authority is legally bound to reply within a specific time frame with a complete and honest answer to the query. Flip to Chapter 8 for more information on the RTI.

Skilled trade shortage

Even with India's massive, well-trained population, there are still some skill shortages worth mentioning. The problem areas are in skilled trades and involve a lack of plumbers, carpenters, masons, and electricians. The root of the problem is a mass exodus of skilled tradesmen from India who went to the Middle East during the oil boom, when demand (and pay) was high. Efforts are being made to educate and train these types of workers to keep up with the dizzying demand for construction in India, but the shortage remains.

Predicting what the future holds

Surveys show that Indian and foreign companies have drawn up ambitious plans for expanding and diversifying their manufacturing presence in India with big investments in the near future. Foreign firms seek to expand their existing manufacturing capabilities, and Indian manufacturers are flourishing and catching the eye of overseas investors.

Manufacturing for Indians, by Indians

India's manufacturing sector is important in two ways: as a manufacturing hub for outsourcing and also as a market for goods that foreign companies can manufacture within the country's borders. The two possibilities feed each other because skilled Indian manufacturing employees are earning money making a variety of products for export, and they're interested in applying that new spending power to goods manufactured by and for Indians. That's a win-win for everyone involved!

The chairman of India's Housing Development Finance Corporation (HFC), who's also a member of the boards of several leading companies, says that if you think business is possible in India, be brave enough to step in. Don't miss the boat. Look around for opportunities, find out when government is allocating funds for infrastructure, and get going. Timing is of the essence.

Checking out the hot areas for manufacturing growth

Several manufacturing industries in particular are poised to experience tremendous growth in India. A few examples include

- ✔ **Automobiles:** Motorized vehicle manufacturing is a core sector in India. The country is one of the world's top motorcycle manufacturers. It's also second in the production of two-wheelers (scooters, mopeds, and so on) and tractors, and fifth in manufacturing of commercial vehicles. Indians also buy a lot of cars, and the country is the fourth largest market for cars (over one million vehicles were sold in 2004 and 2005).

- ✔ **Biotechnology:** Predictions indicate that biotech could soon generate five billion dollars per year in revenue. India's biotech industry is the third largest in the Asian region (including Australia).

- ✔ **Gems:** India has always been on the cutting edge of gem production. Many Indians work in the diamond cutting and polishing industry, which is a world-class sector in India. It is believed that 9 out of 10 diamonds in the world pass through India.

"Bus"ting at the seams

High demand for products in India is driving the country's manufacturing boom. A wide range of Indians now enjoy increased spending power and are looking for ways to improve their quality of life. And India's economic growth in general is helping to increase the need for manufacturing.

No company knows this better than Volvo, whose bus division recently set up a joint venture with Jaico Automobile Engineering of Bangalore. The several million dollar deal calls for the production of 1,000 bus bodies a year for the Indian market. One look at the mass of Indian travelers hanging off an overstuffed bus indicates where the demand for more buses comes from.

Look who's coming to India

More heavy hitters in the manufacturing sector are currently eyeing future operations in India. Advanced Micro Devices (AMD) and Intel have committed to setting up manufacturing bases in the country. Dell, a recent entrant, is so excited that it plans to double its team in two years. U.S. giant General Electric is also eyeing India with glee. These companies are only a few of those that have recently acknowledged India's potential. In fact, GE has identified India as its fastest growing market and has big plans for its presence in the country. Some of the areas that interest GE are infrastructure, materials, and energy. Many others have also finalized massive expansion plans. All this hype is very confidence-boosting for those who're waiting to enter this market. After all, if the biggest, most profitable companies in the world are coming to India, the country must be doing something right!

✔ **Pharmaceuticals:** Pharmaceutical manufacturing in India was estimated at eight billion dollars in 2005. Exports accounted for almost 40 percent of that figure.

✔ **Textiles:** India has always been a hot spot for textiles. Its muslins and silks have always been in great demand and have wooed traders to India's shores for centuries. Textile manufacturing still accounts for a significant amount of foreign exchange and provides a huge amount of jobs.

Indian Commerce and Industry Minister Kamal Nath reports that the manufacturing sector grew 12 percent in September 2006, compared to the 8.9 percent increase achieved in September 2005. From April to September 2006 the sector grew 12.1 percent compared to 9.5 percent in the prior year.

Exploring the Manufacturing Preliminaries

Any business entry into India requires legwork and research, and manufacturing is no exception. You need to make sure all your ducks are in a row before you can press "start" on your state-of-the-art robotic assembly line, or even before you dig your first shovel full of dirt at the ground-breaking for your new factory.

In this section, I help you understand the tasks you need to complete and the decisions you need to make before establishing your manufacturing presence on the ground in India.

Choosing an entry method

You have a number of entry options available to you in India, and you should consider all of them when deciding how to best establish your manufacturing presence. You can read about the various entry methods in Chapter 5, but check out this quick recap:

- ✔ You can set up your company as a solely-owned or as a branch/liaison/project office.
- ✔ You can choose to incorporate manufacturing subsidiaries in India as companies with limited liability, which is the option many foreign companies choose.
- ✔ You can enter into a partnership, such as a joint venture.

Manufacturing investors can set up shop in India as a foreign company or part of an Indian one. Indian companies can be either joint ventures or wholly owned subsidiaries, and as a foreigner you're allowed to hold 100 percent equity, though caps do exist in some sectors. (See Chapter 5 for detailed information on these caps.)

As far as joint ventures or partnerships go, you can either sign a long-term contract for supply or enter into an agreement for process technology.

Before you enter into a joint venture or partnership for manufacturing in India, run a check on your prospective partner for quality and size of operation, as well as his operating style and reputation in the market. You may incur some expense and time, but the expense will be nowhere near what you'll have to face if you find out later that you've made a wrong choice.

Choosing a location

After you've decided on the best entry method for your manufacturing start in India (see the preceding section), you need to choose a location. An overseas company needs to carefully plan and implement its production strategy for India, and the location of the production facility is a huge part of that planning.

I write extensively on the factors to consider when choosing where to set up shop in India in Chapter 5, but when it comes to manufacturing, you need to think about tax concessions, raw material availability, access to a skilled workforce, and infrastructure benefits (power, water, and transport).

Although in reality it may be impossible to find a location that satisfies all of your needs equally, you can prioritize and make a sound selection. If all things seem equal between two locations, decide on the appeal of a particular city for your expatriate management team. Sometimes, when a number of locations meet the important business criteria, the final balance can be tipped by the presence of an attractive feature like access to good international schools.

Land selection

Land for industrial enterprises is readily available throughout India. Industrial zones have been distinguished near all major cities and towns, with an eye on availability of raw materials and minerals and other logistics concerns. Facilities for manufacturing or assembly are provided by the government in most cases. Land can be bought directly from private owners, but it has to be registered with the local government agency.

The Indian government is eager to encourage economic growth — manufacturing growth included — in a variety of areas throughout the country, and it could offer you some attractive incentives to locate your facility in a particular spot.

Help the government in its efforts to speed development in a specific area by agreeing to set up shop there, and you could be looking at subsidized funds for your business or extensive tax breaks (more info in the next section).

Tax concessions

Location-specific tax concessions in India bring up a flurry of acronyms, including EOUs (Export-oriented Units), EPZs (Export Promotion Zones), and SEZs (Special Economic Zones). Industrial and IT Parks are part of the scene, too. (Flip to Chapter 5 for more information on how to ladle your way through the acronym soup.)

The Indian government has set up various zones and areas that offer outstanding tax benefits to lure businesses hunting for a good place to locate their operations. If you choose to capitalize on the offer and locate your business accordingly, you'll be much less exposed to the Indian tax man's advances.

EOUs are among the most common of the special zones, and you can actually set one up anywhere in India, but automatic approval to do so depends on things like minimum value addition (MVA), cost of production, insurance, freight value of capital goods, foreign technology import agreements, and more. If possible, leave the specifics to your Indian colleague or counterpart.

If you choose to go the SEZ route, you have to be a net foreign exchange earner, but you can enjoy the advantages that come with it. You won't be restricted by MVA requirements, for example, and there's no fixed minimum export figure you have to keep (SEZ units work on a self-certification basis for imports and exports).

If you want to manufacture goods for sale to the domestic market in India or the DTA (domestic tariff area), your unit can be set anywhere in the country, and all normal laws apply. Concessions aren't usually available on import duties, but you can export your products and make use of the special Export Promotion Capital Goods (EPCG) scheme offered by the Ministry of Commerce, which lets you avoid import duty on capital goods you're going to use to keep your export commitments.

Used plants and machinery in good shape with a certified residual life of ten years can be imported without being hindered by the special import license that's necessary for importing new machinery. These items attract the same import duty as new equipment. If you're interested, you can secure a certification from an authorized chartered engineer in India.

Seasoned veterans say that channels are available at all levels to address problems. They advise newcomers to avoid unnecessary escalation, and put pressure on the lower levels and work your way up for the best results. If you're left with no other options, go straight to the top. And remember that you may have to cut through some red tape due to the cumbersome nature of the administrative process, but the steps are being streamlined all the time. See Chapter 8 for more details.

Understanding licenses and technology transfer

Soon after India earned its independence from England, Indians only looked inward. Self-sufficiency was the goal back then, and India took care to make it as difficult as possible for foreigners to bring their manufacturing businesses into the country. Several pieces of legislation actively discouraged foreign industry, and if a foreigner still chose to proceed, the paperwork and licensing processes that followed provided a thorny deterrent.

But things are far better now, and the Industrial Policy of 1991 has succeeded in fostering economic growth in India. Industrial licensing has become much easier, as has technology transfer. And many industries that were reserved for the public sector have also been generously opened up.

Although the situation has improved in recent years, the multiplicity of approval processes in India does pose a challenge. Some foreign companies have to knock at many doors to get the appropriate approvals, and a few give up along the way. One company approached the Reserve Bank of India (RBI) in Mumbai and was promptly asked to go to New Delhi. After going there, they were sent to the Securities and Exchange Bank of India. Finally a consultant put them on the right track. That company and many like it will give you the same advice about the approval process: Get advice from the experts. See Chapter 7 for more information.

You can get automatic approval for 100 percent Foreign Direct Investment (FDI) in a variety of sectors, and industrial license for manufacturing activity is necessary for only a few, including

- ✔ Industries reserved for the public sector
- ✔ Defense-related industries
- ✔ Railway transport (partially restricted)
- ✔ Atomic energy
- ✔ Industries reserved for the small scale sector

The small scale sector has a list of industries, which includes units that don't need capital of more than Rs 10 million (including plant and machinery). If the business you seek to start doesn't appear on the list, you can still make reserved items if you equip yourself with an industrial license and promise to export half of what you produce. Even in the off-limit segments, private participation is permitted in some specific areas, such as mining, oil exploration, refining, and marketing. For more information, visit www.smallindustry india.com.

For example, one overseas manufacturer wanted to produce and sell plastic PVC footwear in India but couldn't because it was reserved for the small scale sector. To get around the problem, he cleverly located his manufacturing unit in nearby Mauritius, and then found a good distribution partner in India to sell the product.

Before you get the ball rolling on an industrial unit in a particular location, check to see if the metropolitan or similar authority in the area permits the setting up of industrial units. Though licensing may not be required, you may still need to gain permission.

Choosing to produce for export, or for India (or both)

Many foreign companies have chosen India as the site for major manufacturing facilities that make goods for export back to their home countries and around the world. The list of corporations that currently churns out key products for export in India is long and varied and is becoming more illustrious all the time. But a number of overseas entities manufacture goods in India for distribution and sale in India. You need to decide early on if you want to produce goods for export or for Indian consumers, or both!

Producing for export

The West has been looking to India for manufacturing for a variety of reasons, including the World Trade Organization's efforts to open up trade, and, of course, the cost-saving advantages of manufacturing in Asian countries. Multinational corporations are quickly coming to appreciate the advantages India has to offer as a sourcing and manufacturing hub. Among the big names that have already established themselves are Hyundai, Toyota, LG, and Ericsson. John Deere, the top tractor manufacturer, has also successfully set up a facility in Pune, in Western India. It exports its tractors everywhere, including back home to the U.S. market.

The early bird catches the worm, so fly in quickly and snatch up the best suppliers and talent for your manufacturing effort. You can also capitalize on advantages doled out by the Indian government to foreigners who set up manufacturing entities ahead of the pack. And don't worry, your contemporaries will follow: Predictions indicate that Indian manufacturing exports will reach the $300 billion mark by 2015.

Pharmaceuticals, specialty chemicals, and industrial electronics are currently hot manufacturing areas. White goods, building construction, automotive, and processed foods are also projected to grow quickly, according to business leader, M. Lakshminarayanan of the Confederation of Indian Industries (CII).

Producing for India

Manufacturing goods for export isn't the only option in India. As multinational corporations move their manufacturing bases to India, several have discovered that there's a need for them to make things for India *in* India. Alcatel, Cisco, Ericsson, Nokia, LG, and Samsung are a few of the companies that are fine-tuning their made-for-India products. I provide some very prominent examples in Chapter 11.

Building Your Manufacturing Presence

The process of going from raw material to finished goods is challenging anywhere in the world, but it's particularly tough in India. Intricacies of the system, from seeking multiple approvals, to enforcing safety norms, to handling changing labor laws, are areas worth discussing and spending time on. This section helps get you started.

Breaking (and covering) ground

Before you can set up your factory in India, you must follow certain procedures and fill out paperwork. The authorities have simplified the process as much as possible, and it all takes much less effort now.

During the process of building a manufacturing facility in India, you need to take many steps while your facility is being built:

1. **Get the drawing plan for your building approved by the Metropolitan Development Authority of the city you're in.**

   One place to start at is the Web site of the Ministry of Urban Development. Check out `www.urbanindia.nic.in/moud/moud.htm`.

2. **Get approval for construction.**

   The legwork for this step and Step 1 should be done by you or your Indian representative.

3. **After you begin the foundation, keep the Municipal Corporation informed.**

   They send out a chief engineer to inspect the plinth (base) area.

4. **After the building is complete, apply for a completion certificate.**

   You get another visit from the Municipal Corporation at this stage.

5. **Secure an okay from the fire department, occupancy permit, and water, sewage, power, and telephone connections.**

   All these areas must be inspected by various authorities, so prepare for more visitors.

Putting safety first

Occupational safety and health (OSH) is a concern in some areas of manufacturing in India. Chemical production and mining are the most significant sectors for safety considerations. However, safety awareness is growing, thanks to some staggering shortfalls that have produced disastrous results in recent years. Indians are, on the whole, much more safety conscious than they have been in the past.

Even outside of the factories, many Westerners find safety a concern. Take Nokia, for example. The company is big on employee safety and found that the process of transporting its staff safely to and from factories by road was a bigger concern than it expected. A two-hour commute from the nearby city out to the factory took the workers through a hazardous highway construction zone, and Nokia had to take extra steps to avoid a dangerous situation.

 In planned manufacturing areas like special economic zones (SEZs), special consideration is given to safety concerns, and setting up a unit in one of those locations is a lot less risky than setting up manufacturing bases in general areas.

Adhering to Indian labor laws

Without labor laws, ensuring that Indian manufacturing workers are being treated in an appropriate manner would be difficult. The Indian government has placed several layers of legislation that help to protect the interests of the Indian worker.

Laws for firing

If for some reason you want to cut down on your staff size or even close down an entire plant, don't try to just up and do it. First, review the Industrial Disputes Act of India. Specific laws regulate the ways in which you can fire employees.

For example, should you find yourself in a situation where you need to lay off employees at your plant with a workforce of more than one hundred, you can't do so overnight or all at once. You have to get approval from the government at least 90 days in advance of such an action.

Laws for hiring

Firing isn't the only sector that's governed by Indian laws. There are rules for hiring that must be followed, too. For instance, if you want to employ a group of contract laborers, make sure to build in a time frame. You can't use those workers as contract laborers for long periods. If your work is likely to take a long time to complete, you have to regularize the laborers and put them on your payroll, which automatically grants them access to several perks.

Hire a local legal expert to advise you on the proper ways to bring temporary help on board. She knows her way around the system in a way that even top legal advisors from another part of the country may not.

General labor laws

India is a founding member of the International Labour Organization (ILO) and has ratified 39 ILO conventions. Of these, eight are core — the ones focusing on forced labor, equal remuneration, abolition of forced labor, and discrimination. For details, visit www.labour.nic.in/ilas/india andilo.htm.

The Factories Act states that each workday is to be 8 hours long, and weekends must be 48 hours. Have an impossible deadline and need your workers to put in some extra hours? Don't lose heart: you can ask your workers to stay overtime. It just means that you have to pay them double. That's the central government's contribution. And not to be left out, various state governments have laws that specify minimum wages, hours of work, and safety and health standards for many sectors. Because it's hard to keep good workers, most factories pay more than the stipulated minimum wage.

Indian labor laws do include a measure of inflexibility when it comes to working hours. For example, elsewhere in the world it might be possible to put in a week's worth of work hours in four days, allowing workers to have the subsequent four days off, but that's not allowed in India.

In SEZs, labor laws are more strictly enforced. Workers have freedom of association, meaning they can form associations, but because of restricted entry (only bona fide workers are allowed in) trade union activity is limited.

Factory inspectors are appointed to make sure that Indian labor laws are followed, but because there are a lot of factories and a small number of inspectors, the inspections aren't always carried out in a strict manner. But don't take it for granted that you won't get a visit from an inspector. One can turn up when you least expect it, and if you're caught breaking any rules, tough luck.

Being green: It's easy and important

If the type of manufacturing you want to do in India runs a risk of damaging the environment, you need to take some steps to stay on the right side of the law. The central government's Ministry of Environment and Forests plans, promotes, coordinates, and supervises the implementation of environmental and forestry programs. Pollution control boards also play an important role.

The government civil servants who head the pollution control boards are usually Indian Administrative Service (IAS) officers — some of the most intelligent folks in India. They take their jobs and responsibilities of protecting the environment very seriously.

Plan your strategy for adhering to environmental laws and regulations as early as you can because the process is important and takes time. Appoint a local as a colleague to do this liaison work for your project, and be sure that they're keeping in mind the rules set out by The Water and Air (Control and Prevention of Pollution) Act, which also aims to reduce pollution in industrial areas.

Avoiding counterfeiting

Many different products are counterfeited in India, including a few that may surprise you. Did you know that more cases of "Black Label" scotch whisky are consumed in India than are actually produced in Scotland? Even booze is subject to counterfeiting!

The fast-moving consumer goods (FMCG) sector, with products that typically feature low retail values, has been hit the hardest. Light bulbs, cosmetics, soaps, and over-the-counter pharmaceuticals are subject to counterfeit. But the problem isn't limited to FMCG. Some high value products like automobile components, software, watches, music, and films are also affected, and the end results are losses for legitimate businesses.

The good news is that the incidence of intellectual property (IP) crime in India is lower than in other countries in the Asia-Pacific region. The bad news: IP crime is definitely still a problem. It's best to keep that in mind when you begin to do business in India.

One Indian businessman wanted to buy a Walkman as a giveaway for his staff in Mumbai, but when he went shopping at the "customs notified store" — where goods are sold with permission from customs — a salesperson offered him counterfeit Walkmans made in Malaysia, Thailand, and China. And all three models had different price tags! Thankfully, the original Sony Walkman is still sold in authentic Sony stores, so he finally chose that option, knowing after-the-sale service would come with the authentic product.

Two of the most critical factors contributing to the counterfeiting are as follows:

- ✔ **Technology:** Indians have access to high-tech equipment, and they know how to use it. Sophisticated machines make it much easier to produce high-quality fakes.

- ✔ **Globalization:** Because of the ease of world trade, you can make fakes in one place and export them for sale in another, distant market.

India does have laws in place to discourage counterfeiters. Although there isn't separate legislation to tackle the problem, the integrity of IP is provided for in the Trademarks Act of 1999; The Copyright Act, 1957; The Patents Act 1970; The Designs Act 2000; The Geographical Indications of Goods (Registration and Protection) Act 1999; and The Customs Act, 1962. The laws exist, but who enforces them and how is the question. A growing numbers of counterfeiters and a lack of public awareness add to the problem being swept under the rug.

To help fight against counterfeiting, you can help safeguard your products' integrity by utilizing the following:

- ✔ **Technology:** It can work for you just as well as it can work for the counterfeiters. Use technology to distinguish your products from the fakes. You could, for example, add a hologram to the product. The additions would heighten production costs, but eventually it would pay for itself by separating your goods from the bogus ones.

✔ **A reliable distribution network:** A well-known, trustworthy warehouser, wholesaler, and retailer are certainly valuable assets in your fight against counterfeiting.

✔ **Regular surveys:** Market research surveys are a good way to reveal counterfeits in the market, in addition to providing useful market information.

Building quality control systems

In India, where almost as if by default, quantity is more important than quality, a system to monitor the quality of your manufacturing is a fundamental prerequisite. Indian costs of production are comparatively lower, but this cutting edge will be completely blunted if a quality management system isn't put in place.

A quality management system (International Organization for Standardization (ISO) 9001:2000 or similar) is the most commonly used international standard that provides a framework for an effective quality management system. The ISO has formulated a family of the most commonly used yardsticks for an effective quality management system, and it gives organizations a rational framework to manage quality at all levels. See `www.bsi-emea.com/Quality/Standards/index.xalter` for more information.

The Bureau of Indian Standards (BIS) was set up by the government to lay down ground rules for industrial and commercial growth and to see that the best possible quality is delivered in the most efficient way. BIS-set standards are created by the joint effort of various groups like manufacturers, testing teams, and consumers, and cover the whole range of issues involved in trade and industry.

If you need to know the specifics for a certain sector in which you're interested in doing business, you can get the information from the BIS, for a price. BIS also has various certification schemes, which allow manufacturers — both Indian and foreign — to use its Indian Standards Institute (ISI) — a former incarnation of the BIS — mark on their products as a symbol of quality.

Apart from its national standing, the BIS is also internationally recognized. It is a National Certifying Body under the International Electrotechnical Commission (IEC).

Considering the Winners and Losers

You can read about many manufacturing success stories in India that can help you envision your future triumphs, and I could fill up the rest of this book with examples. To give you an idea, though, I provide a few examples from various sectors in this section. The successes far outweigh the failures, but for the sake of balance I also include a few manufacturing losers and tell you why they ended up that way.

Indian manufacturing successes

India's economic environment is extremely well suited for successful manufacturing. You can find companies that have taken advantage of the fertile manufacturing ground across many sectors and industries.

The automobile sector

Liberalization has really changed things for this sector in India. From a time when Indian children knew to identify only the Ambassador of Hindustan Motors, Fiat's two models, and the Standard Herald (produced by Standard Motors) there's been startling progress in the market. Cars of so many different makes and models now clog the streets. Many names exist like Ford Ikon, Tata Sumo, Qualis, Opal Corsa, Honda City, Santro, Indica, and the fashionable compact car Suzuki Elisio.

Ford Motor Company is one of the most impressive success stories. Ford came to India initially as a joint venture, but acquired a majority stake in the enterprise and renamed the company Ford India Limited in February 1999. Ford has so far poured in over $350 million into the project, which exports CKDs (completely knocked down kits), which are reassembled in their destination countries such as South Africa and Mexico. To add to its manufacturing success, Ford also built a phenomenal presence with their service and financing in India. Ford introduced Quality Care, a branded service initiative, and set up Ford Credit to provide financial solutions and services to those who bought their cars. Take a page from their book and be sure to cover all of your bases, even beyond manufacturing!

Another piece of business wisdom that you can take away from the Ford example is the importance of working with local Indian companies. Ford has developed a good arrangement with Hindustan Motors, which now manufactures engines and transmission units for Ford cars.

The consumer electronics sector

Here, Samsung India can teach you a lesson or two on leveraging the Research & Development (R&D) strengths of this country. It set up an R&D unit at NOIDA near New Delhi, and its success has been so huge that it has now evolved into the regional center for not only India but also the Middle East and South East Asia. In the process, Samsung, which came to India in 1995, has managed to earn a name for itself in diverse segments of high-tech consumer electronics and home appliances.

Samsung has also leveraged India's focus on IT and its love affair with mobile telephony by setting up Samsung Electronics India Information and Telecommunications limited in May 2000. This outfit makes PC monitors — the slim and sleek flat screen that reduce desk clutter — and related paraphernalia as well as mobile phones. It has also set up a software operations unit in Bangalore.

As an offshoot, the telecom sector has seen such triumphs as Motorola and Nokia. These giants have shown the way by their stress on timely entry, a willingness to change with changing needs, an ability to study the Indian psyche and use the knowledge to remove hurdles, and importantly, the capacity to persist.

The food processing sector

PepsiCo, with its soft drinks and snacks, entered India in 1989 through a joint venture. Post liberalization, it took matters into its own hands, and has since grown to great heights. If you study its success, you can understand the value of developing a local management team. That was the game plan to which the company owes much of its success. Indian managers have impressed this global major so much that it has even nominated an Indian woman CEO, who's rated as one of the most powerful women in the world!

Also, figure out how to extract maximum benefit from setting up shop in earmarked backward areas. PepsiCo has eight greenfield sites in such areas.

A few manufacturing failures

Most of the cases that have failed in manufacturing have done so because of lack of persistence. They didn't do their homework and stick to a checklist.

For instance, a British glass company, which came into the country with very high hopes, ran out of steam quickly when it came up against a number of hurdles. The British businessmen didn't have a clue about how to change things in their favor, and couldn't get their local contacts to do it either. After knocking on several doors that remained stubbornly closed, they gave up and went home. This negative ending could have been avoided if the company had equipped itself with full knowledge of the prevailing situation, worked out what the problems were, and also how to get around them.

On the other hand, a French glass company appointed an Indian managing director and used its deep pockets to ply the project with resources. Now it is a runaway success and is this year holding its multicultural team-building workshops for new managers worldwide in India.

Here are some examples of other hurdles that you may run into:

- ✔ Your joint venture partner doesn't have the power to hold out because their pockets are not deep enough. Consider throwing in a higher amount of capital than you planned to keep things going, and you may earn profits eventually.

- ✔ The market perception of your product is not as classy or targeted at your segment of the audience. Rebranding may be needed.

- ✔ The raw material or process you need is simply not in the region for suppliers to finish your product. Don't give up, explore close-by markets. One telecom company had the same problem and was able to access needed materials in Sri Lanka.

If you find that something in your business system doesn't work, find out everything you can about the subject, analyze the flaws, find a workable solution, and then put forward a proposal to the appropriate authorities (in or outside of your organization). Chances are, when the people concerned are presented with not only a problem but also the way out of it, they'll have something to work toward, and you'll get there in the end. Those who've made a success of doing business in India have found that it's not that people are unwilling to make changes, it's just that they have to be told what changes to make. The British glass company which quit earlier is back in India now, exploring a brand-new setup in another state.

Chapter 13

Legal Landmines

*H*istorically speaking, India is a peace-loving country. Keep in mind that India has never started a war with anyone. Even when India was invaded, it responded primarily with submission instead of aggression. But don't assume that Indians are pushovers when it comes to business dealings or that business relations with India are guaranteed to be smooth and go off without a hitch.

With such a massive population, India contains businesspeople of all stripes, from quiet in the south to more aggressive up north. It's best to understand that problems are as likely to crop up in India and to have a rough idea of the options for dealing with legal issues, including contractual disagreements, court proceedings, arbitration, and intellectual property rights.

Contract Conundrums

Putting the details in writing is standard procedure pretty much throughout the world. India is no exception. Take care that whenever you come to an agreement or seal a deal with Indian colleagues you have the specifics set out in a contract. In this section, I explain the ins and outs of contracts in India, and let you in on a few possible problems that you may encounter.

Contracts aren't always binding

Even though contracts are important to record your business dealings, any Westerner looking to do business in India must understand that a contract doesn't mean everything. In India, just putting something down in black and white doesn't mean that it's going to be honored down to the last letter! I must warn you here that there have been cases where contracts have been blatantly breached.

Indians have a relaxed view of contracts. That's because they're used to constant changes in the environment and have a tradition of giving more weight to personal relationships than the written word. As far as Indians are concerned, only in a controlled set of conditions can a contract be binding. If the conditions change in any way — if the infrastructure disappears or breaks down or there's a change in government policy — then the conditions set out in the original deal are subject to renegotiation. As a Westerner who may be used to contracts being the final word on a business deal, India's almost happy-go-lucky approach to written agreements may shock you.

If you feel that the Indian stance on contracts is unfair, I can only suggest that you try to view the situation through an Indian's eyes. Remember that in business, Indians are comfortable with a bit of uncertainty and open to the idea of change. If you can embrace these qualities, you may save some headaches down the road, and you may even use your understanding to leave room for negotiation in the future.

This blasé view of contracts in India has been bolstered by the long-windedness of the country's legal system. Cheeky as it may sound, contracts are sometimes breached in India by parties who know that it's going to take the other side forever to seek justice through a somewhat bogged down, circuitous legal structure.

If you're interested in avoiding situations in which your business partners try to make a little wiggle room in your contract, the solution lies in researching your partner before the deal. Be sure to vet a potential partner's background — including their track record for reliability — thoroughly before committing to any deal, in writing or otherwise.

Concerns when drafting contracts

Great care must be taken while drafting contracts in India. Even the smallest details in a contract can have a huge effect on your bottom line. The advice in this section can help you avoid future disputes.

The "acts" of life in Indian contracts

India's legal system is broadly based on the British system. Most of the commercial laws were drafted before independence, and they're based on English principles of contract. The three most important pieces of legislation relating to contracts are the Indian Contract Act, 1872, the Sale of Goods Act, 1930, and the Negotiable Instruments Act, 1881.

The Indian Contract Act, 1872, sets out the basic principles of contract in India, and for the most part they're the same as what you're used to in the United States and the United Kingdom. In other words, both the contracting parties must have the capacity to contract, the object and consideration of the agreement must be lawful, and any agreement to do an act which is prohibited by law or against public policy is void. Only agreements that satisfy these requirements can be called contracts.

The general principles of contract deal with offer, acceptance, and consideration. These principles explain how a contract should be performed, what circumstances are a lawful excuse for not adhering to or terminating a contract, and how the damages should be determined in a breach of contract situation.

You should read up on some Indian acts as you begin to do business in India. Check out the following acts:

✔ **The Sale of Goods Act, 1930:** Deals with the transfer of movable property for monetary consideration

✔ **The Transfer of Property Act, 1882:** Focuses on the transfer of immovable properties, mortgages, and leases

✔ **The Negotiable Instruments Act, 1881:** Deals with checks, bills of exchange, and promissory notes

When working to draft a contract in India, consult an advisor who has been through the contract process dozens, if not hundreds of times. An advisor can fill you in on the best ways to lock in the most critical aspects of the contract and help to minimize the "wiggle room" I speak of earlier in this chapter (see "Contracts aren't always binding").

A senior advocate in India says that parties interested in drafting a contract should first prepare a term sheet that sets out what they intend to do for a particular project. The rights and duties of both contracting parties should be briefly detailed. Using the term sheet as an outline, the contract can then be drafted as simply and succinctly as possible.

Deciding what to include in your contract

Every contract is different, but any contract in India should contain and focus on a few critical points. Experienced businesspeople in India suggest that when creating a successful contract you should follow these pointers:

✔ Ensure that there's no ambiguity in any aspect of the contract. Clarity in wording is immensely helpful when resolving any disputes.

✔ Include a clause specifying arbitration as per the London Court of International Arbitration (LCIA).

✔ Include a clause for governing contract law according to the English legal system. The Indian courts are overburdened, and the addition of this clause helps speed any necessary legal actions.

✔ Make sure the *force majeure* clause is as detailed as possible. Clear, thorough wording comes in handy in the event of a dispute.

✔ Make sure that the language of the contract and the arbitration proceedings are in English.

Negotiating the contract

As you gear up to hash out the details of your contract with your Indian business partners, keep in mind that the concept of bargaining or negotiating is firmly ingrained in the Indian psyche.

Begin your contract negotiations on a friendly level because Indians respond better if you can begin the conversation with some casual banter. Ask about an upcoming religious festival or perhaps a famous Indian dish from the part of India where you'll be doing business. And try your hand at a few words in the local language.

After the ice is broken, make it clear early on that you have a thorough grasp of the project for which you're seeking to draft the contract. Indian business-people appreciate foreigners who've studied up and know the most up-to-date project data and developments.

When you really get into the negotiations, ask for a lot at the beginning of the discussions. Figure out the points of the contract that really matter to you, and then ask for those *and* half a dozen more that aren't as important. That way you can concede the latter and insist on the former!

Throughout the negotiation process, remember that on the whole, Indians aren't overly aggressive negotiators. Be as courteous as possible, and you can earn the respect of your Indian business partners, greatly decreasing the chances of disputes down the road. If your partners value you as a person and see your relationship as long term, they may often yield to your contractual demands. If you come on too strong and make unreasonable demands, the negotiations may be over before they really even begin.

Avoiding unwritten agreements

Avoid unwritten agreements at all costs. Doing business in India today is far from perfect, but it's much more transparent and professional than it used to be and there's no need to look under the table for business deals.

Until just a few years ago, standard operating procedure was to have "unwritten agreements" when doing business with countries like China, India, and the former Soviet Union. These somewhat questionable business arrangements were pursued based on the fact that international trade with these countries was handled by government-controlled agencies, which were supposedly willing to play ball if one of the contracting parties needed to massage certain terms to avoid a financial blow. Although that did happen in a small number of cases, the unwritten agreements more often ended in acrimony and grief.

After the contract: How to get (and keep) the ball rolling

Even after the contract is signed, you still have some hoops to jump through to keep the ball rolling. In this section I offer advice on how to do just that.

Getting an Indian advisor on your side

India is a melting pot of different societies, and it has a wheels-within-wheels culture. Many of the country's cultural intricacies may surprise and confuse you, so bring a local agent or office on board to act as an advisor and help you with the details. You may also benefit from an affiliation with certain influential members of the Indian government. To know more about them, flip to Chapter 8 where I speak more on this subject.

As soon as you begin work on a contracted project — or possibly even before that — make it a high priority to find a local Indian advisor who's familiar with the area in which you'll be working. Ask around, and find yourself an advisor from a well reputed local firm.

The influence of religion, language, and caste on the inner workings of business in India is undeniable, and as a foreigner you may be faced with a good deal of difficulty in accounting for these differences. A local Indian advisor is well equipped to navigate the tricky cultural waters, and can think of ways to leverage the differences that may never occur to you.

Take Adam Quinn, an executive in a leather company doing business in India. He was recently starting a new project that involved working with a new partner from Mumbai, although Adam was unaware of this detail. However, as soon as the early discussions began, one of Adam's Indian colleagues saw that the businessman's last name ended in "kar" — an obvious (to him) indication that the man was from the Mumbai region. Adam's Indian colleague immediately began using key phrases from the Marathi language, which is prevalent in Mumbai. That little bit of cultural expertise was a huge benefit to their dealings because it got everyone off on the right foot and cut down on the time and excessive paperwork.

The importance of bringing an Indian advisor on board is directly related to the size of the project or investment. If you're just working on a small joint venture with an auto parts manufacturer or software company, you won't need to worry as much about finding Indian guidance. But if you're making a bigger splash — buying land, for example — you need to seek Indian help pronto because you don't want to have to deal with the central and state governments and local bigwigs on your own.

Consider the story of a Dutch company that was looking to buy a 10-acre piece of property for a new factory in India. No less than 52 farmers from a nearby village owned land within the 10 acres in question, and the Dutch were faced with a real estate negotiation nightmare. After they convinced a few villagers to sell their plots, the other villagers who owned land between those plots knew that they could demand a higher price, knowing that the Dutch would need all the pieces to make a rectangular area. The situation was saved when the Dutch, through their realtor, hired a local village head to finesse the negotiations.

Fostering a relationship with an Indian bureaucrat

Indian governments are elected to power and voted out, and Indians bemoan the constant turnover by saying *aaya Ram, gaya Ram* (Ram came, Ram went — Ram being a common Indian first name). But the unchanging bedrock of the system, the real power center, is comprised of the bureaucrats, or *babus*. I explain the details of these powerful government officials in Chapter 8.

In terms of getting things done in India, you can't beat a babu. Cultivate a relationship with a babu or two. If you do, your business paths can be much smoother and concerns can be nipped in the bud before they develop into major problems. But how can you come in contact and develop a relationship with a babu? See Chapter 8, where I deal with networking and organizations like the Federation of Indian Chambers of Commerce and Industry and the Confederation of Indian Industry, both of which provide good contacts that can lead you to a babu.

Labor and Allied Laws

India has an elaborate system of labor laws. Some are federal laws, which are applied by the central government, and the others are enforced by the state governments. The labor union movement has substantially declined, and strikes are far less common. The important labor laws you should study include the following:

✔ Factories Act, 1948: This law addresses the security and welfare of workers by requiring safe working conditions in factories.

✔ Industrial Disputes Act, 1947: This law governs industrial relations, including retrenchment, closure, and layoffs. Prior government permission is required to lay off workers or close down businesses employing 100 or more workers.

Getting such permission is no simple matter, but that could be changing soon because the Indian Parliament is considering raising the ceiling on the number of employees that necessitates the need for government approval before layoffs. The Parliament is also looking at putting in place strong deterrents against strikes and lockouts.

✔ Laws relating to provident funds, gratuities, workmen's compensation, employee state insurance (for medical relief), and apprentices.

After you've made certain that you're obeying all the relevant laws with your Indian employees and colleagues, consider all the ways you can keep those teams together and keep them motivated. I include a great deal of that information in Chapter 7.

Unions and labor disputes are a fact of life in India. Indian workers have the right to form or join unions of their choice. Unions represent less than one quarter of the workers in the organized sector. And the majority of those workers are in government sectors. Most unions are linked to political parties. Though unions did present a big problem to the overseas investor not so very long ago, the new, investment-hungry India is different. The number of workdays lost due to strikes and lockouts has been steadily declining.

Much of the IT sector is also leaning toward union formation, so there could be trouble brewing. Keep an eye on the business news for further developments and plan accordingly. Nothing can slow down your endeavors in India like problems with unions or labor disputes. Try to avoid these types of difficulties at all cost.

Settling Disputes through Court or Arbitration

You may be hard pressed to find a business or industry that doesn't run into disputes at some point. Disputes can and will arise while you do business in India. You may even find that the contract you drafted as carefully as possible is being challenged if one of the involved parties can't meet its obligations.

It's always best to try and settle these problems amicably, and arbitration is one option for resolution, but should the time come when kindness and courtesy fail and you find yourself with no other option but to take legal recourse to solve a dispute, you need to know something about taking (and surviving) legal action in India. (If you're interested in India's broad legal framework, have a look at Chapter 8.)

This section gives you an overview of using the courts to resolve disputes and also presents arbitration as a viable alternative.

Settling disputes in India's courts

India places much emphasis on the rule of law, and its courts are known for their just and equitable decisions. Very heartening, you may think. But there's a downside. The legal process in India is excrutiatingly slow. There's a constant and heavy backlog, and, like many of the country's court buildings, the path to justice is old-fashioned and littered with piles of dusty case files.

If you resort to legal action to settle a contract dispute, you may have to wait. Even simple contractual issues can still take years just to be heard. Consequently, contracts are often interpreted very liberally by all concerned parties while waiting for the wheels of justice to start moving.

If you can find a good way to settle your business disputes without calling in the legal eagles, do it. Over-the-table negotiations are a good idea. Work out the limits to which you're willing to compromise beforehand, and have Indians on your side whom you trust to give you good advice.

India has the world's second largest number of lawyers. It also has the largest number of laws, at the central government and state levels. I go into detail on India's legal system in Chapter 8, but in this section I offer a few tidbits that are particularly relevant for settling disputes.

An overview of India's court system

Each Indian state has its own hierarchy of courts, starting with courts at the village and district levels. Most of these deal with civil and criminal cases. In most major cities, the civil and criminal courts are separate. The courts are extremely backlogged, and you can expect substantial delays, although the length of those delays varies from state to state. The total cases pending in all courts in India is over 30 million. What's remarkable is the fact that the average Indian still has faith in the judiciary.

Litigation typically starts at the District or Lower Court, and then moves to the High Court (each state has its own High Court). The next rung up the ladder is the highest: the Apex or Supreme Court. This is the highest Court of Appeals in the country and is located in the capital city of New Delhi.

For commercial disputes, you have to approach the courts (at the appropriate level, depending on the magnitude of the dispute) based on where the matter of dispute took place and the place of the defendant's residence. For guidance, turn to your Indian legal advisor.

Apart from these three tiers of courts, a number of special courts and tribunals have been created in India to deal with specific disputes. These are the following:

- ✔ Tax tribunals
- ✔ Consumer dispute redress forums
- ✔ Insurance regulatory authority of India
- ✔ Industrial tribunals
- ✔ Debts recovery tribunals
- ✔ Company law board

Unlike courts in the U.S., Indian courts don't award outrageous amounts as damages. So stories of people in the West being sued for millions of dollars leave Indians astounded! Because of this difference in expectation, what Indians think is adequate or lawful may seem paltry to an American.

Foreign judgments

According to the Code of Civil Procedure 1908 (CPC), judgments delivered abroad are binding in most cases. In true legal style, few exceptions exist, which can be explained by your legal advisor.

The CPC treats foreign judgment as binding unless it is passed by a court that doesn't have the necessary jurisdiction or is obtained by fraudulent means. Generally, a foreign judgment is treated as conclusive between the parties and is enforced by Indian courts without reopening the issue. Thus, judgments delivered by courts in the U.S. or the U.K. have been enforced. A foreign judgment can be in a commercial case or even a divorce decree.

Hiring professionals to help

Numerous Indian legal firms focus on commercial law. Consider seeking the guidance of an Indian legal professional as you set up and run your business in India. It's well worth the cost.

In addition to strictly Indian firms, foreign and international firms also operate in India, often in formal or informal relationships with well-established Indian firms. You have plenty of choices, and my advice to you is to hire a professional to help you avoid disputes and legal problems.

Criminal courts

India has an elaborate system of criminal law. The three main pillars are the Indian Penal Code, the Criminal Procedure Code, and the Evidence Act. The lowest rung of the hierarchy is the Magistrate's Court, then the District and Sessions Courts (for grave offenses). Appeals and revisions go to the High Courts, and final appeals go to the Supreme Court. India abolished the jury system more than 40 years ago. For tax offenses, the criminal law makes an important departure from the basic principle that every man is innocent until proven guilty. In most tax laws, it's stipulated that if the company is found guilty of an offense, then every director or officer-in-charge of the business is deemed to be guilty. It's up to the director to prove his innocence. However, very few criminal cases prosecutions are filed against company directors or corporate tax offenders.

Legal delays, and how to deal with them

Despite the fact that the Indian legal framework is fundamentally sound and well organized, you may still have significant delays if you choose to take legal action or if legal action is taken against you. The backlog of cases is unlikely to be cleared significantly in the near future.

The best ways to cope with the delays caused by backlogs are avoiding seeking official legal action altogether and seeking alternative dispute resolution options.

Unfair disadvantages

As a foreign businessperson, you may notice that the playing field isn't always completely level. For example, the legal system puts a number of restrictions on the transfer of land, which can make buying and selling real estate difficult. Your status as a foreigner may also make it tough for you to use property as collateral in India.

Despite some restrictions, the playing field has become more level in the last ten years. Liberalization has given foreign companies and investors much more flexibility. In several industrial sectors, 100 percent foreign investment is permissible. Some restrictions exist on investment in agricultural plantations and a few other sectors.

In many cases relating to trademarks, several foreign companies have filed suits for infringement and have been successful. For example, Daimler-Benz successfully prevented a manufacturer of underwear from using the brand name "Benz." Similarly, Glenfiddich was able to prevent an Indian distillery from marketing a single malt whisky with a deceptive label. Novartis was able to enforce its Exclusive Marketing Rights (EMR) — under the Patents Act — against leading Indian pharmaceutical companies for its anti-cancer drug Glivac.

Alternative options for resolving business disputes

A number of options exist outside of India's court system that you should keep in mind when problems arise. Alternative dispute resolution schemes and specialist tribunals have been set up for this purpose, and they've proved very successful in distributing justice speedily.

The *Lok Adalat,* or People's Court, is one such system that has been very efficient in settling community disputes. It can also be used to bring a speedy end to minor commercial disputes. The catch is that heeding a Lok Adalat summons is totally voluntary. And you can take the matter to the traditional court system if you're not satisfied with the verdict.

Resolving disputes through arbitration

Although it's rarely a pleasant situation, you're bound to run into some sort of arbitration during your business's life in India. The dictionary defines arbitration as "hearing and determining a dispute, application of judicial methods to the settlement of international disputes."

The basics of arbitration in India

You need to be familiar with arbitration in India and international arbitration if you're to succeed with this sometimes frustrating aspect of doing business in India. Despite some shortcomings, the arbitration process is much faster than an ordinary civil suit.

So maybe it wouldn't surprise you that the number of arbitrations have increased substantially. More and more issues involving corporations are being sorted out by this means. And if you're not satisfied with the verdict, you can always go to court. The party who loses the arbitration still has the right to appeal to a higher court of law. The bad news is that there is a backlog of appeals in some high courts, and the original arbitration award may be the one with the maximum influence in a verdict.

The key comfort clause in a contract that involves an Indian corporate entity is the arbitration clause. It's probably the most underrated clause in Indian contracts, especially when a foreign business partner is involved. In the event of hitting a major business contract roadblock, it offers an alternative to the issue languishing in the Indian legal system.

Under Indian law, some differences can't be settled by arbitration. For those problems, approach the civil courts. Ask your local legal advisor for details.

The Indian Arbitration and Conciliation Act 1996 is based on the model suggested by the United Nations Commission on International Trade Law (UNCITRAL) in 1985. It deals with the entire gamut of arbitration, from the arbitration agreement to enforcement of the award or an appeal against it. In addition, it outlines the appointment of and powers of arbitrators, as well as the enforcement of New York Convention and Geneva Convention Awards. It also adopts the UNCITRAL Conciliation Rules of 1980.

International arbitration

The Indian Arbitration and Conciliation Act 1996 applies to international arbitration, too. The Arbitration and Conciliation Act is an effective piece of legislation for holding arbitration in India. As it follows the United Nations model, foreign businessmen need not worry about unexpected provisions giving them shocks.

India has bilateral investment treaties with several countries, including France, the U.K., Germany, the Netherlands, Australia, Japan, Korea, and the overseas private investment corporation (OPIC) of the U.S. These relationships allow investors in India and those in the other countries to sort out their differences through negotiation, conciliation, or arbitration.

The Arbitration Act provides for international commercial arbitration in cases where at least one of the parties is a foreign national or incorporated in a foreign country. Its scope includes contracts and is therefore an invaluable tool in settling disputes related to contracts. Check out www.lcia-arbitration.com for more information. Chapter 16 has more stuff on this.

Intellectual Property Rights

Intellectual property (IP) laws in India cover trademarks, patents, copyrights, and designs. The country's patent laws were originally framed by the British, in line with the laws prevalent at that time in England. These laws have been amended now and again in India, and, with growing awareness of the importance of IPR, the efforts to enforce laws governing these issues have also increased. Copyright laws are also in place and being enforced, and trademarks are protected, too.

Two areas to be wary as far as India and IPR are concerned are pharmaceuticals and software. However, even in these areas you should have no cause to worry if you ensure that you check the credentials of your prospective partner.

Another factor that could be of interest to you is the fact that in India, the amount of IPR-related litigation is far less than what you see in the West. That's probably because IPR awareness in India doesn't yet match that of the West. But this issue has been given a lot of media coverage lately, and the average Indian is growing more aware of trademark, copyright, and patent protection, and concerned citizens are promoting fair practices.

The state of intellectual property rights in India

The scope and sternness of IP laws have been increasing in recent years: All the laws were amended in 1999 and 2000 to conform to the WTO's Trade-Related Aspects of Intellectual Property Rights (TRIPS), and Indian courts frequently follow English and U.S. judgments in trademark and patent cases. In the major cities of Mumbai, Delhi, Kolkata, and Chennai, complaints on violation of trademarks and patents are filed directly before the High Court.

Authorities are taking steps to ensure maximum compliance with IP laws, having realized that violations can damage India's appeal as a business destination. India is party to the Geneva Convention for the Protection of Rights of Producers of Phonograms and the Universal Copyright Convention. It is also a member of the World Intellectual Property Organization (WIPO) and UNESCO. The law now provides national treatment for foreign trademark owners and statutory protection of service marks. And the Indian Copyright (amendment) Act 1999 completely reflects the Berne Convention on Copyrights.

The intrinsic problems of the Indian judicial system can make it difficult to exercise intellectual property rights established by law. For more info on the legal system, check out Chapter 8.

Although as recently as a decade ago patents were unfamiliar and uncommon in India, they have been gaining visibility. Now many Indians are aware of the importance of IP and the need to protect it. People from all walks of life are asking how to go about obtaining a patent. They may be seeking protection for anything from the quirky to the life saving, but there's awareness, and that's the important part. India has gone from a country where patents were unheard of just a few years ago to a land where every hopeful teenager working on a science project dreams of having his invention patented.

Protecting your intellectual property in India

Intellectual property rights in India are getting stronger. The Patent Office in India, which has branches at several locations throughout the country, grants patents according to the country's rules. These rules have now been streamlined to make the process quicker and more inventor-friendly. Even if patent applications are pending in your native country, you can file applications for patent protection in India. For more details, visit http://ipindia.nic.in/.

Progress with intellectual property rights is being made in India, but for now, don't assume that your trade secrets are totally safe in India. Most people like to stick to the WPO's Trade-related Aspects of Intellectual Property Rights (TRIPS). Stay on your guard when it comes to your intellectual property. For example, be careful when transferring technology or patents to your Indian business partners. State clearly in your contract that it is expressly forbidden for the proprietary information to be made available to outside entities.

Part IV
Ensuring an Indian Success Story

The 5th Wave   By Rich Tennant

"Oh, quit looking so uncomfortable! It's a pool party! You can't wear a cape and formal wear to a pool party!"

In this part . . .

I try to help level off your potential stress about doing business in India. Knowing the important behavioral patterns gives cutting-edge knowledge to increase your output as you foster effective business relationships in India. Help is at hand in these chapters — discover proper Indian etiquette and dodge the craters in your road to success.

Chapter 14

Understanding Indian Culture

. . . .

In This Chapter

▶ Discovering Indian collectivism

▶ Realizing the role of emotion in business

▶ Overcoming communication challenges

▶ Appreciating cultural differences between India and the West

. . . .

*O*ne of the best ways to evolve important business opportunities is to do your best to build positive, lasting, productive relationships with your Indian counterparts and colleagues. Building relationships is all about seeing both sides. As a global player, if you're unwilling to try and see both sides of an issue, you may have problems communicating effectively.

So now that you've decided to build a business relationship with India, you need to know how to go about seeing that it's a pleasant experience for both you and your Indian counterparts. In order to accomplish that, you have to look at the components of the Indian psyche and figure out the best ways you can cater to it to develop strong relationships.

Getting a Sense of Indian Collectivism

Collectivism is a term used to describe any moral, political, or social outlook that stresses human interdependence and the importance of collective instead of separate individuals. Understanding the Indian sense of belonging can be a huge asset for you as you begin to do business in the country. You need to have great respect for certain bonds in order to build useful, lasting business relationships, and knowing how Indians relate to each other helps you to relate and avoid confusion.

There's a big difference between the social make-up of India and that of the West. Indians still think in terms of clans, at least subconsciously. This has a bearing on various levels of Indian society. For starters, Indians may feel that they belong to a certain caste, community, or religion. They may also have a geographic sense of belonging, from living in the same village, city, or state. Then there's the clanship of extended families — responsible for powerful ties — and, above all, the kinship of simply being Indian.

All these different levels of connection means that if you put any two Indians in a room together, chances are they'll discover some commonality. That's pretty amazing, considering the teeming millions that make up the country. And though the old system of large joint families sharing homes and responsibilities is disintegrating — thanks to the booming growth of cities — many Indians make a conscious effort to touch base regularly.

Indians take their bonds to other Indians very seriously. For instance, members of humongous families originally hailing from the state of Kerala who have moved away to Indian cities hold regular "meetings of the clan" in their new homes. They may not keep in touch throughout the year, but will make the effort to join up for the annual get-together.

In this section I explain for you the ins and outs of the Indian sense of collectivism.

The importance of family

Family ties are the ones that bind in India, and you may see that as soon as you step foot in India. The crowds gathered outside the terminal and airport gates are there to greet you to welcome you back if you're returning from a trip abroad. (I once counted 20 people in a receiving committee for a relative returning from overseas!)

This commitment has an upside: Indians are conditioned to work as a team. The trait is a throwback to India's agricultural ancestry, where each member collectively tilled the land, reaped the harvest and lived off its bounty, and the whole process ran smoothly.

Collectivism is so deeply ingrained in India that decision making, from the trivial to the corporate, is a combined effort. No jokes! Indians rely on their families for everything from arranged marriages, to buying a house, to what to name a child.

Time off for family ties

Indians place an enormous amount of value on family relationships, and those bonds reach out to extended family members. So don't be surprised when an Indian employee asks for time off to travel to the other side of the country for a distant cousin's wedding. That's the Indian way! However, when you combine these surprising family ties with the obstacles presented by the language barrier, the results can seem shocking — and hilarious! The following are a few funny examples of requests for time off that have been circulating around corporate India recently:

"Since I have to go to my hometown to sell my house along with my wife, please sanction me one week's time."

"As I want to shave my child's head (for a religious ceremony of tonsuring), please leave me for two days."

"As I am marrying my daughter, please grant a week's leave."

The language barrier makes these requests sound ridiculous, but the reality is that you'll face these types of requests, and you need to oblige your employees, or at least meet them halfway.

The wisdom of age

The elders are usually consulted before making important decisions, and their approval is vital. If a decision is made despite the disapproval of the family elders, it usually causes some tangible unease in the rest of the family.

A recent, widely publicized example in corporate India featured the two sons of the leading business family deferring to their mother's wishes (after their father's death) in order to resolve a dispute over the division of one of the largest industrial conglomerates in India.

All in the family

India still doesn't have a formal Social Security system, meant to take care of the financial needs of the elderly after retirement. Indian culture expects the adult son(s) to take care of elderly parents in their sunset years.

It's still commonplace to find senior citizens and sometimes three or four generations of one family continuing to live with their adult children — typically sons — as normal practice. This is often quoted as one of the classic contrasts between an oriental versus Western culture.

In Chapter 7, I explain the bearing that strong family ties have on other areas of Indian culture.

Hierarchy rules

The idea of hierarchy is deeply etched in the Indian psyche. It's been ingrained into the Indian mind down through many generations. Hierarchical relationships are particularly important in the business context. You need to pay close attention to the hierarchies of the businesses and regulatory bodies with which you're involved, and speak to the authorized people if you want results.

Working "through proper channels" is highly emphasized in India, too. For example, if you're looking for quick results regarding your license application take time to study the hierarchical set up of the office where you've submitted the application. If you respect the office hierarchy, you're work gets done faster.

Assessing power distance

India is a country of high power distance, and you can see examples of that throughout Indian society, particularly in business. Superiors are often inaccessible — they have a secretary to intercept visitors and a large office that is off limits to most. Managers usually have and expect to have privileges and status symbols, too, such as a driver for their car, a special lunch room, even a management toilet that subordinates don't use.

Inequality between individuals is expected, and perhaps even desired in some situations. But that, of course, would provoke a very different reaction in any lower power distance culture where inequality wouldn't be tolerated.

Being unequal

An American shoe manufacturer once asked me, "Why does a perfectly intelligent mid-level manager come to ask me for direction on how to do this or that or what to do first? He is capable of doing it on his own, I know. In our country it would have been thought of as juvenile."

That sort of behavior is habitual in India. Hierarchical relationships mean that bosses tell their subordinates what to do and how to do it, and seeking permission from those above is a sign of respect. If you want the employees below you to be more independent and not consult you on every detail, you have to make that clear.

In India, bosses are seen as benevolent dictators who look out for their teams. In less hierarchical cultures, bosses are thought to be more democratic in their management of others, and generally resourceful and capable of offering input in a variety of situations. For example, Indians, when they get a chance, may discuss a wide range of topics with their boss, from office politics to their son's college admission. In turn, their bosses are patient and helpful.

Showing Emotion in Business

In order to build successful and lasting business relationships in India, you may need to be more communicative and emotional than you're used to. When sticky situations arise, you can't leave important words unspoken, assume that everything will fall into place, or rely on other theories. Those tactics rarely work in cross-cultural relationships, and that's especially true in India. It's worth going the extra mile to make certain that important relationships are preserved and on the path to growth.

If you do things wrong in India, hopefully it's due to a lack of knowledge or cultural savvy, not unwillingness to comply. Most Indians understand that, and are fairly forgiving by nature. You can always say, "I don't really know and don't mean to offend, so as we go along do help me understand your ways." Indians admire such humility and honesty, and if things go wrong and you commit a faux pas, they'll guide you. And you can also be up front with your Indian colleagues from the beginning, letting them know that you'll be respectful but also work to improve certain areas (quality, timeliness, integrity, and so on).

To do your part in building successful relationships with your Indian colleagues, be sure to participate if you're asked to be a part of family or festival time events.

Turn off your cultural preconceptions

Cultural preconceptions can color your vision in India. You may interpret an Indian showing up late for a meeting as having a lack of respect for your time. But an Indian would see this lateness as "he must have had a reason, and he's here now, so let's get down to business." If you see the motive behind the Indian's thinking, you may be able to accept or forgive certain actions.

If, on the other hand, you persist in seeing this habitual disrespect for punctuality through your own particular cultural lens, then you may have a problem on your hands, because it isn't very easy to change the Indian mindset, particularly if the people aren't your employees or people whom you can train and control. However, if the Indian on your team is helped to understand that you view tardiness very seriously, he'll be better able to adapt his approach and align it more to yours although a hundred percent match is rare. Things will go much easier with both sides trying.

Pay attention and be sensitive

Train yourself to listen with your eyes and mind, as well as with your ears. Otherwise you could take offense where none is intended, or you could acquire an entirely unwarranted opinion of your partners or colleagues, which may affect your future dealings.

Sometimes in India body language indicates respect, but the word "please" doesn't go along with it. You may think that not saying please is insulting, but an Indian would see it as perfectly polite. For instance, "Just pass me that pencil" would be rude to a Westerner — "Would you please pass me that pencil" is what you think of as polite. But an Indian will crinkle his eyes, use singsong speech, or modulate his voice differently so the listener if he's Indian too, understands and feels the respect even without the word *please*. Be aware of the difference, and remember that it isn't any indication of disrespect.

There are two principles at work in cultural situations that make it important to be sensitive to a new culture. One is being aware of what is there, and the second is seeing things the way they are meant in the correct context. For the former, you need to know that something exists — a gesture, word, or phrase that really means something. For the latter, you need to be able to interpret what you see in the way that locals do.

Teambuilding and multicultural workshops are critical in any international business relationship. Do invest the time and cost on a similar workshop, and you'll see that it pays off down the road.

Reciprocate goodwill

The Indian code of conduct is all about reciprocity. When an Indian goes out of his way to help you out, your simple "thank you very much, I really appreciate it" won't be enough. He expects you to remember the gesture and return the favor when his time comes.

Return goodwill gestures as long as it doesn't compromise your core values and ethics. For instance, invite Indians back when they invite you to a meal, return gift for gift, receive them at the airport (occasionally or at least when you meet for the first time) if they received you. Invite the core management of your Indian team to a meal or out for a drink with no specific business agenda. Just go to develop the friendship! If you can't return a favor, explain how you would have liked to but aren't able to.

One of the greatest ways to return a favor is to ask for an opinion from one of your Indian team members. This gesture makes Indians feel respected and often exceeds their expectations, and doing such things go a long way in ensuring your business success in the country.

Challenges in Communication

As you work toward building great business relationships in India, there are a number of potential communication problems you need to understand, and I explore those issues in this section.

Understanding the "yes" and "no" nuances

Few words are more definitive for Westerners than *yes* and *no*. In India, however, you need to watch out for the numerous meanings that each of those words can hold. For example, Indians may not want to give you bad news and say that no, they can't deliver something you want. Instead they may say yes, but it's because they're worried about your reaction and straight "no" answers in India are considered rude.

Sometimes, under the influence of a misguided desire to please, an Indian may say yes to you, but in his mind he really means "yes I will try my best." To avoid that confusion, make it known that it is okay to say no and that you value that straightforwardness more than you disapprove of an inability to meet a commitment. The lack of a straight answer may also just be the individual's verbose style. Help such a person come to the point by saying "So what you are trying to say is . . . ."

Other nuances to Indian uses of yes and no include the following:

- ✔ If an Indian says yes, it could mean "yes, we have every intention of trying," as in the case of delivery of products or services.
- ✔ When an Indian says no, she can actually mean yes. This occurrence happens often in the case of refusing food or drink the first time someone asks.
- ✔ If an Indian says yes, he can mean "I don't want to say no right now because I need to save face." You may run into that when you ask "do you understand?"

When it's your turn to say no to an Indian, follow the Indian style and make your rejection less direct and more polite than you would in the West.

In the West, definitions and meanings can be very black or white. But in the East (India included), more shades of gray exist, which can make it difficult for Westerners to understand the meaning and implications of certain words and actions.

Questions and doubts

Choose your words carefully when in India, but the importance of careful wording works both ways. Indians use phrases that you may not interpret correctly. For example, Indians often say "I have a doubt" instead of saying "I have a question." It's just a turn of phrase here, but it could get you into a tangle in your official dealings, as Tom, a Western businessman, found out.

"In our call center, which was to go live in one more week, we were baffled when the head of the team said 'I have a doubt.' Was he doubting the whole viability of this project at this late stage? My heart sank, until I realized that I had misunderstood him. I asked him to clarify what he meant, and he said, 'No, I don't have any doubts. I was just asking if we should serve coffee and cake or wine and cheese at the groundbreaking event.' That was a relief!"

I once worked with an executive from a German company that was going to set up a large manufacturing facility in India. The executive's family was in the process of moving into their new home in India. Deadlines for completing the house had long passed and the delays went on and on. "We have never faced this lying and cheating and taking of our money before. We were not prepared for this side of India," our German client remarked. My first thought was that those were harsh terms to bandy around when all that happened was a delay to the project schedule. But when I re-examined the client, I realized the difference. In his experience, you said yes if you could do something, no if you couldn't. If you said yes and couldn't do it, you then forewarned people.

Minding your language

Be conscious of how you come across to Indians, and craft your language accordingly. It's okay to help your Indian team understand new methods and systems to make things more efficient, but remember that they may not appreciate the "I am here to teach you how to do it right" attitude. You can convey that attitude by choosing your words carefully.

If Indians feel you treat them as inferiors, they may avoid you or grow silent. Self-respect is their most cherished value. Indians, especially those who are less literate, read your body language, feelings, and attitudes pretty accurately.

Watch out for the following language pitfalls:

- Speed of speech
- Fluency/correctness of English

> ✔ Indianisms ("kindly" instead of "please" would be one example)
>
> ✔ Accent (regional accents can be heavy and difficult to comprehend)

When in India, never use foul language, even lightheartedly. Indians find curse words deeply offensive.

Asking the right questions

When you ask questions in India, you may notice that sometimes the answers you receive aren't the ones you asked for. It sounds bizarre, but it's not uncommon.

There are a couple of reasons for this strange behavior. An Indian may give you an alternate answer if she doesn't understand what you said. Instead of losing face and asking you to repeat it, she may just try and guess the answer you wanted. And if she doesn't know the answer at all, she may immediately start talking about a totally different subject to distract you or buy herself some time.

The best way to handle this odd situation is to simply persist and ask the same question (rephrased if necessary) until the best response is provided. Politeness and persistence pays!

To help Indians understand what you're saying, you should memorize a few of the unique words of Indian English and add them to your everyday vocabulary. If you want to move up a meeting time, ask to "prepone" it. If you're going out of town, tell your Indian colleagues that you're "going out of station." If you plan to take a few vacation days, say that you're "going on leave." Remember to be more precise than asking an Indian colleague if he'll deliver something to you in a "couple of" days. Couple doesn't exactly mean two but a "few" in India. Finally, you would ask an Indian to "tick off" something from a list, not "check it off " as you may say. No anger is involved.

Paying attention to non-verbal communication and body language

One of the most confounding problems that arises whenever international or cross-cultural communications take place is that of body language. It's tough enough to tackle the verbal language barrier, but with countless variations to gesturing and body language, connecting can sometimes seem too daunting for even the most adept communicators.

High and low context cultures

In high context cultures, communication is indirect and what is said may have multiple interpretations based on body language, tone, and words used. In low context cultures, communication is direct and what you say is what you mean.

India is definitely a high context culture. People develop close connections over a long time and know each other well. They value relationships more than the business at hand. People know what to expect of others so they don't really state everything explicitly. It's like a family situation, where you know what to do and think from years of interaction.

Many Western countries such as the U.S., the UK, and Germany belong to a low context culture. In these societies, people may have many connections, but they're of shorter duration or only for some specific purpose. So when Westerners from those countries travel to India, cultural behavior must sometimes be explained so that the proper meanings are conveyed. You would need to balance between asking explicitly what was meant and recapping understanding when they speak, and being careful to couch your direct approach with pleasantries first when you speak.

Though the influence of non-verbal communication in conveying a message is well known, Indians typically are highly sensitive to the way something is said, to the point that sometimes *what* is being said can be masked. "Reading between the lines" is second nature to most Indians.

Non-verbal communication can be especially confusing in India when you ask a specific question and need a particular answer. Here are a few examples:

- ✔ Head nodding can indicate yes or no.
- ✔ Listening can appear like disagreeing.
- ✔ Pointing can be with the chin when you'd expect a finger.
- ✔ Clicking sounds of the tongue or parted lips can be a sign of sympathy or agreement.
- ✔ Touching someone with the foot can be sign of disrespect.

For more on these gestures, see Chapter 15.

Dealing with an Indian's divided attention

Another problem Westerners face in their business relations with Indians is not being the center of attention during conversations or meetings. You need to realize as soon as possible that Indians are multi-taskers and are eager to please, so you may not get undivided attention in the way you're used to getting it in the West.

While you're talking to an Indian, he may answer the phone on his desk, respond to a text message on his cell phone, and look at a computer screen, all while performing some task for you. You may find it frustrating, but remember, Indians don't mean to undermine you. They value relationships, but the catch is that they value *all* relationships, so they try to please all the people all the time.

Respecting Cultural Differences

If your goal is to foster and develop good relationships with your Indian colleagues and partners, make a concerted effort to respect the differences between your cultures. If you view Indian tendencies and methods with a Western eye, chances are you'll be washing your hands of India sooner than you think. But if you look at things from the Indian point of view, you may soon realize that things aren't really that bad; you can, indeed, achieve a lot here. It's simply about wearing different cultural lenses to see the same world.

In this section, I illuminate some of the cultural differences you need to consider.

Coming to terms with India's flexible working hours

Indians work, then play, then work, and then play together. They work very long and hard, putting in many hours and sometimes sacrificing weekends, but they don't necessarily make the most efficient use of their time. It can be quite different than the American style of work, which features periods of very hard work broken up by quick breaks to recharge and prepare for more hard work. You may be surprised by the Indian coffee breaks, the chats around the water cooler, and the stop-and-start style of working in India. Indians may not understand your objection to their going home for lunch and coming back after 90 minutes because they're willing to stay late to make up the hours.

One of my employees makes for a terrific example of an Indian's perception of flexible working hours. I have a great colleague that has been with me for many years. However, he always shows up an hour late in the morning and always goes home for a 90-minute lunch break. To make up for it, he always stays late, works from home on the weekends and is on call. He's a trustworthy, reliable employee, but he's always backlogged! But I have no way of sorting him out; I can't live with him and can't live without him. Indians put up with this type of behavior in the interest of honesty. I put up with it because this employee's quality of honesty and trustworthiness is invaluable to me while in the West it wouldn't be possible.

If you don't think you could handle the flexible Indian working hours, remember that you call the shots and you can make stricter rules regarding working hours.

Understanding the ways of the Indian working world

The important issues and concerns in the workplace can vary greatly from India to the West. The critical traits and values that you're used to may not be quite as crucial in India, and if you're not prepared for the differences, you could be in for a healthy dose of frustration. Table 14-1 features a number of Indian and Western perspectives on work. Check it out to gain a better understanding of what to expect.

Table 14-1	Indian and Western Working World Perspectives	
Issue	*The Indian Way*	*The Western Way*
Initiative	Not as common as a "do as directed" approach.	Taking initiative using acquired skills and resourcefulness is greatly valued.
Supervision	No sensitivity to being checked on; supervision is expected.	Emphasis is on responsibility, accountability, and independent work.
Management Technique	Good bosses care about employees and their families. They praise good work but are strict when necessary.	Good bosses offer inspiring leadership and give employees the space they need to prove themselves.
Employee Performance	Good employees work hard, don't watch the clock or take too much leave, don't quarrel with their teams, and are honest, soft spoken, and reliable.	Good employees meet deadlines, think for themselves, take the initiative, and are reliable and smart.

Indians are super sensitive about a few areas, such as class, poverty, and the land under dispute with Pakistan. Take every precaution to tread carefully in these areas.

Cultural differences between India and the West

Tons of cultural differences exist between India and the West, particularly the U.S. These differences are by no means insurmountable — look at all the businesses that have already set up shop successfully in India — but if you're aware of them, your entry into the country and workings within it will be much easier.

Table 14-2 offers a useful sampling of cultural differences between India and the West, particularly the U.S.

Table 14-2	Cultural Differences Between India and the West
The West (U.S. in Particular)	**India**
Good public education	Inadequate education opportunities
Jobs disperse population and dilute family bonds, creating nuclear families	Lack of jobs keeps extended family physically close and dependent on each other
Nuclear independent family	Larger interdependent families
Fiercely independent	Nurtured interdependence
Highly mobile	Mobility based on necessity
Professionally opportunistic	Professionally less opportunistic
Abundant jobs, low population results in low unemployment rates	High population creates high unemployment/underemployment
Highly employed workforce creates premium for time	Underemployed workforce makes time inexpensive
Labor is expensive	Labor is cheap
Punctuality demanded	Punctuality is lax
Freedom demanded by people at all times	Sovereign freedom cherished, control/loss of freedom tolerated in day-to-day life
History has molded intolerance of incompetent authority	History has molded tolerance of incompetent authority
Organization and planning held high	Take things as they are

(continued)

Table 14-2 *(continued)*

The West (U.S. in Particular)	India
Humor is part of culture	Serious and conventional
You get what you pay for	You get what's available
Everyone is equal	Hierarchy is a way of life
The great American Dream that nothing is impossible and anyone can succeed if he works hard	The class system that places Indians in certain classes based on birth and limits their upward mobility
Direct, almost appearing rude to other cultures	More subtlety and complexity compared to other cultures

Cultural differences within India

As if it weren't difficult enough to grasp all of the cultural differences between India and the West, you also have to be aware of the differences *within* India. To keep life interesting, Indians have cultural differences from region to region, state to state, and city to village. In this section, I offer you some pointers about how people from the different broad areas of India differ in matters of dress, language, and outlook.

Differences between southern and northern India

As India is a vast country in terms of landmass, it should come as no surprise that there are a number of differences between Indians in the southern part of the country and the northern portion.

✔ **Northern India:** Several languages are common in northern India, including Hindi, Urdu, Gujarati, Marathi, Punjabi, and Sindhi. As far as dress is concerned, women in the north wear sari and *salwar-kameez, chudidar-kurta,* and *lehenga-kurta.* (The last three are variations of the same theme — a sort of pant, either loose or tight, with a long top over it). Men wear *pyjama-kurta* and *dhoti-kurta.* (The first is a more austerely cut version of the salwar-kameez, while the latter is a long, broad section of cloth wound around the midriff in varying styles, coming down to the ankles and topped with a type of shirt, either very long or just below the waist.) North Indian culture is more showy and aggressive. A lot of importance is given to status and outward display of wealth. The Northerners are great businessfolk and are excellent, gracious hosts.

✔ **Southern India:** Indians in the southern part of the country speak primarily Tamil, Malayalam, Telugu, or Kannada. Women wear pavadai-blouses, half-saris with a blouse, and saris. (The pavadai is a long, billowing skirt, worn with a blouse which comes down to the hip. The half-sari is this same skirt worn with a short tight blouse reaching only the midriff, and a length of cloth draped over the chest and over one shoulder. The sari is a grown-up version of the half-sari.) Men can be commonly seen wearing veshti or lungi with a Western style shirt in the merchant community. (The veshti and lungi are the southern versions of the sarong-like dhoti of northern India, but the styles of wearing it are distinctive.) In the business community, the dress code for men is semi-formal Western wear, and elegant casual wear is the norm for women. South Indian culture is more modest and underplays its wealth. It is typical of this region to be humble and subdued even if folk are part of the mega-rich. The southerners are warm as a people and make friends easily.

Eastern and western India also have unique cultural characteristics, although they're not as pronounced as the differences between the north and the south. The western part of the country has a strong merchant community, and communism has played a contributory role in the development of east India. The western and eastern regions are more like northern India than southern.

Differences between urban and rural India

Generally speaking, rural areas exhibit more traditional, conservative behavior, while urban areas reflect more liberal, less conservative values.

In India, the urban north is modern, class conscious, cosmopolitan, aggressive, confident, full of well-educated people pursuing a flashy lifestyle, multilingual, and using mostly English as a business language. In the urban south, people are laid back, traditional, provincial, passive, and respectful, yet questioning in terms of business. English is the predominant business language. The people are on the whole friendly and helpful.

On the other hand, the rural areas in both places have people who are class and caste conscious, conservative and more overtly religious, with low literacy rates.

Is your head spinning? Well, here's something to cheer you up. There are common characteristics you can count on for almost all Indians. In the business context, these include the following:

✔ Highly informal styles of business — written contracts aren't common, and verbal agreements are fine.

✔ Punctuality isn't seen as a virtue.

✔ Family life supersedes business concerns, absence from work for death in the extended family is common.

✔ People are generally non-confrontational.

✔ Indians are hospitable and welcoming.

The influence of Hinduism on Indian culture

Today, India is a pluralistic society where multiple religions, cultures, and languages coexist, largely peacefully. So writing about factors that apply to all Indians is extremely difficult. However, it can be safely said that Hinduism is the predominant religion in India: About 80 percent of the population is Hindu. Based on that, I can say that a large portion of the population is influenced by the important beliefs and values of Hinduism. You may be exposed to these beliefs, so it's worth knowing their ins and outs to gain a fuller cultural perspective.

Hinduism is a way of life. It believes in one God but worships his many forms based on personal preferences and gives a variety of choices. The main trinities to be aware of are Brahma the Creator, Vishnu the Preserver, and Shiva the Destroyer of Evil.

The concept of destiny

Indians in general are instilled with the concept that this life is just one in a long cycle of births and deaths, not all of them necessarily human. The concept of reincarnation is therefore an inherent part of the Indian psyche, and it indirectly influences a lot of other beliefs, and consequently, cultural behavior. The belief in the life-cycle lends itself to the corollary that whatever actions have been done in earlier human lives could have their consequences in this life, and the consequences of actions performed in this lifetime may have repercussions in not only this but also future lifetimes. The timing of such manifestation of consequences is believed to be beyond the individual's control, since it is governed by a cosmic law or theory of karma. This is the basis of the widespread Indian belief in destiny. There are two ways this belief translates to overt behavior:

✔ Destiny could lull a person to apathy and inaction, because he could interpret this as the futility of all action and exercise of free will. This, however, is fortunately the view of only a small minority in India.

✔ The more prevalent effect of the belief in destiny, however, is the ability to take life as it comes and not be buffeted by its ups and downs. Understanding the law of karma enables the Indian to change what can be changed, accept what cannot, and have the wisdom to know the difference. The Indian is thus able to put in the best effort possible and take the results of such efforts in stride, without getting unduly euphoric or disappointed about them. Prayer, meditation, and yoga provide the balance between doing and being.

Comfort with the irrational

Indians are prone to believing in the supernatural and in matters of faith. This is part of their upbringing, which doesn't require a rational or scientific explanation for everything that's taught to them. This trait has its roots in the mythology in India, which abounds with characters having supernatural powers and superhuman forms. Though the reasons for such depiction could be traced to the need to inculcate a sense of awe and reverence in the individual, it has also resulted in making the Indian comfortable with the irrational. This trait has also expanded to encompass the Indian's widespread belief in sciences such as Astrology, Numerology, and Vaastu, to name a few, and the details of each are as follows:

✔ **Astrology:** This science plays a major role in shortlisting and selecting a spouse in the traditional "arranged" marriage in India, where the parents concerned are involved in the pre-selection process, and later introduce their respective son and daughter to each other, either to approve the union, or exercise their "veto" power, so to speak. Astrology is also a key determinant of the time any "auspicious" activity is scheduled to begin, whether it is a religious ritual, a building project, or even a movie production.

✔ **Numerology:** Numerology incites Indians to pay large sums of money to buy certain number sequences in their automobile registration plates, modifying the usual way their names are spelled in order to conform to a more conducive spelling from the numerological perspective, and so on.

✔ **Vaastu:** This code is the ancient Indian building and interior architecture code, has recently become a prime factor in design and marketing of real estate, specifically buildings. Vaastu experts are consulted before a prospective buyer decides on a house or commercial building. Any unfavorable factors are corrected in order to prevent undesirable consequences. New buildings are certified "Vaastu compliant" in order to command better market value, though such certification does not have any legal or official sanction.

Relationships, relationships, relationships

At the end of the day, relationships matter most in India, and the proof is in the language. The things that a culture truly values comes across in the its language. Eskimos, for example, have numerous words for ice and snow. Africans have several words for grass. In India, there are distinct words for specific relationships.

In English, your mother's older sister is called your aunt; her younger sister is aunt; your father's sister is aunt; and your father's brother's wife is also your aunt. But each Indian language has different terms for all different types of familial relationships. For example, in Hindi your father's sister is called *bua;* your father's brother's wife is *chachi;* your mother's younger sister is *masi;* and your mother's older sister is *badi ma.* Each aunt has a special descriptor showing respect for that relationship. And the same is true for all other relatives.

Getting a grip on the Indian sense of right and wrong

The sense of right and wrong can be fuzzy for Indians, especially when they try to rationalize something that's favorable to them but unfavorable, frowned upon, or even illegal in the larger context of society. To help you be wary of that, I present the following examples:

- ✔ If an Indian's umbrella is mistakenly picked up by someone else, he may swipe an identical umbrella from an umbrella stand.

- ✔ Families can be seen to blithely litter in public places such as movie theaters or beaches, despite knowing that they are making it less enjoyable to the public at large.

- ✔ Compliance to road rules in India is often contingent on an officer of the law being present in close proximity. This explains why often so many drivers — at all levels of society — opt to exercise their discretion during off-peak hours when it comes to deciding on whether to stop at a traffic light.

These examples illustrate the Indian's tendency to define right and wrong depending on the context, without adopting a rigid and uniform code. This is not to imply, however, that this behavioral trait is unique to Indians. In fact, it can be found throughout Asia.

Chapter 15

Being on Your Best Behavior: Indian Etiquette

· ·

In This Chapter

▶ Making the right impression

▶ Speaking with your colleagues

▶ Giving and receiving gifts and hospitality

▶ Avoiding mealtime faux pas

▶ Respecting the religious side of business

▶ Managing your Indian employees

· ·

*W*ith its unique, vibrant culture, India is a world to itself. It's a country that has sent satellites into space, but it's also a country in which you may have to wait for days to get your phone line fixed. To do business in India, you need to set aside your usual expectations and instead try to work out what's reasonable in the Indian context. You may encounter different concepts of time, different procedures for firing employees, and even different ways of conducting yourself at the dinner table (you can forget all those lessons about which fork to use). Bottom line: Patience and acceptance are important tools for doing business in India.

Understanding the unwritten codes of etiquette and decorum in India is vital to the success of your business venture. Chapter 14 helps you get a grip on how relationships in India work. This chapter shows you how that sense of culture plays out in everyday situations. It explains how to behave appropriately with Indians in various business and social settings. And as you figure out how to mind your manners, this chapter also guides you in how to maintain your patience and be accepting of a new, fascinating culture.

Making a Good First Impression

First impressions are important all around the world. Yet in an unfamiliar setting, it's easy to take a wrong step and end up in an uncomfortable situation. The good news is that Indians welcome the opportunity to work with foreigners, making your adjustment much easier. Remembering a few crucial points helps you easily roll with the cultural punches and conduct your business smoothly.

Greeting colleagues

Using a gracious greeting shows your new Indian acquaintances that you're committed to being respectful and courteous. The traditional Indian form of greeting is the *namaste,* which literally means "I bow to the divine in you." Sure beats a "Hey, how ya doin'?," doesn't it? The namaste is used for greeting, for taking leave, and also to seek forgiveness.

To greet someone with a namaste, bring your hands together with palms touching in front of your chest in a graceful fashion, as shown in Figure 15-1. Different languages may have different names for the namaste, but the gesture remains the same throughout India.

Greeting your Indian business colleagues with a namaste is considered a compliment, and it sets the right tone for the rest of your meeting and shows that you've taken time to understand Indian exchanges. But offering a handshake isn't looked down upon. In fact, many Indian businesspeople offer a handshake to show that they're familiar and comfortable with greeting foreigners. However, if you're greeted with a namaste and don't reciprocate, Indian colleagues take that as the equivalent of a "cold fish" handshake!

If you offer a firm handshake, don't always expect to receive the same grip in return. Not all Indians give firm handshakes because a limp handshake is a sign of respect, not of weakness.

Playing the name game

The hardest thing about using and remembering Indian names is their length. As you move from the north of the country to the south, the names get longer and longer.

Indian names are fascinating in what they can convey to Indians. From a name, Indians can tell which region of the country the person belongs to, what clothes he wears at home, what language he speaks, whether he's fair or dark-skinned, and probably even what he ate for breakfast! An Indian name holds a whole world of meaning. Most Indian names have a specific meaning or are associated with a particular God. But be wary of making inquiries about these hidden details — not everyone knows the meaning of his or her own name!

The trick to remembering a name is to see it written out and then to break it into syllables. For example, the name Sivaramakrishnan is actually three names — Siva, Rama, and Krishnan (the names of three Indian deities) — strung together. Also if you stress the first syllable of an Indian name you usually pronounce it right.

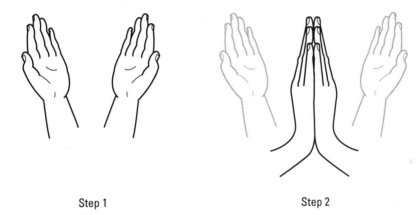

Step 1   Step 2

Figure 15-1:
How to
do the
namaste.

Step 3

When speaking to Indians, keep in mind that Indians start relationships and use of names on a formal basis. Use Mr., Mrs., or Miss (Ms. isn't used in India) and the person's last name. And you can't go wrong with Sir or Madam by themselves without the last name even, especially if the person is older than you. If you're invited to use an Indian's first name, asking for help with the pronunciation is appreciated.

Typically, Indians don't use the name of the person they're talking to during a conversation. This behavior is a mark of respect and not a sign of unfriendliness. They even may be unsure of how to pronounce your Western name and don't want to offend you. Take the time to help your Indian acquaintances get your name right even if they're too shy to ask.

Swapping business cards

Indians like to give out and receive business cards, so if you don't hand one over of your own accord when you meet someone, you may be asked for it. Contacts and networking are very important in India, and jogging the memory with a business card can be extremely helpful.

So what should appear on your business card? It should list your

- Name
- Company name
- Title
- E-mail address
- Other information such as your company mailing address and company Web site as well as a reference to a doctorate or similar degree that you hold

Think twice about including your mobile phone number on your business card. If you give an Indian your mobile number, the lucky recipient will use it freely! Indians handle this by writing out their mobile numbers on the cards they give to a select few.

And don't worry, English cards are fine, whichever corner of India you're in.

When it comes to their own business cards, Indians believe the more titles, the merrier; the business title on the card is of great significance to Indians. And don't be surprised to see educational qualifications on many Indian business cards. The longer the string of acronyms behind an already lengthy Indian name, the better! See Figure 15-2 for examples of thorough Indian business cards.

E-mail: drharii@yahoo.com
Ph (O) : 0413 - 2525325
(R) : 0413 - 2423425
Cell : 94339 93942

Dr. K. HARI M.B.A., Ph.D.,
M. Phil., (Mgt.), M. Com., PGDLL, AMIMA

Professor in International Business
School of Managment, Madurai University
Madurai - 606 123

Res : Plot No. 45, 85th Cross, Kurinji Nagar Extension
Lawspet, Madurai - 606 123

T.N.Gopal

M.Sc.,(C.Sc.).,M.Phil.(C.Sc.).,M.Sc.,(Maths).,PGDCA.,B.Ed.,

Placement Officer &
Head, Department of Computer Science
Krishna College for Women,
Annamalai Nagar, Pondy - 605 018

e-mail: krishnaplacement@yahoo.co.in
Tel.: 0432 - 2787492 Fax : 0432-2709423

Figure 15-2:
Examples
of Indian
business
cards.

Some Indians' business cards even carry former job titles, such as "Ex-Incharge Govt. of India Veterinary Hospital, New Delhi." To you, this detail may be amusing, but the "ex-factor" is very important in India because it provides another boost to a person's credentials.

Most young professional or older, well-traveled Indians don't fill up their cards with acronyms, and you can follow their lead. But Indians place a great deal of emphasis on academia, so if you hold a doctorate or similar degree, do note it on your card.

Wearing appropriate clothing

Indians appreciate formal Western attire at business meetings. They go out of their way to dress smartly for the occasion and respect a business partner who does the same. Up north, there's more emphasis on formal business wear — suits and ties — than down south, where people tend to go for chinos and short-sleeved shirts that are more in-tune with the weather. There's nothing like a blazing Chennai sun to make a businessman rethink his choice of a three-piece suit!

Formal pressed trousers with a collared shirt and closed shoes are fine for both men and women at business meetings. Women may also wear skirts or dresses, but remember not to show too much chest or leg. For the evening, women who wear ankle-length or below-the-knee dresses fit in well. Avoid spaghetti straps or off-the-shoulder dresses, except when you have a chance to attend that Bollywood party!

Here are a few other tips for dressing:

✔ White shirts often turn yellowish in Indian wash — don't ask if it is the water or sun! Dodge the problem by wearing colored shirts.

✔ Westerners tend to find the Indian air-conditioning too cold, much to the surprised delight of Indians, so bring along a jacket or a sweater to a meeting.

 After the meeting, you step into the sweltering streets of most cities, so get used to this change in temperature. Dressing to be in and out of cold and heat is definitely a challenge you face when in India.

✔ You can never be overdressed in India. You may receive an invitation to a casual lunch with friends where women turn up sparkling in silk and jewelry. Don't take *casual* literally and turn up in jeans and a t-shirt. Buttoned-down formal shirts and trousers are considered casual for men.

✔ Always dress elegantly in India. Indians like a well-dressed Westerner. But crushed clothes appear unkempt and Indians may look at you as a "hippie" — remnants of those who came to India in the '60s.

✔ If you wear Indian clothes, make sure you have a classy Indian friend help you choose an outfit or recommend where to buy one. It's easy to fall into the trap of buying something too touristy and making the wrong impression.

Sometimes you may encounter situations in which it's customary to remove your shoes before entering a room or building. Shoe removal is common throughout Asia and has its origins in keeping the outside dirt outside where it belongs. But unlike other Asian countries, in India there is no slipper or indoor slip-ons to wear instead. At office inaugurations or ceremonies such as groundbreakings (explained in detail in the later section "Ceremonies for office openings and groundbreakings"), you may be required to remove your footwear as a sign of respect. There usually isn't a designated area for this, but a pile of other shoes is always a good hint that you should remove yours. When in doubt, ask others. And leaving your socks on is fine.

Sari *does* cut it

The sari is a 6-yard rectangular piece of cloth, often brightly colored, that's draped around the torso in a specific way. The sari and the salwar kameez (a loose pant worn with a long shirt) teamed with a scarf make up a typical ensemble for Indian women. As a Westerner, you may find these clothes pretty but hopelessly impractical. But we Indians do everything in them, from riding scooters to cooking, running businesses, and climbing mountains!

To get full cooperation from your employees, do as the Indians do or at least let them do as they're used to doing in matters of dress. If you just can't, try for a workable compromise. When a leading car manufacturer set up a factory in Chennai, it had the hardest time convincing the women not to go on to the factory floors with floating lengths of cloth. A compromise was finally reached when they agreed to wear Western-style uniforms over their Indian clothes.

Ladies be warned: If you must wear high heels with long trousers, it's best to check beforehand to find out if the office you're going to (such as some audio and sound studios) asks people to leave their footwear outside. If it is, you may want to rethink your outfit instead of risk tripping over your long trousers as you walk around the office!

Conversing with Your Indian Colleagues

Successful business depends on a sense of trust between colleagues. Establishing a healthy rapport with your Indian coworkers, employees, and clients is an important first step in building that crucial comfort level. If you can understand and implement the basics of Indian interaction, you'll be well on your way to becoming socially savvy.

Carrying on a conversation

Although many Indians speak outstanding English, their conversational patterns can differ greatly from what you're used to.

Indians often insert Indian filler words into their otherwise impeccable English conversation. Don't be surprised if a north Indian says *Haan* (which means *yes* in Hindi) several times during a discussion, or if a southern Indian uses *illai* (which means *no* in Tamil) the same way. You're safe just ignoring these words; they're just fillers and mean nothing in particular when used in this manner.

Noises with specific meanings are also common. You may hear an Indian making a sort of "tch" sound using his tongue and lips. Don't be alarmed — he's not making rude noises; he's using a common expression for *no*. The same goes for a clicking sound made with the tongue. You also may hear an Indian make a *pccchhhh* sound, which is used to express sympathy or concern.

Gesturing during a discussion

It's common to begin a business conversation with a few pleasantries and maybe even a joke or two. As you joke, however, be mindful that certain Western gestures commonly made while telling jokes — winking and whistling in particular — send an inappropriate message. Winking at colleagues (especially those of the opposite sex) to emphasize a punch line is more likely to elicit a furrowed brow than a chuckle.

After you exchange pleasantries and your meeting is underway, you may be startled to see your Indian companions shaking their heads firmly while you enthusiastically outline your fine business ideas. Don't lose heart! They aren't disagreeing or implying failure even before you start. When an Indian moves his head from side to side, he's not refuting what you're saying; he's indicating that he's paying attention, in the same way a Westerner would by nodding his head up and down.

To signal "yes," Indians often tilt their heads and wobble them as if they've temporarily lost control of their neck muscles. It's a unique movement that can be quite confusing for a Westerner who's seeing it for the first time.

When your meeting concludes and it's time to part ways with your Indian colleagues, be careful not to wave goodbye. Waving your hand up and down and curling your fingers downward in India indicate that you'd like someone to come over to you. You may be waving goodbye, but Indians think you're beckoning them! And it's always a safe bet to bid someone farewell with a namaste (refer to the earlier section "Greeting colleagues" for a namaste tutorial).

Be on the lookout for other unique Indian gestures because recognizing and understanding them can help you to better communicate with your colleagues. For example, Indians often point at something using their chins or the palms of their hands. If an Indian is motioning toward something with his chin, have a look! It's quite all right to stop and ask for a clarification of what a gesture means if you're in any doubt.

Don't use the curled finger to beckon; I have known of Indians who take offense when American drivers have used this gesture, allowing the Indian pedestrian to cross ahead. Use your whole palm instead.

Putting your best foot forward

Be mindful of your feet while in India because actions involving the feet may imply more than you think. In India, a person may fall at your feet or bend down as if she's about to do so in order to seek a blessing. But if an Indian touches you with her foot accidentally, she quickly touches you with her hand and places that hand over her eyes or heart. This is done to seek forgiveness because a touch with the foot — regarded as the lowest part of the body both literally and figuratively — could be seen as disrespectful.

A Generous Hand: Gifting in India

Who doesn't like receiving gifts? Indians are no different from the rest of the world in this regard. In a business context, it's quite appropriate to take along a small gift each time you meet someone.

You can limit your gifting to the CEO, but if you're meeting with two people of the same standing, make sure that you don't leave one of them out.

Giving an appropriate gift

Giving gifts in India can be a challenge for the new visitor or expatriate who has to deal with a complex culture. To complicate matters, India is a heady mix of tradition and modernity, and on the corporate front, it's a mix of multi-national companies with multinational personnel, traditional family businesses, and companies with a distinctly Indian corporate culture.

The best way to work through the maze of potential gifts is to identify how well you know the recipient. In general, maintain a level of formality with your gifts unless you know the person really well. Indians appreciate a gift that's typical of the giver's country, but you should refrain from giving tourist souvenirs.

Here are some of the safest gifts:

- Chocolates
- Cognac, whisky, or champagne (if you know that the recipient is a drinker)
- Floral bouquets
- Items from your country

- ✔ Paintings
- ✔ Perfumes
- ✔ Watches

The following don'ts apply to gift-giving in India:

- ✔ **Don't expect Indians to open your gifts in front of you.** They're uncomfortable with this and say only a pleasant "thank you" when the gift is received.

- ✔ **Don't wrap your gifts in black or white, which are considered unlucky colors and are associated with mourning.** Green, red, and yellow are auspicious colors that you can't go wrong with using.

- ✔ **Don't give Indian Muslims toy dogs or gifts with pictures of dogs.** They believe that dogs are unclean.

- ✔ **Don't rely on products made from animal hides.** Conservative Hindus don't use such products.

When you give a gift, you can certainly expect to receive a gift in return. It could be something made of silver or bronze or maybe even gold. Gold and silver are a sign of great respect in India. When you receive a gift from a colleague, feel free to open it and show your appreciation. Following up with a thank-you note or — even better — a personal telephone call to thank the colleague for the gift goes over well.

Many multinational corporations are very concerned about being seen to conduct business in India with absolute integrity. Therefore, a foreign businessman may feel compromised when he receives lavish gifts from suppliers and partners during festival times like Diwali. (I discuss festivals in detail later in this chapter in the section "Enjoying Indian religious festivals.") Keep in mind that it's customary to give such gifts during important festivals, and as long as there's no under-the-table implication, you should accept such gifts with grace. Otherwise you leave your Indian business friend feeling insulted. That said, don't hesitate to put your foot down if you feel uncomfortable with the gift; do it gently and firmly, appreciate the thought, then apologize and explain that it's against your company policy to accept such things.

Winning ways

A lot can depend on a gift in an Indian business scenario. An Australian who joined an Indian in a business venture took along an artist's figurine of a kangaroo when he went to visit his partner. Prior to the Australian's visit, the Indian had found that the venture wasn't going well and had decided to pull out. But when the Australian gifted him the kangaroo, the Indian took it as a mark of high regard and found he couldn't sever the relationship.

DISTILLED WISDOM

Loosening your grip on self-reliance

Here's how Canadian Norm Mainland described his first tussle with courtesy, Indian-style:

"Preparing for my first visit to India, I was determined to be a beacon of cross-cultural awareness and sensitivity. I vowed to be a shining example, someone to whom our other functional managers would look for guidance on how to navigate the uncharted seas of Indian culture. But the way to Hell is paved with good intentions!"

"The company driver picked me up at the hotel and drove me to the factory to meet our staff. As I stepped out of the car, I made my first mistake.

A teenaged office boy stepped forward and grasped the handle of my briefcase as his senior managers waited to greet me. Being a self-sufficient person, I didn't wish to impose upon anyone and preferred to carry the briefcase myself. The boy and I then engaged in a brief tug-of-war until, mercifully, my brain engaged and I realized that it was his job to assist and that I was embarrassing him in front of his managers by not letting him carry out his duties. I released my grip, he took my briefcase, and I enjoyed all the wonderful introductions to our Indian staff!"

Accepting Indian courtesies

Indians take courtesy to an extent that Westerners don't easily understand. A concept of the guest as a demigod and a deep-rooted sense of hierarchy influence the expression of courtesy to the country's visitors. Be prepared to set aside your ideas of self-sufficiency and a culture where each person is expected to fend for himself or herself.

Indians happily do all they can to make you feel at home, including the following:

✔ Serve you and let you eat before they eat

✔ Attend to you and see that your needs are met

✔ Fetch you at the airport and see you off

✔ Organize a dinner in your honor

✔ Arrange a sightseeing trip

The rule of thumb is to go with the flow of these extensive courtesies because resistance often is futile. Indians really are that welcoming! Recognize that they're seen as having failed if you rebuff their courtesies. If you're truly opposed to accepting this kind of treatment, however, you can offer a firm "no thank you," and add again "I appreciate it, but I apologize that I'm unable to accept."

Mean what you say, say what you mean

Indians mean every word when they say "don't hesitate to ask if I can help," and they don't separate professional help from personal help.

Tim, an American, told his Indian friend in a spirit of camaraderie, "Don't hesitate to ask if I can help you." His friend Shiva nodded, pleased, and Tim thought no more of the episode. Some time later, Tim got a call from Shiva asking for an introduction to an officer Tim knew in the U.S. Consulate. Shiva wanted a visa for his son and had remembered Tim's offer to help. Tim, however, didn't want to make use of his connections in this manner and told Shiva so. Shiva was deeply hurt, and Tim realized that a casual remark intended merely as a mark of friendship had been taken literally.

The moral of this story is that you shouldn't say "ask me for anything" if you don't mean it literally.

An Australian who started a business in India found himself stifled by the attention Indians heaped on him. He couldn't break them of the habit and was at his wits' end until he thought of a compromise. He came to an understanding with his Indian colleagues that the first time he visited a particular city, he would permit himself to be met and waited on. But on subsequent visits, he would be left to his own devices.

Here are some tips on gaining self-reliance without insulting your Indian hosts:

- ✔ When offered help that you don't really need, assure the helper that he or she is very kind.
- ✔ Explain that you're really not used to such outstanding treatment and would prefer to do it on your own.
- ✔ Use small talk to explain your position on self-reliance.
- ✔ If the same person repeatedly offers to help you, use humor to decline, but stick to your guns.

Eating: The Indian Way

Food is an integral part of any society, and each culture has its own culinary and dining traditions. In India, meals are a major preoccupation and a yardstick of hospitality. The country has a range of cuisine as varied as its rich geography, history, and language. In fact, each region has its own distinctive food traditions.

You're likely to share business related meals with Indians in restaurants or country clubs. They like to entertain and host. Offering food is an integral part of Indian hospitality. And hospitality is an integral part of building business relationships. Depending on how close you are to your colleagues, you may get to enjoy a meal in an Indian home.

Getting the lay of the table

Indians don't do business over breakfast or lunch primarily because they expect that their Western guests want to have an alcoholic drink with their meals and Indians who drink usually do so in the evening before dinner.

Indians are very gracious hosts, and they lay a fabulous table. Buffet dinners either at a private room in a hotel or at the host's house are common among business partners. People eat with spoons rather than forks and knives, although these pieces of cutlery are sometimes provided. It's also possible that you may be expected to eat with your hands (see the section "In good taste: Eating with your hands" later in this chapter).

At an Indian banquet, you can expect

- ✔ A seating arrangement that segregates the sexes
- ✔ A lot of drinking before dinner
- ✔ Whisky or hard liquor rather than wine
- ✔ A beeline for the food when dinner is announced
- ✔ Many dishes of delicious food and plenty of hospitality
- ✔ Approving smiles if you pile up your plate (and more smiles if you take seconds)
- ✔ Deliciously sweet desserts that make your teeth hurt
- ✔ An exodus as soon as the meal is served and eaten

Indian liquor is more potent than what you may be used to at home, so I recommend that you go easy on the drinks if you don't want your senses fuddled. And if you don't drink, it's okay to ask for a soft or cold drink, which in India indicates a nonalcoholic beverage.

Indian parties, business or otherwise, tend to go on and on because Indians like to get their drinking done before starting on the food. So don't be surprised if you're kept waiting for hours before the food is served. If you don't have that much time to spend at the party, politely make that clear as soon as you arrive or suggest that you drop by for dinner another day when you have more time.

If you're going to a restaurant for your business dinner, rest assured that the experience is similar to eating out in other parts of the world. One difference is that you may need to eat with your hands. If that's the case, high-end restaurants provide finger bowls with warm water and a slice of lemon to help you keep your hands clean and fresh. Medium- or low-end establishments have washbasins for the same purpose. After the meal is over, keep in mind that 10 percent gratuities are adequate.

Recognizing foods of India

Low-carb meals aren't exactly synonymous with Indian food. Indian cuisine can be pretty starchy, but that certainly doesn't mean it isn't delicious! Simplicity isn't the norm, either. Providing a good spread is paramount in India; multiple dishes indicate a good host or hostess. And it's easy to enjoy a fantastic Indian meal, especially when you aren't the one doing all the cooking!

Mix and match as you see fit, but keep in mind that the norm is rice or wheat as the main dish and meat and/or vegetables as accompaniments. Rice is the staple diet in the South, and wheat is the staple in the North.

Here's a handy primer of common foods, techniques, and general terms used in Indian cuisine:

- **Biryani:** A rich and spicy rice dish with meat or vegetables
- **Dosa:** A southern breakfast food that resembles salted crepes
- **Idli:** A southern breakfast food that tastes like dumplings
- **Lentils:** Seeds (called pulses in India) of which India has 18 varieties!; the primary source of protein for vegetarians
- **Makhani:** Gravy with butter sauce generously added
- **Murg:** Chicken (as in murg makhani, murg kabab, and so on)
- **Naan, roti, puri, bathura, and parattha:** Some of the varieties of the yummy breads of India
- **Paneer:** Cheese that's a little like ricotta
- **Pulav:** A lighter version of biryani (mildly flavored rice).
- **Rasgolla, gulab jamun, jalebi, peda, and kheer (payasam in south Indian languages):** Sweet dishes
- **Sambar:** A spicy stew of lentils and vegetables that goes with idli, dosa, vada, and rice
- **Samosas:** Deep-fried savory snacks with meat or vegetable fillings wrapped in crispy, flaky pastry

- ✔ **Tandoor:** A special way of cooking pieces of meat or vegetables skewered in a coal oven

- ✔ **Vada:** A savory doughnut

- ✔ **Yogurt:** A great accompaniment often used to tone down Indian spices

I've seen my British clients pore over menus looking for their favorite Indian dishes. However, "curry" isn't the name of a dish in India — it's a way of preparing different kinds of meat or vegetables with sauces and spices. Truly authentic Indian food rarely makes it over to Western countries, so you should take advantage of it while you can in India. Authentic Indian dishes feature freshly ground spices, and the seasonings — curry leaves, cilantro, and lemon, to name a few — are all far more intense than in other cuisines. Also try *rumali rotis* (bread that is as thin as a handkerchief), vegetables like *tindora* or *covaka* (they look like little gherkins), fried jumbo prawns, and crab or lobster in Indian *masalas* (spices). These treats are guaranteed to thrill an Indian foodie.

Indians use a lot of red and green chilies in their cooking. The green chilies pack a stronger punch than the red, and in both varieties, the thinner the chili, the hotter it is. Some dishes can be an inferno for the inexperienced!

When your tongue is on fire from sampling a particularly spicy Indian dish and you don't want to make a scene in front of an Indian colleague, quietly slip a spoonful of yogurt into your mouth. There's nothing better to dowse the flames!

Many Indians are vegetarian but tolerate others eating meat. That tolerance may be less common in traditional homes or smaller towns, but eating meat is okay in business situations. However, if your host is vegetarian, you can earn brownie points by sticking to vegetarian dishes and remarking on how easy it is to be vegetarian in India.

In good taste: Eating with your hands

For the most part, Indians can't understand how it's possible to enjoy food without feeling its texture. For an Indian, to use the hand to eat is to relish the meal. After you get used to this practice yourself, you may not want to give up the habit. Indian dining etiquette is very fulfilling because it means doing everything your mother taught you not to do — touching your food, licking your fingers, slurping at the table, and so on. But Indians do it with panache!

Here's some general advice on how to eat (bet you didn't think you'd need to figure that out again at this point in your life!):

- ✔ **Eat with your right hand only.** If you're left-handed, sit on your left hand to prevent it from getting in on the action!

- ✔ **Break bread, or *roti,* by holding it down with your forefinger and tearing off a bit with the thumb and the other three fingers.**

- ✔ **After your fingers touch your mouth, don't touch any other food with the right hand except what's on your own plate.** When you need a refill, serve yourself with your left hand.

- ✔ **Pass food with your clean left hand.**

- ✔ **Hold your drinking glass with your left hand.** Drinks are placed on the left side of the place setting (as opposed to the right in a Western place setting) so you can use your clean left hand to hold your glass.

Making small talk over a meal

When it comes to small talk over meals in India, you have to ease your dinner partners into their comfort zone. The following topics work well:

- ✔ A person's city of origin in India

- ✔ Children's education

- ✔ Cricket

- ✔ Family

- ✔ Indian cinema

- ✔ The region of origin of the food on the table

- ✔ Travel overseas or in India

Conversation topics to avoid include

- ✔ Caste system

- ✔ Money matters

- ✔ Politics

- ✔ Poverty in India

- ✔ Sex

When you dine in someone's home, compliment the food but don't ask for the recipe. Many people employ cooks to prepare many of the meals, so it's quite possible that your host or hostess won't know the ingredients or how it's made!

Toasting isn't natural in Indian business meetings, but as a Westerner, you may compliment an Indian by raising a toast. If you reel off a simple Indian sentence or two, you may get a round of applause!

For more tips on Indian communication, flip to Chapter 14.

Playing host

One Indian saying that's sure to endear you to your colleagues is *athi-thi devo bhava* (the guest is God). Indians are wonderfully enthusiastic hosts, but they're willing guests, too.

After you've enjoyed the hospitality that's heaped on you by generous Indians, you may feel moved to reciprocate by hosting a meal. I encourage you to do so! Go ahead and be the host with the most!

If you or your company has an apartment or house in India, it should serve as an excellent venue for hosting a meal. If you're not yet that far along, a private room in a hotel also suffices. For the food, you can book an excellent catering service at a reasonable rate.

Invite your guests to the meal personally or over the phone instead of sending a card. If guests have already confirmed their attendance, mention their names when inviting others (especially if you know that the confirmed guests appeal to the invited ones). If a potential guest can be assured that he'll be in good company, he's much more likely to attend.

As for the gathering, Indians are pleased if you

- ✔ Serve buffet-style meals to avoid complicated cutlery.
- ✔ Encourage your guests to mix but don't force the issue if you notice a segregation of the sexes.
- ✔ Offer plenty of food and encourage multiple servings.
- ✔ Provide plenty of alcohol to drinkers.
- ✔ Serve dinner late rather than early and keep some appetizer-type foods (called small eats in India) flowing. Indians do all their drinking before dinner, and an early dinner signals that you're playing Scrooge with your expensive scotch!
- ✔ Label vegetarian and nonvegetarian dishes clearly, and keep the two in separate sections of the same table or even on separate tables if possible, with separate serving spoons.
- ✔ Suggest some games to liven up the party.

Religion in Indian Business: Giving the Deities Their Due

Eighty percent of Indians are Hindu, so Hinduism is a way of life in the country. Separating religious life from public life is practically impossible. Most Indians are deeply devout; some are even deeply superstitious. To conduct and foster Indian business relations, it's crucial that you understand the role of religion. I focus on Hinduism in this section because of its prominence and because Westerners tend to know less about it than the other religions — primarily Islam and Christianity — found in India.

Bowing to the Supreme Being

In Hinduism, the goal is to reach an ideal through an idol. Hindus have myriad varieties of the one formless and omnipresent Supreme Being they believe in. (I lost count at 33,000!) It's quite common for an employee to keep a picture of one of these gods or goddesses in an office or on a desk. Indians make a daily routine of bowing before these pictures (or sometimes symbols or statues) before beginning work. Figure 15-3 shows Ganesha, the elephant-headed God whose blessings are sought at the beginning of all ventures; he's the favorite deity of most Hindu businesspeople.

Figure 15-3:
A typical depiction of Ganesha.

Varun, who was raised in Mumbai, educated at New York University, and works as a Goldman Sachs researcher in Bangalore, practices this blessings routine daily and with sincerity. He's a prime example of a Westernized, educated Indian who's a complex mix of the traditional and the modern. Although it may be unfamiliar to you, respect this practice and Indians will respect you in return.

Attending and participating in religious business ceremonies

Religion is a way of life in India, and religious business ceremonies are common occurrences. Everything a Hindu does is an act offered up to God, and emphasis is placed on the acts themselves, not rewards for the acts. So each new beginning is dedicated to the Gods to seek their blessings, and new beginnings associated with business in India are no exception.

Ceremonies for office openings and groundbreakings

Two of the most common business events that include religious ceremonies are the opening of new offices and the breaking of ground for new facilities. These ceremonies are very important and can be quite lengthy. Indians appreciate your participation, but don't feel that you have to be present for the whole show.

I know of five Westerners who stood for two hours in the blazing sun participating in the opening ceremonies of their new gas plant in northern India. Their Indian colleagues were very keen that they come and were pleased to see them in attendance. But what the Westerners didn't know was that it would have been okay for them to ask for the time of the main *muhurat,* or finale, and attend only that portion of the proceedings. Little did they know that they could have been there for a fraction of the time and still enjoyed the benefits of standing through the entire ceremony!

Indians don't take offense at being asked for the time of the muhurat of a business-related religious ceremony. Show up for that portion and you can satisfy your colleagues without conceding a large chunk of your time.

A full groundbreaking ceremony is likely to proceed as follows:

1. **A priest recites ancient scriptures in Sanskrit.**

2. **A hole is dug in the ground and a sapling (usually a mango tree) is planted to symbolize growth.**

3. **Bricks are laid to symbolize nine planets.**

4. **A coconut, the symbol of plenty, is offered to bless the project.**

5. **The manager is asked to place bricks in the ground as a mark of respect to mother earth.**

6. **Holy water is sprinkled on guests as a blessing of nature.**

Food is always served after any ceremony, so expect plenty to eat.

The launch of a factory is also cause for a ceremony. A priest chants in Sanskrit about lucky beginnings, and machines and tools are honored. Eager to see that everything functions as it should, factory workers are pleased to see such blessings bestowed upon their equipment. The elephant-headed God Ganesha, remover of obstacles, also is worshipped. And (of course) guests eat, or at least enjoy plenty of sweets.

Office prayer ceremonies

Another common religious business ceremony is an office *puja,* or prayer ceremony. At a puja, stand with your palms folded in front of your chest. If lighted camphor is brought to you, hold your hands palms down over the flame for an instant and then gesture as if you're touching your closed eyes. Watch how others do the action before you, or ask for help if you're unsure. Indians take your interest as a compliment.

Holy water or fruit may be offered at a puja, and if it is, keep in mind that refusing it would be rude. Sprinkle a few drops of the spoonful of holy water on your head, letting most of it run to the ground discreetly. Raise the food in your cupped palm (right hand only or right hand supported by your left below) toward your closed eyes in a gesture of reverence before you eat. If you don't want to eat it, put it away discreetly *after* the gesture of reverence.

Remembering a Goddess

On special occasions such as *Ayudha Puja,* which is celebrated with verve and style in southern India around September, Indians show respect to tools of trade with a unique religious business ceremony. At such a ceremony, it's customary to place an auspicious dot of sandalwood paste and/or kumkum powder on doors, filing cabinets, computers, and other equipment. The dot is a sign of respect for the Goddess Saraswati, the muse of learning. Respect this tradition but remember that it's okay to ask your Indian staff to go easy on the placement of the dots. If necessary, the next morning you can quietly ask your maintenance staff to do a thorough clean-up job.

At an official ceremony, bowing along with your Indian counterparts is a touching show of camaraderie, but you're not expected to follow suit.

The core of India's spiritual wisdom

The world comes to India for its trade and teachings, and Indians have always been merchants and monks. The Bhagwad Gita (Celestial Song) is the jewel in India's tradition of spiritual wisdom. It has 18 chapters and 700 verses of pure advice on how to live your life. It teaches three main things:

✔ Do your duty without looking for results.

✔ There is a common divinity in all beings.

✔ The real goal of life is salvation.

Most Indians are raised in this philosophy.

Enjoying Indian religious festivals

As a multicultural society that incorporates adherents of many religions, India celebrates a multitude of holidays of various faiths and special interest groups (see Table 15-1 for details). Indians gladly participate in festivals of other religions because they view the ceremonies as social functions, and your participation in the festivals associated with these holidays can endear you to Indians. So expect a hurt or confused look if you turn down an invitation for religious reasons! Here's some advice to see you through religious festivals:

✔ **Remove your shoes.** For ceremonies at home or at the office, the first rule is to take off your shoes at the door. (Keep your socks on if you wish.) You can easily tell where to leave your footwear — just look for a jumbled pile of shoes, sandals, strappy stilettos, and the odd bathroom slipper.

✔ **Follow the crowd and listen to instructions.** Go with the flow if you notice a male-female division in the seating arrangements. If you prefer to sit with your partner, go to the back of the room. Follow instructions when possible, but if none are forthcoming, take a peek at what others are doing and act as they do. Be prepared for the limelight; as a visitor and a Westerner, you may be seated prominently, and you could even be invited on stage and asked to speak!

✔ **Engage in conversation.** Ask your host or neighbors questions about the ceremony. (Work out an escape route beforehand — you may get more information than you bargained for!) Quiet observation may be regarded as being aloof, so get involved. Don't expect dignified decorum. Everyone will be talking and laughing, so join in. It's fun!

✔ **Graciously accept gifts and offerings.** You may be offered a garland if you're the guest of honor or if you're visiting a temple. Bow down to let someone place it around your neck and comment on its beauty. After that, it's perfectly acceptable to take off the garland and carry it on your arm or place it respectfully close by (that may be taken as a sign of humility). When you leave, take the garland with you to show your appreciation.

Similarly, you may receive an offer of *kumkum* (vermilion powder) in a little box or tray at any ceremony. Delicately dip the tip of your ring finger into it and place a small dot of it on your forehead. Someone may want to apply this for you; if you feel uncomfortable, you can wipe it off discreetly after the person leaves or you move out of sight.

✔ **Don't be alarmed at the ritual actions of other guests.** Many Indians bend down on both knees and bow their heads to touch the ground to seek blessings before elders or at an altar. Men may even fall flat on the ground facedown. In the north, people don't go that far; they just make a quick dip down toward the person's feet. Expatriates and visitors aren't expected to do it. Just don't jump backward if someone bends down before you. You may encounter this act on someone's birthday or wedding if they're seeking your blessings, or, as businessman John McGreggor found, if someone seeks your forgiveness. John's gardener, whom he had fired, fell at his feet and asked to be taken back. If someone bends down before you, swallow your alarm, hold your palms together in the namaste style (explained in the earlier section "Greeting colleagues") and say "God bless you."

Table 15-1	Important Festivals Demystified		
Festival Name	*Purpose*	*What Is Done*	*Holiday Status*
Bakrid	To commemorate sacrifice	The patriarch of Muslim families sacrifices a goat and shares with the poor in a symbolic gesture.	A sectional holiday (businesses are closed in regions with many Muslims)
Christmas	To celebrate the birth of Jesus Christ	Christian church and carol services are rounded off with feasts that combine Western tradition with Indian cuisine.	A national holiday
Diwali	To celebrate the victory of good over evil	Oil lamps are lit in homes, and fireworks boom through the night. Rich Indian sweets are distributed.	A national holiday

Festival Name	Purpose	What Is Done	Holiday Status
Dusshera or Durga Puja	To mark the death of the demon Ravana; in East India, to commemorate the goddess Durga	In north India, a ten-day play, Ramlila, commemorates the epic battle between Rama (symbolizing good) and Ravana (evil); On Dusshera a giant effigy of the ten-headed Ravana is burned to much celebration.	A holiday in Eastern India
Eid-ul-Fitr	To mark the end of Ramadan	Celebration in Muslim homes with the eating of biryani and sharing with other friends.	An optional holiday in some states
Gandhi Jayanti	To celebrate the birthday of Mahatma Gandhi	Debates and speeches are organized in schools, and no alcohol is served in public areas.	A national holiday
Gokul Ashtami or Krishna Jayanti	To celebrate the birthday of Lord Krishna	Hindus worship Krishna. Homes and altars are decorated, and traditional sweets are enjoyed.	A holiday in most of India
Holi	To commemorate the arrival of spring	Social and age barriers are breached, and people have fun smearing each other with colored powders.	A very important holiday in north India
Indian Independence Day	To celebrate India's independence	Parades wind through the capital and flags are hoisted in schools and government offices.	A national holiday
Republic Day	To celebrate India becoming a republic	The president watches a military parade in New Delhi.	A national holiday

(continued)

Table 15-1 *(continued)*

Festival Name	Purpose	What Is Done	Holiday Status
Vinayak Chaturthi	To celebrate the birthday of the elephant-headed God Ganesha	Hindus worship clay idols of Ganesha. Huge statues adorn street corners and days later are removed in a procession and immersed into the ocean. Ganesha's favorite foods are made and enjoyed.	A holiday in most of India

Managing Personnel Relations

You can expect your relationships with Indian employees to be different than what you encounter in a Western office. The dynamics are worth exploring, and it helps to know what to expect so that you're not caught off guard.

Offering constructive criticism

Personal and business personas are intricately intertwined in India, and many Indians find separating them difficult. When you criticize someone's work or ideas, be aware that the employee may take it as a personal attack. Contrary to the Western habit of calling a spade a spade in business dealings, in India it's normal to sugarcoat the bitter pill.

Pair criticism with praise. Begin by saying that you generally appreciate the person you're talking to and then work your way toward mentioning the one small thing you want changed. Like anyone, Indians appreciate the consideration.

Here's an example: To bring your tardy Indian secretary up to snuff, say "I know how hard you usually work, but you didn't deliver this project in time. I'd like to see it on my table Monday." In the West, just the last sentence may be enough to do the trick, but it won't work in India.

DISTILLED WISDOM

Getting up close and personal

In India, personal questions are just a way of showing sincere interest and trying to understand other people's lives. For instance, consider the Dutchman, newly arrived in India, who told his Indian friend that he'd just bought a new house and had moved in last week. "That's lovely," the friend replied. "How much did you pay?" Completely floored, the Dutchman remarked that no one so far had asked him that question, not even his mother. The Indian friend apologized and said, "In India, I would have asked my parents, my uncle in Mumbai, my aunt in Bangalore, and my cousins, too, before making a big decision like buying a house. It's a permanent step, you know!"

You may eventually end up taking such conversations in stride. Consider this: Mark and Cathy had just signed a lease on a new house in India and were talking with their new landlord. "Do you have any issues?" the landlord asked.

"Issues?" Mark replied. "No, none at all." He looked at Cathy. "We don't have any issues do we? We're all set." Suddenly, realization dawned that by "issues" the Indian landlord meant *children*. "Oops," Mark said. "We don't have any children yet." "Oh, I wish you all the best in the new home," said the landlord. "And may you have a hundred sons!" A son was born to Cathy and Mark the next year, and the landlord and the new parents celebrated life together.

Taking it personally

Taking an interest in the personal lives of your employees and coworkers is considered polite in India. To you, this sort of attention may seem nosy. You may receive questions on matters you consider extremely private, but you have to remember that the questions are only an indication of your Indian colleague's healthy interest in you. The sidebar "Getting up close and personal" illustrates the sometimes confusing nature of these inquiries.

Reining it in: Letting off steam in private

Indians regard ranting and raving as a personal relationship accusation and not just a work-related tirade. So you may feel ballistic about an employee's poor performance, but you need to hold your fire.

Indians consider emotional outbursts by expatriates demoralizing and disrespectful even if you're motivated only by your zeal in getting the work done right. Such behavior is never excusable or necessary in Indians' eyes.

Never, ever use swear words in conversations with your Indian business colleagues. Foul language may be a casual, meaningless part of your vocabulary, but it's greatly resented in India.

Doing damage control

Until you're familiar with the ins and outs of Indian business etiquette, you may tread on some toes. But damage can always be undone. Here's how to mend the fence with an Indian colleague:

✔ Show appreciation for or compliment your colleague.

✔ Use humor to wipe his frown away.

✔ Make a joke about yourself or try some self-deprecatory remarks.

A simple and sincere apology to the offended party, particularly within earshot of someone he or she values, goes over very well in India.

Firing an Indian employee

Indian managers give unsatisfactory employees room to wriggle out and hand in their resignation rather than be fired. An Indian boss who has to fire someone makes an effort to cushion the blow by giving a notice period or money in lieu of the notice even by suggesting where the employee can look for another job. Try taking the same approach with your employees if it doesn't go against your company's policy.

One technique is to ask how you can collectively resolve the problem; point out that you need *this* whereas the employee in question needs *that*. Usually the employee says, "Maybe you could find someone else." And you readily agree!

This is how it works for professional staff. For blue-collar workers, "due processes" are required, and firing these employees is quite cumbersome. I talk more about terminating staff in Chapter 7.

Working on Indian Time

Many Indians have a sense of time and urgency that's quite different from that of the Western world. Because Indians have lots of sunlight and daytime hours, they consider time to be plentiful. Indians may arrive late, digress from a topic, meet you at short notice, give you all the time you need, take

The vagueness of time

Mike, an American businessman, was planning a meeting with his Indian counterpart, Sunil Das. Mike asked about the time of their meeting the following day, and Sunil replied, "Oh, 10:00 or 10:30 is fine." Mike was confused. "What do you mean? Is it 10:00 or 10:30?" Sunil replied, "Yeah, in that timeframe."

So Mike arrived at 9:50, was shown into the plush visitors' meeting room, and declined offers of coffee, tea, and water. "But have a little," pressed his host, Sunil. "The coffee is freshly ground and very good." Mike, who really didn't want any refreshment, accepted a cup of coffee to be polite. The coffee arrived, they drank it, and still the other participants invited for the meeting didn't arrive. Sunil plied Mike

with questions about his flight over and the hotel he was staying at and asked who had come with him, what his wife and children did back home, and so on.

They continued to drink more coffee as the clock crept to 10:25. One member of the team still had yet to arrive. Mike shifted in his seat and asked, "Do we know why Kavita isn't here?" "Oh, she said she was stuck in traffic," Sunil replied, "but she'll make it in 10 or 15 minutes." The talk veered to the recent elections and cricket.

Finally, at 10:45, Kavita arrived, commented that the traffic was unbelievable in the morning these days, and the meeting finally started!

the time they need to respond to something, and not think of it as a big deal if they need additional hours for a project or activity. As long as the objectives are met, what's a little give-and-take of time between colleagues? If you're consistently punctual, however, your Indians colleagues and acquaintances will get the message sooner or later.

Carry your laptop or Blackberry to get work done while you wait for colleagues. Having something to do passes the time and also keeps you relaxed. You don't want to start your business meeting tense and uptight while the other members of the team can't understand what's bothering you.

In the workplace, double-check on important things long before the deadline to avoid last-minute disappointments. Educated or Westernized Indians and those who have worked for multinational companies have figured out how to monitor themselves and meet their deadlines more responsibly. But be prepared to adjust to a different concept of punctuality with patience.

Chapter 16

Avoiding Potholes on the Road to Success

● ●

In This Chapter

▶ Getting a feel for possible problems

▶ Identifying and avoiding contractual trouble spots

▶ Taking action when plans go awry

▶ Understanding Indian idiosyncrasies

▶ Making preparations to exit business in India

● ●

Recently, I was driving an American client down an IT corridor in a major Indian city. He kept gasping, "Wow, look at all the growth!" as we passed sleek glass and steel structures built by Microsoft, Dell, Infosys, Tata, and others. He was amazed. But never once did he say, "Hmmm . . . look at the potholes in this road," although we were bumping over several. I was delighted, but our trip made me think how important this chapter was going to be. It's easy to get excited about the success and possibilities in India, but the potholes need to be taken into account, as well.

Doing business in India can be satisfying and very rewarding, but it's not always just smiles and handshakes and healthy profits. You encounter obstacles, as well, and it's imperative that you figure out to first guess where the potholes are likely to be on your road to success, and to then negotiate them so they don't hold you up or stop you in your tracks. In this chapter I point out some of the potential problems on your road to a successful business venture and clue you in on how you can effectively dodge them.

Planning for Common Pitfalls

Problems in India come in different shapes and sizes. Some may be familiar to you, others may fall outside your realm of experience, and still others are completely unique to India. You can't plan for every single hazard, but you can develop a defensive plan to counter the most common problems, and that strategy pays off in the long run.

Avoiding unsafe assumptions

One of the most important rules for doing business is don't make assumptions. You need to constantly remind yourself that you're operating in an alien scenario, where certain perceptions and needs are completely new to you. Many practices, standards, and patterns you're used to in the West simply don't exist in India. Assumptions can wreak havoc in a variety of areas, and I've included a few important ones in this section.

When making your Indian business plans, remember that a desk survey or simple Internet research doesn't reveal all the business information you need. If at all possible, you should dispatch a senior executive or other key employee (if not a team) to assess first hand the real flavor of the Indian business scenario.

Accounting for differences: CPAs and CAs

One example of how assumptions can lead to trouble in India can be seen in the different ways an accountant in the country reviews a balance sheet as compared to a similar analysis from a Western counterpart. You may assume that an accountant in Chennai and one in, say, Boston would evaluate a business's balance sheet in the same way, but that's not the case.

Indian accountants are called CAs (chartered accountants), and their intimate knowledge of the Indian economy and business environment gives them a clear advantage when it comes to thoroughly analyzing a balance sheet over a CPA from the United States. A CA evaluates costs and predicts profits with a much higher level of accuracy.

Make sure you consult an Indian CA for your accounting needs, or better yet, find a CPA-qualified CA. These diamonds in the rough are Indian CAs who have successfully passed CPA exams. If you want accounting analysis in a familiar format but with an Indian viewpoint, find one of these professionals. Many major multinational corporations are tapping them already, and although they're still a rare breed, a high-end head-hunting firm should be able to help hook you up with one.

Making sure you insure

Don't assume that the Indian facility you rent for your business is adequately insured. You may be able to assume that back West, but in India you'd be a fool to take that leap of faith. This reality has provided more than a few rude (and costly) awakenings for foreigners who see their Indian facilities damaged and have nowhere to turn.

Be sure you take the time to confirm the details of your facility's insurance before you take possession, and if everything isn't up to snuff take action immediately to set the situation straight.

Weighing the options for export errors

Regular compliance checks aren't a sure thing in India. For instance, you may assume that for exports, weighing equipment at ports all over the globe is checked accurately and can be counted on to produce reliable measurements. Not so in India. In order for weighing equipment to work properly, it must be checked and calibrated regularly by a competent professional agency. In the port of Kandla, Gujarat, the equipment is checked just once every six months by a government agency. The Port Trust authorities don't even allow a reputable private agency to examine and calibrate the equipment! And that means that the weight measurements there are a crapshoot at best.

Dealing with inadequate infrastructure

Distribution is perhaps the biggest challenge any manufacturer faces. Don't make the assumption that just because your product is a winner and your target audience is eager you're going to bring your goods to market effectively.

The unorganized market in India is characterized by inefficient distribution systems and profiteering by intermediaries. The producer of goods and the consumers both suffer in the process. A lack of infrastructure (cold storages, roads, transport systems, and distribution networks) and bureaucratic indifference also lead to inefficiencies in distribution, and the end results are massive losses and waste. For example, more than 20 percent of the food items in India are wasted because of lack of proper storage, transport, and processing facilities. India, incidentally, is the largest producer of food grains and milk and the second largest producer of fruits and vegetables in the world, so the waste is tremendous.

Reaching every corner of India and its dispersed markets is a distribution challenge, but it can be overcome. Think creatively about your distribution problems, and consult with your Indian colleagues for solutions. Many inventive companies have developed resourceful modes of distribution, like three-wheelers that deliver goods right into the villages without needing any roads.

Coping with corruption

Corruption exists in the world, and in India it's more of a problem, or at least it's easier to spot. The levels of corruption in India range from very serious to not so serious. The vast majority of instances fall in the latter category. The promise of increased profits and new channels may entice you to consider unsavory business maneuverings, but please resist the temptation.

You may also find a member of the clerical staff demanding a small tip to speed your file through a permissions process, for example. Although the sum may seem trivial and the violation minor, stick to your guns and play it safe. The straight and narrow is the way to go if you're interested in long-term success. Join hands with avant-garde Indians who work tirelessly to eliminate corruption. Many, if not all, multinational companies I have seen stayed squeaky clean and have enjoyed much success with their projects.

If you're wary of corruption in a specific situation, consult your Indian agent or partner. He can better judge what's appropriate and what's not.

Avoiding a mixture of business and politics

Politics and business, as the saying goes, make strange bedfellows. Yet attempts at combining the two are made regularly in India, as elsewhere in the world. In India, though, things may take a slightly more bizarre turn. There have been several cases where the government has encouraged the setting up of industries or the creation of special economic zones without so much as a shred of business logic or social awareness. This happens when a local politician (the area's elected representative in the State Assembly or Parliament at the Federal level) is anxious to earn brownie points for his "progressive" thinking.

If you jump on board and support such a politician, your business could be in rough shape if the opposition wins out. Your files may be carefully scrutinized and other aspects of your business may be under the microscope.

This scenario isn't unique to foreign companies. One Indian smelting company wanted to set up shop in Ratnagiri, Maharashtra. Some political finagling allowed the plans to be moved forward quite quickly without concern for the plant's effect on the area. Quite a few documents were signed and sealed, and machinery was even shipped. However, at the last moment, serious public outcry halted the project. People said that plant emissions would kill the prestigious Alphonso mango trees — their fruits are a staple export of Maharashtra — and the smelter wasn't built. The entire project was moved to Tuticorin in southern India, where it's now smelting away profitably. If the company would have taken official routes from the beginning, that costly last-minute move could've been foreseen and accounted for or even avoided.

Making security a top concern

As you begin to do business in India, plan to be vigilant about security. Security breaches and other problems can curtail your success and shake your business to its core. I provide some information in the next sections to make sure that you're aware of and prepared for security issues at the micro and macro levels.

Securing at the micro level

Intellectual Property Rights (IPR) are the rights of persons who have created and own intellectual property such as a specific manufacturing process, an invention, an original piece of writing, or an identifying trademark or business name of a product. Such intellectual property is protected under trademarks, patent, and copyright laws. These laws prevent unauthorized use or sale of the protected intellectual property for a specified duration.

Intellectual property rights are being protected now more than ever before, but many of the safeguards are implemented on a large scale, not on a smaller, everyday level. There are laws to enforce intellectual property rights in India, but the backlog is currently clogging up the legal system.

To help avoid intellectual property rights problems in India, insist on thorough background checks for potential employees during the recruitment process. In addition to background checks, you can use technology to your advantage and install several layers of protection for your most important files, documents, and communications. Don't skimp on the necessary equipment, and you're much safer in the long run.

Recently reports indicate that India has some unsavory employees leaking confidential information, from engineering drawings and advertising campaigns to customer credit card information.

Looking at the macro level

India has had stable central governments for at least a decade now, and the results are evident in the economic progress the country has made. But having a federal system of governance has its cons as well. (For more details, flip back to Chapter 8.)

Friction does exist, and though political instability isn't a major threat to your business, it can't be completely ruled out, either. When governments shake and fall, bureaucracy and policies change, which may affect your business plan. So keep abreast of happenings and trends, either personally or through a consultant.

On a smaller, day-to-day scale, there can be minor hiccups that can affect work to a lesser extent. For instance, take a look at protests. These outbreaks can happen about anything — from a government policy to the perceived callousness of officials in a local road mishap — and can escalate into *bandhs* or *hartals* (strikes that can cause a shut-down of normal life). Business establishments don't work, shops close down, and government offices, schools and colleges even close. Most times, bandhs last either 12 or 24 hours and are announced in advance so you can make adequate arrangements. But sometimes they come out of the blue, and you can be stuck with business delays and interruptions.

This pothole is one you can't fill. Simply just ask your staff not to open your office when a bandh is occurring and then ride out the trouble. Because even though non-violent protest is the stated goal, things can go wrong very quickly, resulting in damage to your property.

Dodging Problems with Your Indian Contracts

First and foremost, you can't underestimate the importance of articulate language in an Indian contract. The reason for this may seem simplistic to you — allow no room whatsoever for misinterpretation — but this needs to be heavily underscored in the Indian context, given the Indian penchant for flowery language. If you sign a contract with an Indian party, and leave it to them to draw up the documents, chances are you and your legal advisors back home can get hopelessly entangled in convoluted phrases and split infinitives. So keep it short and simple.

Make sure you're on the same wavelength as your partner when working on a contract. Are you both looking for a long-term relationship, or is one of you interested in a short-term arrangement? Indians usually prefer a longer-term partnership. Also, are you on the same page in regards to priorities and focus?

Testing the waters with a pilot project is always a good idea before signing a long-term contract. Before you sign on the dotted line with your Indian partner/agent/supplier, agree to a trial run. This time not only gives you a chance to assess whether you can work with each other, but also it can reveal potential problems, which you can then eliminate.

The rest of this section contains a few other core concerns you should consider when working on your contracts. (I don't include any information on commercial terms, which are of course unique to each contract). Check out Chapter 13, where I discuss the ins and outs of nailing down a good contract for your business dealings in India.

Delivery date and time

When including a detail about delivery timing in a contract, be as precise as possible. For example, if the delivery date happens to fall on a public holiday when everything is closed, how does that affect delivery? Your contract should include a provision that addresses that situation. Nailing down an extremely specific delivery date and time cuts out the possibility of frustrating wiggle room.

Governing law

Make completely certain in your contract which laws are set as the governing laws. This detail is vital in the event of non-performance or default.

Mediation and arbitration

If something goes wrong in a big way (if a contract is seriously breached, for example), some companies do opt for legal action. But the legal path in India is slow and tortuous, and arbitration and mediation are more efficient ways to resolve contract disputes. Some companies go to court but are also open to a negotiated settlement, and often that is the best course of action.

Arbitration is the process by which an arbitrator, who is a neutral third party, usually a qualified lawyer, reviews a dispute between two sides, according to a previously agreed-upon set of rules, and gives a decision. The two sides are allowed to present evidence and cross-examine the other's witnesses, just as in a regular court. The arbitration hearings are usually held in the arbitrator's office. You can add an arbitration clause in your contract, specifying the governing laws. Recourse to this means of dispute resolution, however, need not be final because the parties have the right to challenge the decision of the arbitrator and take the matter to regular Court.

Arbitration is an adversarial process where one side may win and the other correspondingly loses the case. The arbitrator decides the case based on the facts and the law just like any judge. The only difference is that arbitration is more informal and the parties are free to choose the applicable law of arbitration. Typically, commercial, construction and shipping disputes are referred to arbitration.

Mediation is also taking root in India. It's recognized by the Arbitration and Conciliation Act. Settlements reached through mediation are enforceable. It's a non-risk, participatory, and solution-oriented choice you can add to your contract in the form of a clause that appears prior to an arbitration clause. Increasingly, inter-corporate disputes are being settled through mediation.

A mediator is someone who, though he is a neutral third party like an arbitrator, merely facilitates an agreement between two disputing sides. He collects information, sets out options, but passes no judgment. Instead, he helps negotiate a settlement between the two parties, often talking to each separately and together. When a settlement has been reached, the two sides sign a binding settlement agreement. Arbitration is adversarial and can be procedural; mediation is consensual and far more flexible.

A successful mediation ends with a settlement that's voluntarily agreed on by both sides. In a certain sense, mediation results in a win-win situation and puts an end to the litigation. In an arbitration, the aggrieved party has a limited right of appeal; in a mediation, the parties resolve their disputes forever and there is no question of going in appeal. Mediation puts an end to litigation while arbitration does not. Moreover, in mediation, any party is free to withdraw itself from the mediation process while expressing his or her reluctance to continue with the case at any stage. All proceedings in a mediation are completely confidential and nothing said during the mediation process is admissible in evidence in a court of law.

Force Majeure

The *force majeure* clause is a standard element in an international contract, and it's often taken for granted or overlooked. This clause more or less frees one or both parties from liability or obligation when an unforeseen or extraordinary event prevents one or both parties from fulfilling their obligations under the contract. Such events include war, natural disasters, and other "Acts of God." In India, however, you need to pay special attention to it and make sure that your contract covers all the important details. I suggest that you pay special attention to the following areas:

- ✔ **Insurance:** Does your force majeure clause cover weight loss beyond an acceptable percentage when weighing equipment? See "Making sure you insure" earlier in this chapter.

- ✔ **Arbitration:** Stipulate that arbitration be held outside of India, so you can ensure a neutral resolution to the problem at hand. I include more information on arbitration in Chapter 13.

Making Adjustments when Your Business Plan Goes off Track

You may experience a time when your business's course varies from your plan. When that happens, don't panic. Instead, focus on analyzing and understanding the reasons for the variances, and think about what you can do to adjust for them.

Market volatility can always impact a plan and can't be accurately forecasted. However, it can be analyzed and understood after it happens. For help with this analysis, seek professional Indian help in the form of marketing professionals. It's worth the time and expense. (I cover the importance of coming up with a solid business plan in Chapter 4.)

But also make sure that you take a look at variances from your Indian business plan that can't be explained by market force volatility. This is where an understanding of a few Indian market idiosyncrasies come in handy.

Delays in customs clearance

For businesses in India that depend on vital imported components, any delay in receiving is a huge cost factor that can considerably impact the profits. Delays are likely, so you need to know about the problems in order to minimize or avoid them.

Incorrect nomenclature of the imported component

More than 80 percent of customs delays are the result of incorrect nomenclature (mislabeled packages). India follows the International Harmonic Code of Classification of Goods, which is hugely helpful, but when it comes to export/import invoicing, companies more often than not get a bit careless. When that happens, Indian customs officials can't correctly classify the goods, and delays start piling up.

In Chapter 11, I talk about rapid changes in technology and the difficulties faced by the Indian Customs Rule Book in keeping pace. This leads to confusion and additional delays, and the best you can hope for is to either establish or cite a precedent to speed things along. You or your agent can study similar cases and find out if you can argue your way out of a tight situation, citing those records. Once you've managed it, you can cite your own precedent. The possibility of delay on this account has to be factored into the business plan.

Weight discrepancies and theft

If you run into weight discrepancies as you import and export goods through Indian ports, incorrect calibrations of the weighing equipment are often to blame. If you have a good Indian consultant or source of reliable information at the port, they can make you aware of the problem in advance. You can also take preventative measures early in the game by writing into your contract for the deal that the weighing equipment must be inspected and approved by a neutral authority.

Theft has also been an issue. Not long ago India was faced with a sudden shortage of cooking (vegetable) oil, and it had to import palm oil from Malaysia. Oil was shipped in bulk loads of about 20,000 tons, which were offloaded into shore tanks. From the tanks, oil was pumped into ten-ton truck tankers which then took the cargo to packaging units where the oil was put in cans for retail distribution. But frequently the tanker truck drivers would siphon off the oil (one method was to fill up empty tire tubes) to sell on the black market! Pilferage from dock areas was also a problem. Commodities like metal powders were stolen so much that importers were at one time insisting on a 150 percent insurance policy for their goods.

Quality control

If manufacturing's your business, nothing's more frustrating than getting a high percentage of rejects at the end of the manufacturing line. And the damage can be severe if the products make it to market and damage your company's image in the eyes of consumers.

A number of companies follow standard techniques for business process improvement, but unfortunately a large number of companies lie at the other end of the spectrum, too. Quality compromises turn up in quite a few places, including machine lubricants, maintenance, and tolerances. These factors and more can contribute to a poor quality finished product, and if proper quality controls are in place, you can experience a high rate of rejected products.

Don't compromise on the quality of your products. Be sure to spell out your standards clearly at the outset, make sure that they are met consistently, and keep tabs on compliance.

Labor problems

Your business plan may also suffer from issues of labor management. This problem in India has been politically managed instead of professionally understood. In government-managed companies, for example, it's virtually impossible for the management to fire a worker. Indian steel plants, avionics, and airlines can attest to that fact. This is where perhaps the role of HR is truly appreciated.

The good news for you is that nothing succeeds like success. Once the Indian workforce has tasted the fruits of prosperity, they are far less likely to pull the trigger on lock-outs and "work-to-rule" agitation, which are akin to the non-cooperation concept and involve workers who won't strike but won't offer any more than the bare minimum effort at work until their demands are addressed. But if your business succeeds and your Indian team is rewarded with the benefits of that success, you have little to worry about when it comes to labor management issues.

Getting Familiar with Indian Idiosyncrasies

A large percentage of Indian workers — even middle and senior management — hasn't had much exposure to international business. Although this fact is changing rapidly, don't be surprised if you end up working with Indian colleagues and partners that seem like they need a crash course in working with foreign businesspeople, particularly Westerners.

In this section, I clue you in on a few Indian idiosyncrasies that you may notice while you're helping your Indian colleagues get used to working with foreigners.

Understanding India-speak

It's true that one of the advantages of doing business in India is the prevalence of Indians who speak English. That said, it's important for you to realize and appreciate that Indian English is probably quite different from your English, and it takes some getting used to before you can comprehend it without missing a beat.

Don't get hyper about hyperbole

One example of India-speak is the Indian fondness for hyperbole (exaggeration). If one of your Indian colleagues says, "I have been to London very often," you may take that to mean that he has been there a dozen or so times. In reality, he may have visited London only twice! He's not trying to mislead you; it's just that the adjective *very* tends to be a bit overused in Indian English.

Other common uses of hyperbole can be problematic in business situations. If an Indian says "I can get that done very easily" or "Things are going very well here," you may think that all is well. But don't be so sure — press for details, probe, and question to make sure that you get the real picture. "I will send it to you in a couple of days" doesn't mean "two" days — it really means "a few" days, so be aware!

Certain words and phrase may pop up the most. Follow up on these examples if you hear them from an Indian employee or partner:

- **Always:** It's *always* on time.
- **Believe:** I *believe* this is true.
- **Must**: It *must* be true because it's in the news.
- **Sure:** I'm *sure* this will be profitable.
- **Think:** I *think* it's all right to go ahead.

What was said and what was meant

You should also watch out for phrases and sayings that are different in India than they are in the West. For example, if you bring up a topic and your Indian colleague enthusiastically asks that you "table it," your first reaction may be to take offense because he's asking to postpone the conversation until later. Not so fast! In India, if someone suggests that you table something, that means that they want to discuss it immediately. Or if an Indian asks you if you "ticked off" the most important bugs on the list, he isn't asking if you got annoyed, he simply means "checked off."

Silence isn't golden

If you're in a meeting and one of your suggestions or comments is met with silence, don't mistake it for consent and agreement. Indians may remain silent and refrain from contradicting you out of respect for you and your seniority, but that certainly doesn't mean you've convinced them.

Why you won't hear "I don't know"

Many Indians have a very hard time saying the three little words "I don't know." Foreign businesspeople doing business in India for the first time are often startled by the fact that Indians won't make that simple admission of ignorance. Instead of saying "I don't know," most Indians choose to express an opinion, however uninformed. They say "I think this is because of . . ." Don't fall for it! Confront them and make it clear that it's better to admit to not knowing something than it is to dodge the situation or save face.

Getting a straight answer

Sometimes, you may feel that you're not getting a straight answer from an Indian colleague. It may seem like they're beating around the bush or evading your question. There may be several reasons for that. For example, Indians sometimes have a hard time relaying bad news or saying "no." A straight "no" is considered rude in India. Sometimes in a desire to please, the person may be conveying what they hope to do. They may say "I will try," instead of disappointing you. Make it clear that you're okay with hearing "no" when it's appropriate. The lack of a straight answer may also be the individual's verbose style. Help your staff member by prompting with "So what you're trying to say is . . . ."

When communicating with your Indian employees, give basic instructions, use simple commands, say "please," cut out flowery language, and ask them to repeat what you said to confirm understanding. And it never hurts to send an e-mail to further confirm that your point was well taken.

Indian acronyms

Modern Indian life — especially the media — is teeming with acronyms, and the sooner you get a handle on them, the sooner you're informed about the important events that can have an effect on your business.

> "RBI raises CRR to 6 percent."

In that headline, RBI stands for Reserve Bank of India and CRR refers to the credit reserve ratio. That news may be important to you, because the RBI (the apex bank in India) changed the credit reserve ration to contain inflation, and anything related to India's economy has a bearing on your bottom line. If you see an acronym that's unfamiliar or confusing, look up its meaning or simply ask an Indian colleague to decipher it for you!

Working on Indian time

Indian businesspeople are notoriously careless when it comes to time and punctuality. This became evident very soon after foreign businesses started flooding into India after liberalization. Thankfully, over the years the situation has improved.

You're much more likely to have an Indian partner show up on time for a meeting today than you would've been ten years ago. However, it's an integral part of an Indian's psyche to be careless with time, so don't go in expecting razor-sharp punctuality. What happens is time is seen as a range rather than an instant. It's flexible and stretched. This attitude can often be a bitter pill for ultra-efficient Westerners to swallow, but if you try and get used to it you can avoid a great deal of frustration and annoyance.

My cross cultural mentor Robert Kohls once pointed out that to Westerners, time is something to be on, kept, filled, saved, used, spent, wasted, lost, gained, planned, given, and even killed. "Don't expect Indians to understand this," he said. The best solution for dealing with these little differences is to keep a keen ear and ask questions when necessary.

Figuring out when trouble is brewing in the Indian workplace

As you slowly settle into your role as a seasoned Indian business veteran, you may start to discover the uniquely Indian cues that indicate trouble is brewing in the workplace. To help speed that process along, I want to bring to your attention a few red flags that are cause for an eyebrow-raising if you notice them in your employees.

You hear no protests, no matter how high you raise the bar

Indians can have a hard time saying "no." This fact can be extremely dangerous because your Indian team could be buried under an enormous pile of work but won't cry uncle when you continue to heap on the tasks. They'd rather save face and accept the excessive responsibilities than risk disappointing you with a negative answer.

As a check, ask your team a few times if they can handle everything you've given them, and also ask if they foresee any problems. You may also offer up some potential problems, and see what they can provide for possible solutions.

Your plans are under excessive scrutiny

If your Indian team is overloaded and needs to buy some time to get everything done, they may try to scrutinize some of your plans. (Remember that Indians invented chess, and they are adept at making you wait until they're ready and able to make a move.) To avoid this situation, ask for clarification and an explanation on what's causing the hold-up.

If you feel that something isn't quite right, don't stay silent and assume that your Indian team will let you know about the problem when they're good and ready. It simply won't happen soon enough. If you have to, play the part of the naive foreigner and say, "I don't understand." You can also send another member of your Indian staff to go and ask for an explanation from the party in question to satisfy the curiosity of the "foreign" boss.

Planning an Exit: It's Hard To Say Goodbye!

Ideally, an exit plan for your Indian business should be something like packing a parachute while taking a flight. It's an obvious precaution, but one that is commonly overlooked. Entering into a business anywhere should involve doing a risk-reward analysis at the outset. If that's done, any foreign investor is fully aware of the inherent risks and potential rewards from the beginning. An exit plan therefore comes into play only in extreme situations where just about everything has gone dreadfully wrong.

Exiting from a business in India isn't much different than from doing the same elsewhere in the world. The financial and personnel heartaches remain much the same. Probably the only significant difference is the legal factor (Chapter 13 points out the Indian legal system.)

Knowing when to say when

If you've tried every trick you know, knocked on all the doors in sight, and your business still isn't taking off, you may start thinking about pulling out. I usually advise my clients to try for at least a year, if possible. If at the end of that time you don't see how you're going to make it work, it's time to call it quits.

But don't lose heart. One foreigner I know came to India with the idea of getting into the leather business. He went all out to make it work, but for one reason or another, he found that he couldn't get the necessary clearances even after a year of trying. So he reluctantly had to abandon his plans. He did have a silver lining though: During the time he spent trying to get his idea to work, he chanced upon some other excellent business opportunities, and he has vowed to come back, next time with a solid plan for an Italian ice-cream company. So even if leaving India does feel like goodbye, it may be more like "see you later" than you think.

Taking care of your workers: Legal obligations

In India you can't just close up shop when you feel like it. There are laws, such as the Industrial Disputes Act and the Industrial Employment Act (see Chapter 13 for more details), which govern closure of organizations with a certain number of employees. Even some downsizing can't be done as a matter of course. "Hire and fire" is still very much a foreign concept.

An exit plan in India should always factor in the trade unions, because the right to association has provided both awareness and power to the working class, and they'll most likely know if they're entitled to something. Make provisions for every eventuality, with legal guidance, while handing out appointment letters and signing employment contracts.

Options do exist for your exploration. One of those options includes voluntary retirement schemes (VRS), where employees can opt to bow out, taking with them a compensation package worked out between the management and the workers' representatives or trade union. Called the *golden handshake,* it's often accepted by employees who feel their growth prospects are limited in the organization or who feel that the cash compensation adequately covers the loss of job security.

These schemes are only purely voluntary — employees can't be compelled to accept them. If you aren't careful, you may find that you're left with just the people you *don't* want. So be sure to study your own particular situation, and make sure your HR department is able to handle the scheme to get the results you desire.

For an overview of the legal angle, see `www.ilo.org/public/english/ dialogue/ifpdial/info/termination/countries/india.htm` or consult your Indian legal advisor.

Part V
The Part of Tens

"It's for people who have been using
'Obsession' too long."

In this part . . .

This classic *For Dummies* part is a perfect way for you to get quick information. In this part, you get information on managing your Indian workforce and managing the cultural quirks of the country, too! But don't forget to have some fun in your free time (make sure you save some time to be free, okay?). One chapter is dedicated just to ways to enjoy yourself while you're out of the office.

I also share with you the wisdom of an Indian business guru who lived 2000 years ago. His words are relevant for you today.

Chapter 17

Ten Tips for Training Your Team India

. . . .

In This Chapter

▶ Considering the best ways to train your Indian team

▶ Finding fun ways to team build

▶ Following up on your training

. . . .

*T*here's a wise quote in Sanskrit, India's oldest language, which says "He who's seeking knowledge should give up comfort; he who's seeking comfort should give up learning. For the knowledge seeker can't get comfort and a comfort seeker can't truly learn." This chapter looks at ways to impart knowledge to your team without getting them too far out of their comfort zone.

Through the years, I've seen businesspeople from abroad who face the task of training their Indian employees in a variety of different areas. Training sessions are essential for getting your Indian staff to understand a different work culture or even a company- or position-specific process.

Training Indian employees is different than training workers in the West, so you need to know a few tips and tricks to get the most out of your training sessions. And that's the point of this chapter: Discovering useful methods that yield positive results as you work to train your Indian team.

Using Real Life Anecdotes

Indians master tasks extremely well through the telling of illustrative stories. When training your Indian team, use stories to get your points across. Those points then stick in the minds of your employees, and they'll apply them in real work situations.

Traditionally, Indians all over the country read books called the *Puranas,* or Epic Tales. These stories feature heroes that have flaws and are as imperfect as the readers who embrace them. Throughout the course of the stories, the heroes learn, grow, and find ways to do things better.

When I train Indian employees about the importance of effective cross-cultural communication, I tell them about my experience trying to confirm an airline reservation in the United States. The airline employee needed the exact spelling of my name, so I spelled it out using words that started with the letters in my last name. I said, "M like monkey, A like Ahmedabad, N like Nagpur, I like ink, A like Ahmedabad, and N like Nagpur." Needless to say, the American who helped me was bamboozled! He said, "Lady, I was less confused before you started to spell that name!"

Using that story immediately earns me the attention of the employees I'm training, and as a result, they're much more receptive to mastering the international spelling code (A as in alpha, B as in bravo, and so on). You can achieve the same result if you take advantage of storytelling in your training!

Incorporating Interactive Games and Quizzes

Indians are serious about education, and they take it very seriously throughout their growing years. But if an element of fun is introduced into adult education, they take to it like fish to water. One way to inject some fun into your training sessions is to incorporate games and quizzes that allow employees to play an active role in the proceedings.

Here are a few steps to get you started:

1. **Divide your employees into teams or groups.**

   Indians are a collective lot, and they love teamwork.

2. **Assign someone to keep score.**

   Indians like to compete, especially if you keep score. As you play your training games, notice that your staff watches the scorekeeper keenly to keep tabs, make sure he's doing it right, and also to see who's winning.

3. **Start with a basic quiz.**

   Ask questions and allow the teams to jump in with their guesses. The questions can be about the material you're teaching or a few cultural tidbits, but either way, make the questions ones that they definitely know the answers too.

When I teach Indians a course on cross-cultural understanding (American culture), I first ask for the three favorite sports in America. They typically get that one right, and that gets them interested in the game. But then I ask them how to correctly pronounce *Potomac* or for the number of states in the continental United States. Those questions tend to stump them, and they really want to know the answer so they can continue performing well in the quiz which is one of the successful interactive games to use. It helps to use multiple choice questions to help encourage guesses too.

Trying Role Play

Indians enjoy drama and acting, and what they perform they remember. They especially like situational role playing. Acting is an exciting way to be taught and not a form of teaching that's often used in formal Indian classrooms.

One of the best uses of role playing I've ever seen came from an American trainer named Tom, who taught an Indian software call center team how to handle tough customers. Tom was playing the tough customer role, and he had one of his students trying to field the faux call. At one point, Tom said, "You guys are always making excuses. You can't really solve my backup problem!" The student was really getting into the situation, and explained, "We are here to help you, Tom, and we can solve the problem."

"Yeah? How?" Tom demanded, continuing the role play.

"We will walk you through your screens, understand the error, and offer solutions," the student said.

"What's different about that? The previous guy did the same things but my software backup problem is back again!" Tom countered. The student didn't have any more tricks up his sleeve, so Tom took over his role and showed the trainees how to deal with the irate customer. His audience was engrossed and soaked up the material like sponges.

Presenting a Trainer in the Right Light

If you choose to bring in an outside trainer to help train your Indian staff, be sure to establish her credibility and standing from the very beginning. Indians are more willing to study a subject and won't challenge a trainer's authority if you clearly explain why she's well qualified to conduct training sessions.

Toot your trainer's horn by listing her degrees, work experience, travels, and professional accomplishments to ensure that your employees are all ears when she begins imparting wisdom. As an old Indian saying goes, "Acharya devo bhava," which means "Treat the teacher as God." Make sure your employees know that your trainer is fit to take on such a lofty role.

Implementing a Useful Demonstration

Indians appreciate being shown how to do a task correctly, so take advantage of that tendency. If your business requires that something be done in a very specific way, set up a demonstration so your Indian team knows exactly what to do.

A major automotive manufacturer wanted to stress the importance of precisely painting its cars, so the plant manager came in to do a live car-painting demonstration for the Indian plant employees. He wore his overalls and showed everyone how to correctly paint one of the company's cars. This session had a positive effect on two levels — it showed the manager's respect for the work the Indian employees would be doing, and it also made clear the fact that the manager had the skills and knowledge necessary to do the job right. The Indians were impressed and inspired, and the session was a great success.

If you show your workers how to do a job correctly and with a sense of accountability, they gladly imitate you and work at a high level. After all, isn't imitation the sincerest form of flattery?

Giving Your Team Their Turn to Talk

The Indian educational system isn't famous for its opportunities to let Indians voice their opinions and communicate openly. At most levels, instruction consists of a highly respected teacher or professor who lectures a classroom full of silent, attentive Indian students. So don't be surprised if, during your training sessions, your Indian employees don't immediately offer much to a discussion. They probably won't offer much feedback or contribute their own experiences, unless you ask them a very specific question.

But just because they're silent doesn't mean that the people of India have nothing to say. Indians would love to speak up and share their thoughts and experiences as you train them. Give them the chance! Take the time to ask questions and spark discussion, and your employees will be extremely engaged and eager to dig deeper and deeper into the training material. And you may just uncover some great business ideas with your prompting.

The trick is to work out a balance between providing opportunities to speak and them getting too verbose! They may want to continue sharing their thoughts and go off on tangents. Keep an eye out for this problem, and nip it in the bud by thanking the long-winded employee and summing up what he said for the entire group in a concise manner.

Offering Specific Feedback

Throughout the course of training, you may want to offer your employees feedback and tips to make sure they're catching on and doing things correctly. This part of the process is important because you don't want your team to misunderstand the finer points of their jobs and get in the habit of making mistakes.

Indian students — in this case, your employees — aren't sensitive when it comes to receiving feedback, as long as you confirm when the training starts that it's okay that you offer pointers along the way. Make sure your staff knows that you offer input, and then your employees can take the feedback in a positive spirit and use the advice to get better.

I recommend giving feedback during a coffee or lunch break. Start by affirming something good about the employee and then point out the area in which he could do something a bit differently to improve his performance. Sometimes I tell my employees that I make (or have made) similar mistakes, and that seems to help the delivery. I practice doing things the right way and am now competent enough to teach others. Making yourself appear fallible helps in developing camaraderie, which you need in your business endeavors.

Using Interactive Q & A

Indians tend to enjoy interactive training, so spice up the sessions with some lively Q & A. Throw out an open question to the team and allow them to chime in with their ideas and answers. Most Indians are naturally competitive and work hard to come up with the correct responses before others in the room. When they do offer up a right answer, be sure to praise them because Indians value praise highly, especially in public and in front of their peers.

As you incorporate the Q & A sessions, remember that it is important to maintain control of the discussion and to steer the responses so that they are made one at a time with the right points being emphasized.

Establishing Your Expert Position

If you've been reading the other sections in this chapter, you know that helping your Indian team get over their shyness and getting them to become active participants in a training program are important, but just as crucial is the process of establishing yourself as an expert at the very start of training.

Your employees need to know that you're the boss and that what you say is important and should be taken to heart. Then your staff should apply your wisdom when they resume daily operations. Otherwise your Indian team may kid around a bit too much or start getting wordy with their responses to your questions.

Following Up on Training

As with any good training program, you need to follow up early and often with your Indian team after the training sessions are over. Because of other habits they developed while rising through the Indian educational system, such as not thinking out of the box or going beyond the scope defined, your employees probably won't continue to discover more about their jobs unless you build in follow-up mechanisms to help them along.

You can effectively follow up on your training sessions in many ways:

- ✔ Send out group e-mails featuring a communication-focused newspaper column to continually remind the employees of the importance of the material covered during training.

- ✔ Point your employees to Web sites or books that emphasize the main points of the training.

- ✔ Have a refresher hour to recap what had been taught and discuss how the team has applied their new knowledge since the training session.

Chapter 18

Ten Cultural Tips

After you dive into India's culture, you may feel a bit of culture shock. And you're not alone. *Culture shock* is a state of bewilderment that you may experience after suddenly being exposed to a new, strange, or foreign social and cultural environment. This phenomenon is as common as the common cold. In India, you get a double dose of shock, thanks to the country's merry mixture of extremes: wealth and poverty, breathtaking beauty and breath-holding squalor, secularism and fanaticism, bullock carts and satellites, superstition and science.

During your first few weeks in the country, you may be fascinated by the novelty of it all. You'll stay in hotels where the Indian staff is exceedingly polite and gracious to foreigners. You'll be shown around town and see exotic sights. You'll feel like you're on a honeymoon. But it will all be over soon.

As you try to adjust, you may begin to feel some hostility toward your host country. Familiarity is thrown out the window, and you may feel lost, desperately seeking some key cultural clues and cues.

To help ease the shock, I've included some helpful cultural pointers in this chapter. These tips should help you make it through the rough spots and become more acclimated to Indian culture.

Don't Touch!

India is a bit wary of body contact, and public displays of affection don't go over well. Westerners tend to like the firm handshake, steady eye contact, or a peck on the cheek as standards for a greeting, but that's not the case in India. Indians use *namaste,* a multi-purpose gesture made with folded hands (see Chapter 15 for details on namaste). A handshake is as much contact as Indians hazard for a greeting, and those run the gamut from limp to quite firm.

If, in a burst of enthusiasm, you embrace your newfound partner, you may have some explaining to do. To cut through the awkwardness, tell him or her that you're sorry if the hug was a surprise but that such displays are common in your culture. That should produce smiles all around.

Mind Your Language

When you're in India, don't use swear words. Even if the words mean nothing or if they're just words you use as a filler, bite your tongue. Swearing is absolutely not appreciated in India. People will clam up, leave a meeting sooner than you expect, or even not want to do business with you if you swear. Rarely will they tell you they don't appreciate it and you'll have to heal with hurt feelings that'll be hard to fix. You may also be looked at as unclassy and uncaring.

Once, on the Cosmopolitan Golf Course in Chennai, I noticed a Westerner ready to swing his club, when a Japanese man walked in front of him. Irritated by the distraction, the Westerner yelled, "Where the #@*^ did you come from?" The Japanese man bowed, and replied in a calm tone, "From Saitama prefecture." He did Asia proud that day, and you would do well to show the same level of restraint when you're in India.

Be Prepared for a Dry Day or Two

In the West, a drink is just the thing you may need after a tiring day at work, but in India, don't think that you can successfully find an alcoholic beverage to wet your whistle at any point of your day. There are dry days, hours, and even states, and alcohol sales are even illegal during certain holidays.

Don't scour the city looking for some place — any place — where you may get just one drink on a dry day. You may end up in hot water. October 2 is a dry day throughout India. Other dry days may be announced if there is a national mourning of some sort. No public consumption of alcohol is allowed, and you risk arrest if you violate this law. People can drink in their own homes or private residences, though no alcohol will be sold that day.

Keep It Official, but Don't Forget the Personal

Indians are basically conservative in social situations, and they may not like the more liberal attitudes of the West. What to you is completely innocent behavior such as winking or touching someone's arm, may seem provocative and unacceptable to an Indian. So keep things official. Joking and friendship in the office are fine but Indians won't always get your jokes right away. Make sure not to include sexual or political overtones to the jokes.

Along the same lines, don't take certain liberties for granted as you would in the West. For example, if you need to make an overseas or long distance phone call from your Indian associate's office, offer to pay for the charges. Even if the offer is declined, don't assume that it's acceptable for you to make several such calls.

Don't confuse Indian restraint with a lack of emotion or sentimentality: Indians are sentimental. There's a thin line between business and personal life, and most people fill their workspace with pictures of family and pets. Comment on the cuteness of the employees' children or talk of their smile for example, and you're sure to get a good response! In fact, Indians think you're strange if, with typical Western restraint, you don't comment on their collection. So do take an interest in their interest. You won't go overboard on this, so don't worry about making a personal comment that you may not do back home.

Shop Around

No matter how busy you are while you're in India, you're sure to do some shopping (or at least try to make some time for it). Take in the complete retail experience. While the elite malls offer you quality goods, don't miss out on the ambience of local markets and pavement shops. Bargaining is expected in India at these places and at fairs and festival markets, but remember to be reasonable.

For example, if a shopkeeper quotes, say, Rs 200 for a shirt, don't think too hard about it. (That's roughly 4 USD.) The price quoted is probably thought up on the spot especially in the open air cotton street markets in major towns, and the shopkeeper may expect you to try and whittle the price down. But don't waste too much energy in bargaining.

When you're bargaining, start by offering 60 to 70 percent of the asking price. If the shopkeeper refuses, settle for 80 to 90 percent, and you're still getting a bargain. This skill comes with experience, so at first, you may want to take an Indian friend or colleague along until you get the hang of things. And then remember to buy your shopping helper something for his time. This token can be as simple as a book at a bookstore — chances are he'll refuse, but the offer goes over very well.

Embrace Your Ancestry

Are you a non-resident Indian (NRI), and do you want to start a business venture back in the home of your ancestors? If so, be warned — foreign returned Indians are viewed with a more critical eye than Westerners are in India. Generally, you come face to face with comments such as, "You're one of *us* — why are you acting like one of *them?*"

For instance, a Westerner moaning about the heat or a power outage may be tolerated, while an Indian-American for example, with the same complaints will be seen as a whiner. If you're an NRI, be sure to establish early on that you've lived out of India for a long time and that you're out of touch.

Respect and Reward Your Staff

If you hire domestic staff in India, your relationship with the staff needs to be one filled with respect. You may not be used to such pampering back home, but in India the domestic role allows your staff to support their families.

Ask around and pay the going rate for domestic services. You may be surprised, but the general pay rate for an entire month is likely to be the same amount of money that a month's worth of toiletries costs you. Don't feel guilty; just be generous with festival bonuses once or twice a year.

Also remember that household staff gain vicarious importance from the status of their employers. Working for a foreign businessperson can actually improve their market value and future employment prospects. Think of that every time you feel a little guilty, and also give them a good testimonial when you no longer require their services.

If you run into trouble with your staff, first look into the possibility that the trouble is probably just miscommunication. Figure out how to laugh and to see the funny side of things. Humor is your best coping mechanism.

If discipline problems crop up or things go missing from your home, then you have every right to first discuss this with the staff and give them a warning. If the problem persists or if you don't want to tolerate it further, then letting them go with some severance pay is fine. I encourage the severance pay just to buy yourself peace of mind and to comply with the Indian way of making the blow soft when giving the pink slip.

Define boundaries and avoid social interactions with your domestic staff. Sharing coffee in the kitchen or appearing in any state other than fully dressed can confuse your help and confuse your roles as employer/employee.

Mind Your Manners

At some point in time, you may be invited to be a houseguest of one of your Indian colleagues or friends.

If this happens, remember these tips:

✔ **Don't make your own bed, do your laundry, or do the dishes.** More than likely, the domestic staff (if they exist) handles these tasks. Just sit back and enjoy being waited on.

✔ **Do offer your help.** Offer to assist with the kids, running errands, or other Indian routines. Your host may likely decline the help but be happy that you asked.

✔ **Do tip the staff of your host.** Shoot for between Rs 100 and 500 each, depending on the length of your stay and what each staff member did for you. Remember that the cook is at the top of the pecking order, followed by the driver if you've been chauffeured around. You can also give your hostess a round sum and request that she distribute it to her staff. Tips are given in one lump sum, typically on the day of your departure.

✔ **Do participate in any festival or ceremony your host family may be celebrating.** There are dozens of these festivals in India, you may find yourself right in the thick of one. If there isn't a festival going on, ask which one may be right around the corner. Take an interest in your host's interests.

✔ **Do take a gift for every family member.** If that isn't possible, take a larger gift that all the family members can share, such as a box of chocolates. In addition, take one age-appropriate gift for the youngest member of the family. Children enjoy a special place in all Indian homes, and it's especially important not to go in empty-handed as far as they're concerned!

Read up on Indian culture and religion before interacting with your Indian counterparts. Indians take a great interest in the world and like it when the world does the same of them.

In particular, familiarize yourself with the Indian trinity. The Hindu trinity is Brahma (the creator), Vishnu (the preserver), and Shiva (the destroyer of evil). I know of one foreign businessman who earned brownie points on a recent visit with his Indian team when he talked about the ten avatars (manifestations) of Vishnu, which is based on the Darwinian forms of life.

Study up on Hinduism by visiting the following Web sites:

✔ www.hinduism.about.com/od/basics/Beliefs_Practices.htm

✔ www.culturalindia.net

You should also become at least slightly familiar with the multicultural heritage and history of India. If you happen to be visiting a Muslim, a Parsee, a Sikh, or a Christian family, do take time to understand those religions and the way that they're practiced in India.

Respect Lifestyle Differences

Life in India is different than life in the West, and Indians may not understand the things you take for granted back home. They may see you as a spoiled Westerner who lives in air-conditioned comfort and travels in chauffeur driven cars with the windows rolled up. Don't be surprised if you receive little sympathy if you complain about things like the weather or your staff.

Your team members' lives may be quite different than your own, and to them a vacation may be hanging out with a large number of family members or going on a pilgrimage. When you come back from a vacation, do chat with your staff about it generally, but don't expect them to understand how relieved you were to be sunbathing and sipping piña coladas in the Bahamas the previous week. Respect these lifestyle differences and avoid bringing them to the fore in conversation.

Chapter 19

Ten Tips from Chanakya, the World's First Management Guru

. . . .

In This Chapter

▶ Considering the wisdom of Chanakya

▶ Bettering your business through age-old advice

. . . .

*I*ndia is a country steeped in spirituality, which has answers to all aspects of life. Indians are resilient and have a "can do" attitude because they have had inspiring leaders throughout the generations. One such leader lived from 350 to 275 B.C. and his teachings make sense for the business world today. This person was Chanakya.

Chanakya wasn't just the advisor to a king, he was actually a king maker. He was a religious scholar, economics wizard, and military strategist, all rolled into one. His military, political, and economic strategies succeeded in fashioning the first nation in the world's history, cobbling together many little kingdoms under one powerful umbrella, thus laying the foundation for the emerging India.

In keeping with the modern management trend of looking back to look forward, Chanakya's master work, the *Arthasasthra* (which can be translated as the "science of material gain or profit") is on par with *The Art of War* and other such works of ancient military and political wisdom. Although centuries old, the *Arthasasthra* can be adapted to offer insight on corporate survival in the 21st century.

In this chapter, I share Chanakya's wisdom on management matters with you.

Strengthen the Seven Pillars of Your Business World

The building that houses your business in India is only as strong as the materials you use in construction. Chanakya had a similar realization about the governing of a nation. He came up with what he called the seven pillars, which, if they were sound, would form the basis of a lasting and effective regime. Although Chanakya was dealing with affairs of the state, the same idea can be transposed to the corporate world. Take away the important parts of the seven pillars of Chanakya:

- ✔ **The king:** The business owner — it is your duty as the king (business owner) to select strong and able men or women as your ministers.

- ✔ **Ministers:** High-level managers. These people can both offer you advice and also implement your instructions.

- ✔ **The country:** Your market. Know your market as well as you can. Discover its strengths and weaknesses, and understand where it can be exploited and where it needs protection.

- ✔ **The fortified city:** Your head office. Run your head office well, and see that it has all that is required to keep those within its walls productive as well as satisfied.

- ✔ **The treasury:** Your finance department (whether it's simply small business accounting software on your computer or a massive accounting department). Keep a close watch over your treasury, and budget for future needs, as money underpins the whole operation.

- ✔ **The army:** Your workforce or team. Handle your army (your Indian team) wisely to win their loyalty and steer them in the right direction.

- ✔ **Allies:** Consultants who work with you. Choose your consultants well, making sure that they understand your needs and are committed to keep you abreast on all important issues. See Chapter 7 for more information on how to select your allies.

If these seven pillars of your business are strong, it can withstand any kind of challenge, internal or external. Finally, as Chanakya says, make sure that your seven pillars are firm and strong before the enemy (in this case, competition) strikes at you.

Understand the Importance of Stability

Growth and progress are the aims of all businesses. But before growth can occur, stability within has to happen. Chanakya says, "The policy, following which he were to see neither the advancement nor the decline of his own undertakings, constitutes stable condition."

As a progressive corporate head, you need to ensure that your organization has financial stability and a focused mission before it can move on to the next rung in the ladder of progress. Another area of concern is fast employee turnover, especially in IT companies. This problem is a particular nuisance in India today, with headhunters on the prowl and the young, upwardly mobile Indian ever on the look out for bigger bucks and designations. You must establish a work atmosphere attractive enough to see that your staff stays with you. There are various ways to do so, and you can find details in Chapter 7.

Keep Employees Happy

Chanakya knew what it took to build a powerful presence, be it military, political, or economic. He emphasized the importance of workers, and of making the most of their contributions. In *Arthasasthra* he states the following:

> "In the happiness of the subjects lies the benefit of the King; and in what is beneficial to the subject lies his own benefit."

Even 2,000 years ago Chanakya realized that happy, motivated employees were one of the most important keys to success. Keep this in mind as you manage your Indian workers! Westerners tend to get excited about the prospect of saving money by taking advantage of lower Indian salaries, but remember that wages and other forms of compensation are just as useful a tool for motivation in India as they are in the West.

In Chapter 7, I describe the various ways you can compensate your Indian employees to keep them happy, motivated, and working extremely hard for you.

Make the Right Hiring Choices

If you want your employees to be happy, you need to be happy with them. And that means you've got to make wise hires. I talk about recruitment issues in Chapter 7, but Chanakya also has something to say on the topic.

He felt that a sound, trainable person is one with the following qualities: ability to listen, ability to think from all angles, ability to reject false views, desire to learn, and intentness on truth, not on any person.

These pointers come to you from 2000 years ago to help you when you're sitting in the interviewer's chair, quizzing prospective employees. You may be inundated with résumés all citing lofty degrees and competencies each more impressive than the last. So how do you select the right person? Frame your questions so that the candidates' potential (or lack of it) in these areas is made crystal clear, and presto, your choice becomes easy.

Mix the Old and the New

You can hire the most able, talented employees in all of India, but even that won't ensure success if your team India is long on talent but short on training. That brings me to the next nugget of wisdom from Chanakya: "One conversant with the science, but not experienced in practical affairs, would come to grief in carrying out undertakings."

India is awash with B-Schools (as business schools are known in India), and management degrees are in fashion. These schools have excellent curricula and the caliber of students is outstanding, but make certain that you hire some experienced staff, too. They can warn you of possible pitfalls and offer advice on what works or doesn't in India. Aim for a sensible mix of the old and the new (particularly those who are eager to be trained) for best results. Good recruitment agencies (look at Chapter 7 for details) should be able to help. And for new recruits, organize mentoring programs to help them get on-the-job training.

Stay in Contact

Check out the day-to-day running of your organization. To do that, you need to communicate with a variety of Indians to keep your business well positioned, supplied, and ahead of the pack. It's all about networking.

The wily Chanakya realized this two millennia earlier. Referring to the role of the king (or business owner in the extended comparison), he wrote in the *Arthasasthra* that "He should establish contacts with forest chieftains, frontier-chiefs, and chief officials in the cities and the countryside." Apply this dictum to the corporate jungle today — it's just as relevant.

Regular contact with your staff is essential for maintaining control and being on top of the important situations at all times. Have a look at Chapter 6, where I talk of running your business from abroad. And also check out Chapter 16, where I discuss potential pitfalls. Both chapters should give you a clear idea of the importance of staying in touch and reading your Indian employees.

Plan Your Travels Carefully

If you have multiple branches or if you're managing your Indian business from abroad, travel and logistics form an important part of your work. In Chanakya's view, it formed an integral part of the king's role too, and he had this advice to offer: "He should start after making proper arrangements for vehicles, draught-animals, and retinue of servants."

These words are valid in today's Indian business context, because transport and logistics hurdles are important ones to see and to clear. Sure, you won't need draught-animals or a retinue of servants, but you do have to plan for your needs: look up plane and train timetables, budget for delays, book your hotel rooms in advance (see Chapter 10), and double check your product distribution and transportation structure. If you don't plan your comings and goings (and those of your products) down to the last detail, you could have to pay heavily in terms of time, money, and frustration.

Manage Your Money

Familiar with the importance of monitoring the financial aspects of an operation, Chanakya stressed the need for consistent accounting and frugality with funds.

He also has this to say: "If the (officer) does not deliver the income that has accrued (or) does not pay the expenses put down in writing (or) denies the balance received, that is misappropriation." That's an important pointer for you in India, because it's related to the problem of hierarchy, something that may seem strange and irksome to you.

Although educated, enlightened top-level management staff in India play fair, you may find that your accountant or someone in the lower rungs of management chooses to exercise power in petty ways like holding back legitimate payment to staff and clients. They may employ delaying tactics, such as saying that invoices haven't been received or processed, sanctions are taking excessive amounts of time, authorized signatories are away, and so on all to keep people waiting. Explain, sometimes many times over, that such practices aren't tolerated. The message will get across.

Gather Information before Acting

Based on the next nugget of wisdom from Chanakya, a version of the SWOT (strengths, weaknesses, opportunities, threats) analysis existed way back in the third century B.C. Chanakya has the following to say about the importance of carefully considering the business landscape before jumping into a new venture:

> "After ascertaining the relative strength or weakness of powers, place, time, revolts in rear, losses, expenses, gains and troubles, of himself and of the enemy, the leader should march."

In today's India, you — the Western businessperson looking to start up in India — are the leader, so before you "march" into your Indian business venture, be sure you've done your research! Pay special attention to the strength and quantity of competition and how your finances can cope with the curveballs that the Indian business environment is sure to throw your way. Check out Chapter 9 on money, for more details on finances.

Attack the Competition

Chanakya knew that a king can't be without enemies. At some point in his reign, he must be prepared to meet the enemy, and his future depends on the outcome of the meeting. Think about this in terms of business, with you — the business owner — as the king. The corporate world is a veritable war zone today, and Chanakya's advice to the king who comes face-to-face with the *Shatru* (enemy) in battle holds true in boardroom and market battles: "If near him (the enemy), he should strike at his weak point."

But how does one strategize and make this move against the enemy (competitor) in today's corporate world? Here are a few tips:

✔ Study the competition.

✔ Discover everything there is to know about your competitors.

✔ Understand the rules of the market and practice well.

✔ After you're confident, go for the attack.

Chapter 20

Ten Ways to Enjoy Your Downtime in India

....

In This Chapter

▶ Traveling around India

▶ Getting involved in the culture

....

*O*nce you've carved out a bit of free time in India, away from the pressures and challenges of the working world, you may need to spend some downtime away from the office. Luckily for you, the options are many and varied — India is a country full of wonders. This chapter offers ten possibilities for you to consider as you choose how to spend your free time while in India. Doing and being are balanced in most of these options, as is the Indian way of life.

Travel to an Indian Temple

India is replete with temples. The vast majority of them date back hundreds or even thousands of years, and they often formed the nucleus of Indian cities that are now thriving. Consider visiting these temples to witness their architectural splendor and experience the sense of sanctity and peace they exude.

Some of the most famous temples in India include the following:

- **The Khajuraho temples** in the state of Madhya Pradesh are known for their erotic sculptures.

- **The Lord Venkateshwara Temple** is the richest in India, situated in the hills of Tirupathi, where pilgrims shave their head as an offering. The hair is then exported around the world for wigs and hair extensions.

- **The Meenakshi Temple** in Maduari features an awesome *gopuram* or temple tower.

- ✔ **The temple at Chidambaram** has one thousand pillars, and was dedicated to Lord Shiva, who took the form of *Nataraja,* the Lord of Dance.

- ✔ **The Jagannath Temple** at Puri once hosted a huge chariot festival that spawned the word *juggernaut* in the English language.

- ✔ **The Bahai Temple** in Delhi is more modern and shaped like a lotus.

You can witness brilliant flashes of Indian culture at its temples. You may see Indian women decked in their finest silk saris and jewelry in honor of the gods they visit. There may also be a child with a shaven head romping about, his parents having vowed to offer his hair in exchange for good health. Or you can see a priest carrying water and fruits to wash and offer the idols. Check out www.indiantemples.com for more information.

Hindu temples aren't the only grand religious buildings in India. In Chennai you can visit a Christian church called St. Thomas Mount, where the apostle St. Thomas lived and was killed. India also boasts famous Islamic pilgrim spots such as the Jama Masjid in Delhi and the Hazrathbal mosque in Srinagar, and you can travel to both. Or you can go to The Golden Temple — the most important Sikh place of worship — and behold its awe-inspiring gold domes. Many Buddhist sites abound.

Tour a National Park

India is the land of *The Jungle Book.* You don't have to dream of "far-away India" anymore — the jungle's at your doorstep! India is home to some of the world's most captivating wildlife. To get a close look at some of these breathtaking creatures, take a trip to an Indian national park:

- ✔ Watch tigers in **Jim Corbett National Park,** the park named after a great naturalist.

- ✔ Visit the lions in the **Gir Forest National Park.**

- ✔ See elephants up close at the **Periyar Wildlife Sanctuary.**

- ✔ Check out the rhinos in the **Kaziranga National Park.**

- ✔ Go birding at the **Bharatpur Bird Sanctuary.**

The options for exotic wildlife viewing are as varied as the countless species that can be discovered within India's borders. Animals are deified in Hinduism and are often treated as demigods. Other important national parks include those at the Sundarbans, Nagarhole, Rathnambore, and Point Calimere.

Visit a Hill Station

The British coined the term *hill station* years ago. It refers to a cool getaway in the hills. When the Indian heat gets to you, these spots are great for some R and R. You have a vast selection of hill stations from which to choose, but if you're the adventurous sort, take the road less traveled. Visit some places which aren't high on the tourist list (though high enough in altitude), and you'll be rewarded with peace and quiet as well as cool weather. The lesser-known hill stations include Chamba, Dalhousie, Coonoor, Kotagiri, Mercara, Horsely Hills, and Haflong.

One sight you won't want to miss is the blooming of the *Kurunji,* a bluish purple flower that covers the Nilgiris mountains on the Kerala–Tamil Nadu border and gives the hills (translated as Blue Mountains) their name. The plants bloom just once in twelve years, and if you happen to be in India for the next bloom period, do yourself a favor and make a visit to the Nilgiris.

For additional information, visit www.hillstationsinindia.com.

Participate in a Major Indian Festival

When you're in India, go with the flow and experience the color, vibrancy, and joy of a major festival. During the holiday times, give yourself a break. Apart from Diwali — the festival of lights and more or less a national event — there are other regional festivals that are celebrated with equal verve. For example, *Holi* is the festival of color. It heralds the onset of spring. To participate in the festivities, let your hair down, wear your oldest clothes, and join the crowds in the streets. You get smeared with colored powders and water and as you dance and twirl you send sprays of colored water flying around everywhere. It's a good way to rediscover the child in you!

Get a Taste of Indian Village Life

Don't leave India without spending at least some time in a village, to get familiar with the real heart of India. It isn't hard to find a village — you have about 500,000 to choose from! You have to do without air conditioners, and you may not have access to shopping malls, but in an Indian village, you get to know the meaning of extended family, and you can see how life revolves around agriculture. Every member of the family, the little ones included, pitches in and does his share.

Enjoy the authentic tastes of India, too. The piping hot, freshly cooked, simple meals are enjoyable and the welcoming nature of families makes you feel at home. As a bonus, you may also forge friendships that last a lifetime.

To arrange a trip to a village, consult your Indian colleagues or friends. Ask them for a recommendation on a good village to visit, and the best mode of transportation for getting there. And then enjoy folk theater, music, and dance, join in traditional art and craft making, and witness the incredibly gifted side of India.

Take a Ride on the Rails

Train travel has become increasingly popular for world travelers visiting India, and the accommodations and service have been improved as a result. India's railway is arguably the world's longest, and you can see much of the country from a train car. Indian railways employ 1.4 million workers and run 1,100 trains daily carrying more than 15 million passengers. They own some of the best real estate in the country and are soon going to develop world class stations and budget hotels like the West. Air-conditioned, upper-class train compartments are clean and comfortable ways to travel in India today. The nicer compartments even include toilet paper, which is missing from most bathrooms in India.

Toilet paper is typically not provided at public restrooms in India. Culturally, there is a perception of washing being better hygiene than wiping, in India. Water jets called "health faucets" are used, and in rural areas a simple bucket of water is all that is available. On most of your travels in the country, be sure to carry your own toilet paper.

Food is often served on these train trips and is sometimes included in the ticket price. The food is usually safe to eat, but unseasoned travelers whose palette is not used to Indian spices or visitors who have just arrived with lower immunity and sensitive stomachs, may want to pack a sandwich. You can also find plenty of bottled water, fresh fruit, and biscuits for sale at train stations. First time travelers can pack and bring along their own food and drink from a reliable bigger urban store or hotel.

Train trips are a surefire way to come in contact with local Indian culture. If you feel outgoing while you're on your train trip, don't hesitate to make friends with other passengers. Indians are very forthcoming and friendly people. Expect to be quizzed on your family, job, food habits, country, and customs, with very little of the Western reserve you may expect back home. You may also get to hear all your traveling companions' life histories and end up with heartfelt invitations to visit them whenever you're in their part of the country.

Shop for Bargains

India is full of bargains for foreign visitors, and the whole country is a shopaholic's dream come true. Shopping is perfectly safe and can be very fun.

The fun comes when you start to bargain. It's common to bargain for a better price while shopping in India, but you have to know where you can bargain and where you can't. Usually Kashimiri shops selling carpets and boutiques in the shopping arcade of five star hotels where tourists shop, are always open to discounts. As a rule, government-run stores and upscale boutiques have fixed prices. If you want to try and bargain at these sites, you may need to ask an Indian friend for help so you can be guided on whether to and how much to bargain. The shopkeepers may also give you a better deal if you're shopping with an Indian. In some tourist stores (the locals can point them out to you) you can ask for a discount, and after it's given, ask for some more. A rule of thumb is to ask for about a quarter of the price off.

Unwind at an Ayurvedic or Naturopathy Center

India has a number of systems of medicine that the world terms as alternative, but these methods were considered the prime systems in the country for centuries. Chief among these systems, and probably the best known outside the country, is *Ayurveda* — a word meaning *Science of Life*. Because of the growing interest in alternative medicine and the West's search for holistic cures, Ayurveda has evolved into a sort of tourist industry, and Ayurveda resorts have sprung up in many parts of the country, particularly in the scenic state of Kerala.

These resorts or centers treat you to body massages, oil therapy, rejuvenation therapy, beauty treatment, stress management programs, weight-loss packages, and much more. The centers are staffed by trained professionals and most make their own medicines. To consider your options, visit www.indiantravelguide.com/ayurveda-travel-in-india/ayurveda-resorts-in-india.html.

Spend a Day at a Charitable Institution

If you want to do something truly fulfilling with your downtime in India, consider volunteering for a charitable institution. Your choices for doing so are vast. Charities handle every section of the needy in Indian society, and some even cater to animals. You're sure to find a worthy cause that fits your interests.

Doing charity work and getting hands-on experience in giving allows you to empathize with India's people and view its idiosyncrasies with more equability. Many institutions (including the world famous Missionaries of Charity founded by the diminutive nun from Albania, Mother Theresa, for the poorest of the poor) offer a chance to do volunteer work for short stints or at regular intervals. Look around and see what suits you best. Are you ready to give your time to the elderly by sitting and talking with them and listening to their reminiscences? Are you good with children? Visit www.charityindia.org/charity_org.asp for ideas and tips on getting started.

Study an Indian Art

If you're visiting India for an extended period of time, consider studying an Indian art form. India is a land of culture, steeped in music, dance and art. Each region has its own distinctive art forms. You can familiarize yourself with Carnatic music in the south and Hindustani music in the north. If you'd rather play the music than just enjoy it, try your hand at the veena or sarod, (both stringed instruments), the tabla or mridangam (percussion instruments) or the nadaswaram or shehnai (wind instruments). If you're interested in dance, you may try to study the basics of Kathak, Odissi, and Manipuri dance forms in the north, or Kuchipudi, Bharathanatyam, and Mohiniattam in the south.

You can also study a martial art like Kalaripayattu in Kerala, or take a course in yoga, which helps you stay healthy while uniting body and mind. If literature is your bag, try out an Indian classic ready for you to devour. (You may want to consider taking classes in an Indian language first — there are dozens to choose from — because translations are only second best to India's original masterworks.)

Index

• D •

[DISCARD